THE DEED

by

Gerold Frank

NEW YORK

SIMON AND SCHUSTER   1963

For Lillian

A NOTE TO THE READER

THIS STORY has haunted me for nearly twenty years. I have not been able to write it before. Now, after having written a number of books dealing with quite different subjects, I have found it possible to put *The Deed* on paper.

The Deed is the story of two boys who gave their lives for an ideal. They killed a man—coldly, calmly, with premeditation. They were caught and tried. They were found guilty and they were hanged.

Neither attempted to deny the act; instead, they used the prisoner's box as a platform to defend it, to accuse their accusers. Their cause was freedom, the freedom of Israel, but the means they chose was the assassin's gun, believing, in the tradition of those who hold with political assassination, that by their act they could change the course of history.

The man they killed was the highest British official in the Middle East, a minister of state, a member of Churchill's war cabinet; the time was the last months of World War II; the place was Egypt. No person, no time, no place, could have been chosen more likely to result in embarrassment to the British, the Egyptians and the Jews. Yet they did it; it was so planned.

These boys, one seventeen, the other twenty-two, were members of a secret terrorist organization in Palestine, denounced by the Jewish community, known as the Stern group. Its active members at one time numbered no more than twenty-six; at most, in the span of our story, no more than 200. The two boys played out their part in their tiny corner of the struggle for Israel and were no longer on the scene when, three years later, the British yielded their mandate for Palestine and the State of Israel was established.

Only historical perspective can assess the importance of the tragic drama in which the two were involved. The full measure of their role—the effect, for example, of the attention it focused upon the sorry situation in Palestine—is a question for future historians. Certainly the independence for which the two were hanged in 1945 would not have been won in 1948 without decades of political activity in England, in Europe, in the United States, in Palestine and elsewhere; without the immigration and colonization and labors of hundreds of thousands; without, in the end, a determined citizenry, a resourceful army and an indomitable leadership. Nor, without all these, would that independence have been maintained in the years that followed.

But there is no doubt that the deed was one of the great irritations, the great harassments, which so annoyed and confused and bedeviled the British that ultimately they gave the problem over to the United Nations—and thus opened the door to the partition of Palestine and the first Jewish state in two thousand years.

I was in Palestine and Egypt in the time of the terror. I attended the trial of the two boys in a high-pillared courtroom in Cairo; I was there as a newspaper correspondent, but at the same time I felt myself the guest of whom Coleridge wrote, fixed by the glittering eye of the Ancient Mariner, held spellbound by the tale.

Since then, while I was haunted by the story, I found myself slowly collecting material relating to it. Writing assignments have taken me back to the Middle East a dozen times since I attended the trial, and each time to the very scenes and places associated with the two boys and their growing up. Each time, too, it seemed that I met or was brought into contact with those who had been members of their tiny conspiratorial group. Elsewhere, time and again—in London, or Paris, or Cairo, or New York—I would meet someone who in some way had been connected with them.

As a result, of the nearly fifty persons involved in the deed, I have met and interviewed in person nearly all of them. I have spoken to all the major conspirators. That is to say, to the boys themselves, to the three men who formed the Central Committee of the Stern group, who passed sentence of death on Moyne; to the man who assigned the two boys to carry out that sentence; to the man who was their immediate superior in Cairo and supervised the carrying out of their mission. I have spent time with the friends, schoolmates, teachers and parents, brothers and sisters of the two boys.

Also, in the course of writing this book, I have retraced the steps of the deed, returning to Cairo and visiting again the Rue Shagaret el Dorf, the scene of the assassination; the Bulak Bridge, by which the two boys sought to escape; the courtroom in which they were tried; the prison in which they were held; the square—Bab-al-Khalk ("The Gate of Creation")—in which they were hanged; and I have stood, too, where the weeping Sadovsky stood over their grave.

As to the underground associates of the two—those who survived the manhunts, the tortures, the prisons—I have interviewed them in half a dozen cities here and abroad. Anonymous now as they were then, they are today middle-aged men and women, many with families, to whom the experiences of those terrible years are sometimes as vague as a dream, sometimes only too vivid, as in a nightmare. These men and women spoke freely to me. Some wished to do so but were unable. One friend, when he began to relate his experiences in the Stern group with one of the boys, found his voice failing him. He could not speak above a whisper. Presently, he could not get the words out at all. Another, telling me of tortures inflicted not on him but on his associates, began to gag and gasp for

9

air, as if the ordeal he was describing was his at that very moment. Still others could recall hardly anything. All had been blacked out.

The writing of *The Deed* has taken two years. It might have taken less had I not discovered that even the historian of such an event can share the nightmare of those who played a part in it. He, too, finds it hard to get the words out. For these were boys belonging to a people who had a tragic history as victims of violence—yet they turned to violence. They were of the People of the Book, living in the Land of the Book—yet they violated its supreme commandment: Thou shalt not kill.

Thus, the story of the two Eliahus, Eliahu Bet Zouri and Eliahu Hakim. I have tried to tell it as one who saw, was deeply moved, and sought in the years that passed to learn how such a thing came to be.

—GEROLD FRANK

New York, Cairo and Jerusalem
1963

CAST OF CHARACTERS

WALTER EDWARD GUINNESS, LORD MOYNE – *The victim*

CAPTAIN ARTHUR HUGHES-ONSLOW – *His aide-de-camp*

MISS DOROTHY OSMONDE – *His secretary*

LANCE CORPORAL A. T. FULLER – *His driver*

SIR HAROLD MACMICHAEL – *High Commissioner for Palestine*

SIR JOHN SHAW – *Chief Secretary, Palestine*

ABRAHAM STERN – *Founder, the Stern group, or the Fighters for the Freedom of Israel (FFI) also known as Lehi*

SERGEANT BENJAMIN GEFNER – *Chief of FFI in Egypt before The Deed*

SERGEANT JOSEPH GALILI – *Chief of FFI in Egypt during The Deed*

ITZHAK YIZERNITSKY ("RABBI" SHAMIR) – *One of three FFI chiefs. Operations commander of FFI, man who gave order for assassination*

ISRAEL SHEIB (DR. ELDAD—*also* SAMBATION) – *One of three FFI chiefs. Ideologist of FFI*

NATHAN FRIEDMAN-YELLIN – *One of three FFI chiefs: successor to Abraham Stern; chief of three-man secretariat of FFI*

ELIAHU BET ZOURI – *Assassin*

ELIAHU HAKIM – *Assassin*

YAFFA TUVIA – *ATS girl, FFI member, Hakim's companion in Cairo*

RAPHAEL SADOVSKY – *Egyptian teacher, key Egyptian civilian in plot, contact man*

11

DAVID RAZIEL – *Commander of the Irgun*

ESTHER RAZIEL – *David's sister, and Bet Zouri's instructor in National Cells*

DAVID DANON ⎫
AMIHAI PAGLIN ⎪
TAMAR VERED ⎪
ADI LANDAU ⎬ *Friends and associates of Bet Zouri*
ADA RON ⎪
DAN KOOR ⎭

DAVID SHOMRON ⎫
BARUCH ⎪
ELISHA ⎬ *Friends and associates of Hakim*
YAACOB BANNAI ⎪
JOSHUA COHEN ⎭

AVIGAD LANDAU – *Commander, Irgun, and later FFI, Jerusalem*

MIRIAM – *Avigad's wife*

HANNAH KUSHNIR – *Eliahu Bet Zouri's girl*

MOSHE BET ZOURI – *Bet Zouri's father*

DEBORAH BET ZOURI – *Bet Zouri's sister*

AVIVA BET ZOURI – *Bet Zouri's sister*

LEA BET ZOURI – *Bet Zouri's sister*

URI BET ZOURI – *Bet Zouri's brother*

SIMON HAKIM – *Eliahu Hakim's father*

PAULINE HAKIM – *Hakim's mother*

MENACHEM HAKIM – *Hakim's brother*

OVADIA HAKIM – *Hakim's brother*

JOSEPH HAKIM – *Hakim's brother*

YARDINA HAKIM – *Hakim's sister*

SHLOMO BEN JOSEF – *First Jew executed in Palestine since the fall of the Temple, 70 A.D.*

JONATHAN RATOSH – *Poet, spiritual leader of the Canaanites*

ASHER LEVITSKY – *Attorney from Palestine*

Moalam MOHAMED SHOURA – *The hangman*

CHUDAR PASHA – *The warden*

MOHAMAD HAIDAR PASHA – *Director General, Prisons of Egypt*
MAHMOUD MANSOUR BEY – *President of Court at trial*
ABDULA FATTAH EL SAID ⎤
TEWFIK DOSS PASHA   ⎬ *Defense attorneys appointed by state*
HASSAN DJEDDAOUI ⎦
MOHAMED TOWAYAR PASHA – *The Public Prosecutor*
LIEUT. COL. SELIM ZAKI – *The Public Interrogator*
CONSTABLE MOHAMMED AMIN ABDULLAH – *The Arresting Officer*
MRS. HELEN BLANCA ⎤
LORD MOYNE'S HOUSEBOY ⎮
LORD MOYNE'S COOK   ⎬ *Witnesses at the trial*
YOUSSEF MAHAMED EL KHADEM, ⎮
    MOTORIST ⎮
SAID SELLAH, CHAUFFEUR ⎦
RABBI HAIM NAHUM PASHA – *Chief Rabbi of Egypt*
RABBI NISSIM OCHANA – *Deputy Chief Rabbi of Egypt*
PROFESSOR HARROUN HADDAD – *Tutor of Mohamad Haidar's nephews*
DR. ISAIAH SELIM – *Physician to Mohamed Shoura, the hangman*
AHMED MAHER PASHA – *Prime Minister of Egypt*
JOSEPH ROMANO – *Cousin of Eliahu Hakim*
MOSES HALLEK – *Uncle of Eliahu Hakim*
J. J. HAKIM – *Secretary of Jewish Community of Cairo*

HAGANAH – *Defense organization of Palestine Jewry as a whole*
IRGUN ZVAI LEUMI – *National Military Organization—one of two outlaw terrorist groups*
LOHMEY HERUTH ISRAEL (THE STERN GROUP) – *Fighters for the Freedom of Israel—the smaller of the two outlaw terrorist groups*

CHAPTER

1

THERE WAS NOTHING that Monday morning, November the sixth, 1944, to single out this day in the life of Lord Moyne. The Right Honorable Walter Edward Guinness, first Baron Moyne, whose family name—thanks to the excellent stout that bears it—is a byword in every English home, had no reason to expect that this would be a day set apart.

He rose as usual a few minutes before seven o'clock and as usual breakfasted alone in his room on grapefruit, rolls and coffee. He ate in his dressing gown, before a window looking out on the green polo fields of the Gezira Sporting Club, for decades Egypt's most exclusive gathering place for British colonialdom—indeed, so exclusive that rare was the Egyptian, save servant or employee, who entered it. Even the trees and shrubs were English: firs from Aberdeen, azaleas from Sussex gardens, beds of lavender from London. At his window, listening to the soft moan of doves outside, Lord Moyne could feast his eyes upon a corner of England itself.

After he had eaten, he dressed in a white linen suit designed to make the Cairo heat more bearable, and descended to the main hall of the rococo two-story villa that was his official residence as British

Minister of State in the Middle East. Waiting for him were the two other occupants of the house, his aide-de-camp, Captain Arthur Hughes-Onslow, and his secretary, Miss Dorothy Osmonde. Both were tall, slim, precise, and they, too, had breakfasted alone in their rooms. Miss Osmonde was poised and fresh in a white cotton frock, and Captain Hughes-Onslow, in his knife-edge khaki drill uniform, was the picture of a Black Watch officer.

They exchanged good mornings (there was among them that cool intimacy which marks people who treasure their privacy but cannot help being thrown together most of the day) and went out to the long black limousine awaiting them. It had arrived at precisely 8 A.M. Lord Moyne glanced at the driver and raised his eyebrows in surprise: the man was new. The latter snapped to a stiff salute: "Lance Corporal Fuller, sir. Sergeant Lamb is ill." Moyne nodded and entered the car. Miss Osmonde took her seat beside him in the back; Captain Hughes-Onslow, his place next to the driver; and the sleek black Humber, its miniature Union Jack flying on the left fender, moved off.

Moyne's villa was in Zamalek, an exclusive residential district on Gezira island, in the Nile. Zamalek, owned by an Egyptian family which traced its title to the land back to the time of the Ptolemies, was connected with Cairo on the mainland by the busy Bulak bridge, a long, low, many-girded arch over the Nile. Now as the car made its way into the teeming morning traffic of the city, Moyne scanned the pages of the *Mid-East Mail,* one of Cairo's two English-language newspapers. As newspapers went, it was a sorry example: published primarily for His Majesty's Armed Forces, its news was sparse and what there was of it, badly written. Far more readable and informative was the *Palestine Post,* published in Jerusalem, 400 miles across the desert. But the *Post* was suspect (one never knew how insidiously Zionist propaganda might be slipped into news items to work its spell on the thousands of British and Commonwealth soldiers in the Middle East), and so it was the *Mail,* for all its patchwork reflection of the world, that was read each morning.

A Washington cable caught his eye. Roosevelt's audacious try for a fourth term had apparently fired the United States; tomorrow

15

millions of Americans would go to the polls. The story had almost driven the war, now in its sixtieth month, off the front pages. At any event, the beginning of the end was very near—Germany's military and diplomatic might was crumbling every day. Hitler had hurled his SS into the abortive Budapest struggle; Tito's Partisans were on the Greek border. The entire world waited for the opening of the Balkans, as if the hour-by-hour details of the Axis downfall no longer mattered. It seemed that three-fourths of the world had poured into Cairo these last weeks—refugees, army officers and diplomats of a dozen countries, newspaper correspondents, UNRRA and OWI officials, OSS agents, spies speaking a babble of tongues —Cairo had become the Lisbon of World War II, a listening post for rumor and intrigue, where peacocks cooed in villa gardens and four royal kings, the reigning and the deposed, might be found chatting together at a reception. . . .

Lord Moyne's car drove along the river to the Kasr-el-Nil Bridge. Crossing it, the car turned right along the bank on the east side of the Nile until it reached the huge barbed-wire enclosure in the center of which was the British Embassy. From here, as highest British government official in the Middle East, as Winston Churchill's chief minister outside London, Lord Moyne dealt with the onerous and frustrating problems of his post.

As he descended from his car and strode past saluting guards to his small, three-room office suite, Lord Moyne was weary, very weary. A spare man, six feet two, sixty-four years old and a widower for more than five of them, he had been appointed nearly ten months before. It had been a relentless period. He took the heat of Cairo badly: that was the first vexation. But these last months had been as arduous as any he had known—more, indeed, than his two preceding years as Deputy Minister of State, and the two years before that as Colonial Secretary.

In neither of these posts had he been as harassed as now. He entertained elaborately, as was expected of a man of his rank who also happened to be one of England's richest men. Through his residence and his weekend villa near the pyramids passed a never-ending procession of distinguished guests. But in this cockpit of bristling nationalisms, it was politics, not pleasure, that exhausted him. In his responsibility to Whitehall for all the Middle East, he faced a hydra-headed monster—now Greek, now Yugoslav, now Egyptian, now Arab, now Jewish. At the moment Greece appeared the most troublesome. Ten days ago he had had to fly to Athens with Anthony Eden to survey the critical situation there. Civil war tore the country apart, inflation had mounted monstrously, starvation and misery were rampant. The retreating Germans had left behind utter devastation. They had blown up bridges, mined harbors, demolished factories, destroyed farms. He and Eden wrestled with these problems alone. Churchill was to have joined them but the air-pressurized plane his physicians made him use was too large to set down in the Athens airport.

Moyne still felt the heavy burden of that meeting.

And add to this the decisions he faced. Perhaps none this hectic summer had been more difficult than the one involving Joel Brand, that strange Hungarian Jew, and his fantastic claim that Adolf Eichmann, Hitler's SS chief in charge of "the final solution of the Jewish problem," had authorized him to negotiate a "blood for goods" trade—with the Jews, the Allies or anyone else. If they would provide 10,000 lorries and a quantity of tea, coffee, soap and other goods, Eichmann would save the lives of 1,000,000 Jews by releasing them from the death camps—5,000 at first, then 12,000 a day.

So Eichmann had been quoted by Brand when British security seized him as an enemy agent in Syria, en route to Palestine to place this incredible scheme before the official Jewish organizations there. Brand had been brought to Cairo, put under house arrest and relentlessly questioned day after day. His presence here had been another irksome problem dropped into Moyne's lap.

Was one to believe Brand's story? It could be a trap. His Majesty's Government could not engage in anything that might be construed as "negotiating with the enemy." Eden was wary of the scheme. Moyne remembered his own brief meeting with Brand and his remark to the distraught man (assuming the offer *was* in good faith): "My dear fellow, whatever would I do with a million Jews?"

17

And if it was not the Jews outside Palestine, it was those inside Palestine—Palestine, always Palestine! The endless acrimony, the insistence with which Jew and Arab pressed their conflicting claims, the hysterical agitation over immigration, over the refugee ships trying to land their human cargo in that tumultuous country too tiny for either Jew or Arab! And the infuriating attitude of the Americans, playing big brother to both sides but refusing to shoulder any responsibility! Over all and above all, the awful threat of Jewish terrorism everywhere in Palestine.

On his desk now lay the final reports from that dour and incredibly exact Sir Harold MacMichael, until a few weeks ago His Majesty's High Commissioner for Palestine. Sir Harold had held a tight rein. He had faced the demoniac hatred of two terrorist outfits —the Irgun Zvai Leumi, or National Military Organization, with some 1,000 members, and the tiny Stern group, some 200 fanatics bent on assassination. Sir Harold and his officials had done all they could: his administration and courts had jailed hundreds of Jews, exiled still other hundreds to Mauritius and Eritrea, imposed house arrest, curfew, fine and hanging: still no British official, from High Commissioner to policeman, slept calmly in Palestine. If he, Moyne, had had a bad time of it, Sir Harold had had it even worse. Almost day to day outrages—soldiers kidnaped, police stations bombed, immigration offices blown up, senior police officials shot dead on the streets, and finally, even an attempt by the Sternists on the life of Sir Harold himself. They had ambushed his car on the way from Jerusalem to Jaffa in a hail of machine-gun bullets and hand grenades. Fortunately, the car had been moving at high speed, the assailants were overeager and Sir Harold had escaped with minor wounds. Bitter mementos to take from the Holy Land!

At least, for all of Lord Moyne's own harassments, fear of assassination was not one of them. Only last night after dining at the home of Pinckney Tuck, the American Minister, he had dismissed his car and walked the mile and a half home alone, unarmed and unafraid, through the deserted streets, enjoying the cool of the night. The Egyptians might rage inwardly at British domination—

Egyptian-British relations were at the breaking point—but anti-British violence was a thing of the past. . . .

Lord Moyne sighed. He pressed a button that summoned Miss Osmonde: on the agenda was a conference with Sir William Croft, his chief of staff, Major Forrestor, his security officer, and Air Vice Marshal Nutting, his advisor. He threw himself into the morning's work.

He could not know that this was the last day of his life.

It had been planned many months before. His every move had been watched for weeks. His comings and goings had been analyzed with scrupulous care. His death had been the subject of involved discussion by men of whose existence he did not dream. Earnestly and with profound soul-searching, they had debated his significance as a symbol of foreign rule; the responsibility of any high government official for the policy of that government; the ethical right to take one man's life for a cause involving the freedom of millions; and the overriding question, beyond good and evil: can any individual act change history? . . . All this had been gone over again and again.

The hours in which Lord Moyne now worked at his desk were the last hours of a career which had ranged over many countries, and had been rich with honors from a grateful King. He who had seen a great deal of the world of his time, who had been big-game hunter and explorer, lecturer and soldier, colonial administrator and political leader, who had served his country in a dozen important roles—he would have been astonished beyond words could he have heard sentence of death passed on him in a narrow room in the heart of Tel Aviv on a soft autumn night months before. . . .

Two men were sitting in quiet conversation in that room on the top floor of No. 24 Achad Ha'am Street. Achad Ha'am Street is a street of three-story, flaking, white stucco apartment houses which winds haphazardly through the center of the city. Its chief distinction is its name, honoring a Hebrew philosopher who warned half a century ago that the Jewish people would disappear as a people

19

unless they established a spiritual center on the ancient, regenerating soil of Israel.

It was almost dusk outside, the quick dusk that drops so sharply in the Middle East. The room on the top floor was dimly lit. Save for a battered wooden table—on which was a bowl of oranges—two equally battered chairs and a half-made cot against the wall, the room was quite bare. Of the two men, one was squat, powerfully built, square-faced and square-jawed, with deep furrows in either cheek. He had a thick black mustache, black eyes under overhanging black eyebrows and a heavy black beard. He was in his late twenties. He wore khaki shorts, three-quarter-length khaki socks showing his bare knees and a khaki shirt open at the collar from which his enormous chest seemed ready to burst. His gaze was direct and unwavering. He was an escapee from the Mazra Detention Camp near the Crusader fortress town of Acre where, under wartime emergency regulations, the British government of Palestine held without charge or trial hundreds of political prisoners—Nazis, Communists, suspected Arab and Jewish terrorists. Hiding in this room, he emerged only at night. Even then it was in disguise: he wore the circular black flat hat, the long black gabardine and shiny boots of the highly orthodox: he became "Rabbi" Shamir, scholar and Talmudic dreamer. Only a handful knew his real identity. He was Itzhak Yizernitsky, one of the three leaders of the dreaded and outlawed Stern group.

The man with whom he was in earnest conversation cut an altogether different figure. In his early thirties, he was slight, frail, with a foxlike face—pointed nose, pointed jaw with pointed goatee—and he carried himself, his whole thin, dried-up little body, with such an air of suppressed passion and dedication, so obviously in the thrall of his own internal ferment, that he seemed like an exclamation point come alive.

He called himself Sambation.

This, too, was an assumed name, taken from a legendary river behind which, it is said, hide the ten lost tribes of Israel. The river, so folklore has it, seethes and boils with hot stones every day save the Sabbath and spews these jagged rocks at anyone who might stumble on it. So, too, Sambation spewed words in his pointed, exclamatory fashion. He was in reality Dr. Israel Sheib, Doctor of Philosophy from the University of Vienna, authority on the Talmud and Schopenhauer: half-mystic, half-Nihilist, he was the second of the triumvirate of Stern leaders. If Shamir was the man of steel, the Stalin of the Stern group, Sambation was its Lenin, its eloquent theoretician.

He was speaking now, his voice in whispers, yet so insistent that it seemed as shrill as the loudest speech. "We end this war with the police, then, with the local administration?"

Shamir nodded. "Yes. We smash the dragon's head, not the tail. He who forms high policy is guilty—not the lieutenants."

Sambation inched forward in his chair. "Now, why do we choose him?" It was a rhetorical question, the answer to which he had obviously worked over time and again, an answer one had to formulate into words if only to stand off to one side and study it. Sooner or later he must explain it to the rank and file. His hoarse whisper took on a kind of measured chant, a singsong, the intonation of a schoolmaster presenting theme and counterpoint. "For three reasons. One: He pays with his own life for his stand. He carries out policy but that policy flows in part from the guidance he gives London. He is responsible as a symbol but also as a personality. Two: The man who succeeds him will think twice before doing the same thing. Three: We have a stage upon which to explain our motives to the world."

Shamir spoke with finality. "It is agreed, then. When the time comes."

Somewhere outside a door creaked, or it might have been the wind. The two men froze, and listened. Below, from the street, muffled by the closed wooden shutters, came the sound of children playing; then the sudden roar of an army jeep speeding by, signifying the beginning of the curfew that would clamp down on the all-Jewish city promptly at 6 P.M. After that hour any civilian found on the streets risked being shot by an over-nervous policeman. The British were engaged in their nightly manhunt and the very air bristled with danger. Two of their prime targets were Itzhak

Yizernitsky and Israel Sheib. They would have been even more tense had they known that at this moment, the third and chief of the Sternist Central Committee—a man named Nathan Friedman-Yellin, with whom the two had been in constant touch—was preparing to tunnel his way to freedom with twenty followers from Latrun Detention Camp near Jerusalem.

Then silence.

Sambation relaxed. He rose. Rabbi Shamir saw his guest to the door. How Sambation would melt into the hostile darkness outside, how he would find his way to the room in which he hid, only he would know.

"Shalom," said Shamir. They shook hands. "I will proceed to organize the action."

"Shalom," said Sambation, and glided out the door.

Cairo is wretchedly hot, even in November. The thermometer can reach 110 degrees. A daily siesta is imperative, and the British followed local custom. At 12:30 that afternoon of Monday, November 6, Corporal Fuller drew the black Humber up before the building housing Moyne's office. From its cool arched entrance came the trio he had driven to the office that morning: Lord Moyne, his secretary, his aide-de-camp. As they emerged into the brilliant sunlight they were assailed by the odors of noonday Cairo, suspended in the motionless air: a mélange of camphor, rancid mutton oil, coffee, musk, stale urine, gasoline fumes—one simply had to become accustomed to it. They arranged themselves in the car for the return trip. Each was busy with his own thoughts. For days Lord Moyne had been expecting a letter from his son, Captain the Honorable Bryan Guinness, stationed in Damascus. One of Bryan's couplets—the boy had already published one book of verse—ran through his head: "Let us despise the dust we are/That could devise the arts of war"—strange philosophy for a military man. Lord Moyne closed his eyes and tried to rest. Captain Hughes-Onslow was looking forward to a quick dip in the Gezira pool and a nap in his room after lunch. They would not go out again before late afternoon—either for a round of tennis at the Gezira Club, if the mood was upon them, or back to the office. Miss Osmonde was thinking of Corporal Fuller, their substitute driver, sitting so stiffly at the wheel before them. She could not get his woebegone face out of her mind. She had chatted with him on some other duty two days before and he had blurted out that his wife had just run off with another man. He was absolutely wretched.

The car moved slowly through the baking heat, retraced its path across the city and finally arrived at Lord Moyne's residence.

The house stood back from the road. Behind a black iron picket fence, almost hidden by shrubbery and bougainvillea, a short driveway led to the ornate, wrought-iron front door. The red brick of the building contrasted sharply with the deep green of the lawn. As the car turned in, Miss Osmonde noticed two boys engaged in conversation near the gate. She thought nothing of it.

The car halted. Fuller got out and hurried around to the rear on his side to open the car door for the minister. At the same time Captain Hughes-Onslow got out and strode toward the front door of the villa. He opened it, turned—and froze. On the other side of the shrubbery two figures had popped up, like jacks-in-the-box, vaulted over the fence and were racing toward the back of the car. Even as his mind registered the fact that they made an odd pair— one dark like an Egyptian, the other blond like an Englishman— and that both were brandishing revolvers, the dark youth had reached the automobile, wrenched open the back door and fired three times at Lord Moyne. Almost simultaneously three more shots rang out. Fuller had leaped at the blond boy standing cover for his companion—and the boy had fired at him, three times. Fuller fell, clutching his side.

Inside the car Lord Moyne lay slumped in his seat, breathing stertorously. Miss Osmonde heard him say, as if in great surprise, "Oh, we've been shot—" and then he lapsed into unconsciousness. One bullet had lodged in his neck, another in his abdomen, the third, meant for his heart, had missed and gone through Miss Osmonde's light frock without touching her. Miss Osmonde, in a state of near shock, found herself getting out of the car. She heard a faint voice, that of Corporal Fuller writhing on the ground.

"Please help me, I'm badly wounded—" She went round to help him and as she bent over him he died. All she could think of— it was ludicrous, it was shameful—was that poor Corporal Fuller could not have had time to change his next-of-kin card, and his army pension instead of going to his needy mother would go to his despicable wife and her paramour.

Now, as in a slow-motion film, the elements of the scene separated themselves. Around a turn in the road outside, an Egyptian motorcycle policeman chugged leisurely into view. The two assailants seized bicycles leaning against the fence, propelled them forward, and as they gained momentum, threw themselves into the seats and began pedaling frantically in the direction of the Bulak Bridge, some two hundred yards away. At this moment the door of the house adjoining Lord Moyne's burst open and a white-faced Arab houseboy who had seen it all from a window appeared. He stood there, an incongruous figure in his red fez and long white nightgownlike robe, his head thrown back, his eyes tightly shut, wailing in a singsong voice, "The high Ingleesee has been shot! They shot the high Ingleesee!"

The motorcycle policeman saw the limousine with its door ajar, the woman bending over the body in the street, and caught a glimpse of the two cyclists vanishing around a corner toward the bridge with Hughes-Onslow in pursuit. He was suddenly galvanized. With an ear-splitting roar of his motor he set after them, shouting, "Stop, murderers, stop!" Half a dozen passers-by milled about uncertainly; the cyclists were on Bulak Bridge, heads down, pedaling madly, the dark one first, the other behind him. The policeman on his motorcycle was almost upon them. Captain Hughes-Onslow was far in the rear. The blond boy turned, fired at the tires of the motorcycle and missed. There was a sharp exchange of shots. He staggered in his seat and lost his grip on the wheel. Rider and bike crashed to the macadam pavement. The dark youth looked behind and made a wide circle to come back to his companion's rescue. The crowd, enraged without knowing what enraged it, pounced on them now, pummeling, kicking, ripping off

24

their clothes. Within seconds the policeman had collared the two. Blood seeped from a wound in the blond boy's chest.

They stood, captured. They offered no resistance as the policeman seized their pistols, searched them and began shaking them furiously. "Who are you? Why have you done this?"

The blond boy spoke. He spoke in Hebrew, with astonishing calm. "We have nothing to say. We await the judgment of mankind."

At 8:40 that night, after an emergency operation by King Farouk's own physicians, Lord Moyne died.

CHAPTER

2

THE NEWS FELL upon the three countries most directly concerned like a thunderbolt. In Egypt, Moyne's death threw the government into an acute state of crisis. Wild rumors spread that the British would seize upon the Moyne assassination to depose King Farouk—that they would put the awful crime at the door of the Egyptians themselves.

Prime Minister Ahmed Maher Pasha, when a student twenty years before, had been suspected of complicity in the murder of Sir Lee Stack Pasha, British Governor of the Sudan, by the Black Hand, an Egyptian terrorist society. The British had retaliated mercilessly. They seized the Sudan, ousted the Egyptian Army and forced the Egyptian government to pay an indemnity exceeding $2,000,000.

What might not London do now?

Ahmed Maher Pasha moved swiftly. He summoned the cabinet into extraordinary session and announced he would take personal charge of the Moyne investigation. Egypt, occupied by the British, was already under martial law, but stringent measures were taken; all planes and trains were searched, guards were redoubled on all borders and the hotel rooms of every Palestinian Jewish visitor in Cairo, Alexandria and Port Said were ransacked by secret police.

In London, Parliament met in a cold fury. Churchill, whose close friend Moyne had been for thirty years, did not trust himself to speak at length. It was Eden who announced details of the shooting to the House of Commons: Churchill would deliver Moyne's eulogy later. King George and Queen Elizabeth telegraphed condolences to the bereaved family. In Commons one member rose to ask if the techniques of the Spanish Inquisition might not be used on the two murderers.

In Palestine the Jewish community was stunned. People stopped each other on the streets to speak in stricken tones. If the Egyptians feared reprisals, the Jews were even more alarmed. They were haunted by the memory of the riots and pogroms after the shooting of Petliura, butcher of the Ukraine, by a young Jewish watchmaker in 1926, the killing of a Nazi diplomat by seventeen-year-old Herschel Grynspan in 1938, the death at the hands of the Czech underground of Reinhard Heydrich, Nazi hangman of Moravia in 1942.

The Hebrew press could not find words strong enough to denounce the deed. It was an "abomination." . . . "Since Zionism began," lamented *Haaretz,* the most influential newspaper in the country, "no more grievous blow has been struck at our cause." The Jewish Agency expressed its horror "at this revolting crime." In London Dr. Chaim Weizmann, who two days earlier had a long, friendly conference with Churchill, said that this shock had been "far more severe and numbing than that of the death of my own son," RAF flight lieutenant Michael Weizmann, missing in action against the Germans. That the revered world leader of Zionism could utter such grief-laden words perhaps more than anything else shocked the Jews of Palestine into a realization of the enormity of what had been done.

Their anger surged. The killers could only have been members of the lunatic Stern group. The fight against terrorism had been going on for months, almost to the brink of civil war: now there could be no half measures. Terrorism must be stamped out. "The bullet that struck down Lord Moyne," wrote a distinguished Zionist leader, "was aimed not only at him but at our own hearts."

In Cairo, the authors of the deed were anything but repentant. From the moment of their arrest they had acted with strange calm. In the car rushing them to Bulak police station they were quite self-possessed, though the blond youth obviously suffered from his wound. They spoke Hebrew when first seized but seemed equally adept in Arabic and English. When Police Captain Hussein sought their names, they were silent. But a key found in the blond boy's pocket led to a room where papers identified him as Moshe Salzman of Jerusalem, a student, his companion as Itzhak Cohen of Jerusalem, also a student.

Captain Hussein barked questions at them: Who, if any, were their accomplices? Where did they get their guns? Who was on their death list?

Cohen stared at him expressionlessly. Salzman simply smiled.

Captain Hussein tapped his riding crop against his palm. They had better talk. . . .

Salzman's smile, under his blond British-type mustache, did not change. Finally he said, quietly, in Arabic, "Look, my Captain. There is no point in our fencing with each other. We are both intelligent men. Please don't ask me to tell you any tall tales and please don't tell me any. I will have my say when the time comes." Cohen added, "Captain, I respect you, I know you have to do your duty, but in spite of my respect I do not wish to talk."

In their cells in opposite wings of Cairo's Bab-al-Khalk prison— the name, with that Moslem fatalism which is part hope, part mysticism, means "The Gate of Creation"—the two remained serene. The dark youth, Cohen, had been cast into a cell completely bare save for a burlap prayer mat on the cement floor. He lay there, curled up and unperturbed. Salzman, obviously the spokesman, had been operated upon in the infirmary for removal of the bullet in his chest. The wound was not a deep one and forty-eight hours after the crime he spoke easily with Colonel Selim

Zaki, the official police interrogator. "As you wish," he said in Arabic, and heavily guarded, followed the other where he led.

Russell Pasha, British Police Chief of Cairo, had asked all newspapers to print photographs of the assassins taken immediately after their seizure, with a request that anyone recognizing them come forward and tell what he knew. Five persons waited in the prison yard to identify them.

One was the owner of the bicycle shop who had rented two bikes to the boys. The second was the Arab houseboy who had witnessed the crime. The third was a private chauffeur, who, seated in his parked car down the street, happened to glance into his rear-view mirror just as the shots rang out. The fourth was Moyne's cook who, as it turned out, at that moment had been carrying garbage from the kitchen to the incinerator behind the house. The fifth was a plump, middle-aged Egyptian-Jewish housewife named Mrs. Helen Blanca, in such a state of agitation that Colonel Zaki questioned her before anyone else.

Yes, she said hysterically, she was almost certain. The blond one. He had knocked at her door at sundown two weeks ago. She remembered it because it had been the day before the Sabbath and she had shopped that afternoon for candles. He had introduced himself as Moshe Salzman of Jerusalem, in Cairo on a brief vacation. He knew her daughter, Judith, a blind girl, who lived in a home for the disabled in Jerusalem. He had brought a gift from her—a nutcake she had baked herself. He had just arrived, he explained, and had asked if he could spend the night. He would go to a hotel first thing in the morning. Mrs. Blanca had found him most gentlemanly and welcomed him into her home. On his return to Palestine, he promised, he would take along any gift she might want to send her daughter. Next morning he was gone, but he left behind a small parcel wrapped in newspaper with a note that he would pick it up in a few days.

Then this morning she had opened her *Journal d'Egypte* and there, on the front page, was his face. It was contorted with pain because the police photographed him before giving him first aid, but she recognized the name.

29

She was ushered into the prison courtyard. Salzman stood against the wall with half a dozen other prisoners. He was barefoot and dressed in prison garb—faded blue shirt over his bandages, faded blue trousers—and when he saw her he exclaimed, "Mrs. Blanca!" And the criminal dared smile at her! As she looked at him, terror-stricken yet overwhelmed at the thought that she was betraying him, he said, still with a smile, "You must not be afraid. You do me no harm. As you see, I am already caught."

Still she stared dumbly.

He turned to Colonel Zaki. "She knows nothing. I told her nothing. She is innocent of any knowledge of us or what we did."

Only then could Mrs. Blanca nod and say, "Yes, he is the man."

Colonel Zaki asked, "And the parcel he left with you?"

She produced it from her handbag and he in turn handed it gingerly to a policeman to take outside and test.

"You need have no alarm," the prisoner said. His voice was matter-of-fact. "You will find only a soiled shirt and in that some sticks of dynamite. They cannot explode as they lack a fuse. You are all quite safe."

For two days this was all the Egyptians could learn. Neither to the Public Prosecutor nor to three senior British police officials who flew down from Palestine the next morning to interrogate them (on the same plane came Captain Guinness, from Damascus, to attend his father's funeral) would the prisoners tell more. What impressed their questioners was the proud, erect bearing of the two. Cohen said nothing: Salzman, plainly the more educated and the more eloquent, was polite but uncommunicative, except to deliver a scathing attack on the British Administration in Palestine and a declaration of his belief in the inherent and inalienable right of the Jewish people to their homeland.

The boys kept silent while the repercussions of their deed, like ripples in a pond into which an enormous rock has been cast, spread in ever-widening circles of fear and outrage. They kept silent while the venerable and almost blind Rabbi Haím Nahum Pasha, Chief Rabbi of Egypt, and J. J. Hakim, Secretary of the

30

Jewish Community in Cairo, called on Lord Killearn, the British Ambassador, to offer their official condolences. Lord Killearn was out of the city; they were received instead by British Minister Terence Shone. The minister received them with icy formality: he remained standing, he did not invite them to sit, and after they had expressed their profound regret, he had them as icily shown out. The boys kept silent while the state funeral for Lord Moyne and Corporal Fuller took place in a hushed Cairo. The flag-draped coffins, borne on gun caissons, moved to the slow beat of funeral drums through the thronged streets, in a procession nearly a mile long, followed on foot by Prime Minister Ahmed Maher Pasha, by turbaned leaders of the Moslem world, by the highest ranking Allied and Egyptian officials, behind them row upon row of men and women of the uniformed forces of a dozen nations, until it reached All Saint's Cathedral, where services were held for His Majesty's Minister in the Middle East.

Suddenly, on the eve of the third day, Salzman composedly turned to his guard and said, "I have a statement to make."

His real name, he said, was Eliahu Bet Zouri, twenty-two, a surveyor, of Tel Aviv. His associate was Eliahu Hakim, seventeen, a student, of Haifa. As had been surmised from the first, both were members of the terrorist Stern group—more formally known as the Fighters for the Freedom of Israel. "We came to Egypt at our organization's order and carried out our assignment according to instructions." Lord Moyne had been chosen because he headed the Middle East division of the British government; he was the symbol of British rule in Palestine; he had been responsible for carrying out oppressive policies intolerable to the Jewish Nationalists of Palestine. Bet Zouri then shut up. He would say no more until the courtroom.

Zaki Pasha was most impressed. With great courtesy he proffered a cigarette to Bet Zouri and lit it for him. "Why not tell us something of your movement," he suggested. "It will make things easier for you."

Bet Zouri inhaled deeply. "I appreciate your question, Colonel," he said, his eyes showing the slightest glint of amusement. "But you know I cannot tell you that."

His interrogator pressed on. "Surely you have colleagues in Cairo who assisted you?"

Bet Zouri only shook his head.

Zaki Pasha sighed. "My dear young friend—" he began. Then for several minutes he urged him in flowery Arabic to disclose the plot. He concluded, "You hold your life in your own hands. You know the gallows awaits you. But if you cooperate, it may be possible—" He gestured delicately. Zaki Pasha had no love for the Zionists, so busy remaking Palestine in their own image, but as an Egyptian nationalist, he had even less affection for the British. "This is still Egypt, not England—"

Bet Zouri's smile was regretful. "I cannot," he said. Then, after a pause, "Do not mistake me, my Colonel." His Arabic was as beautifully turned as the other's. "I love life and I love it well, but honor first must be served."

Zaki Pasha knew when he was defeated.

"So be it," he said, and withdrew.

In Palestine, as the terrible truth was confirmed, the cry rose: excommunicate the terrorists! The Jewish Agency exhorted the population: drive them from their places of hiding, flay them from their jobs, pluck them out of the schools, tear out this cancer which shames us before the world!

At the same time flying squads of British police struck villages and towns, cordoned them off, set up huge wire cages into which they herded all Jewish males to be questioned and searched: they threw into prison hundreds even vaguely suspected of contact with terrorists. Steel-helmeted officers armed with tommy guns, assisted by British troops, patrolled Jewish areas in armored cars, and from 6 P.M. to 6 A.M. a curfew was imposed on all Jewish quarters in the major cities of Palestine.

"Our very existence is at stake," warned the Jewish Agency, as the community tensely awaited Britain's reaction to the crime.

32

They could not know that for many hours Winston Churchill had debated whether to halt summarily all Jewish immigration into Palestine—and finally abandoned the idea lest it only drive more Jews into the extremist camp.

On November 17, 1944, eleven days after the deed, Churchill delivered his eulogy to Moyne in the House of Commons. He spoke heavily and bitterly. The Jews of Palestine, he said, had lost a far better friend than they knew. "This shameful crime has shocked the world," he went on. It had affected "none more sharply than those, like myself, who in the past have been consistent friends of the Jews and constant architects of their future." He spoke slowly, choosing his words with care. "If our dreams for Zionism are to end in the smoke of assassins' guns and our labors for its future to produce only a new set of gangsters worthy of Nazi Germany," then many, like himself, would "have to reconsider the position we have maintained so consistently and so long in the past."

In Jerusalem Dr. Leo Kohn, political advisor to the Agency, turned to a group of correspondents who had been listening with him to Churchill's broadcast words. There were tears in his eyes. "When I think how proud we have been that Zionism could come before the world with clean hands as a creative movement of the highest order, and when I think of what these boys have been led to do—" Helplessly he clenched his fists. "It is something so exasperating, so awful and dreadful—" He could not go on.

In their separate cells in Bab-al-Khalk prison, cross-legged on their prayer mats, the boys awaited their trial. They would not recognize the authority of the Egyptian courts; their deed was one whose implications were so broad that they extended beyond the boundaries of any one country—they must be tried before a supranational court, a true international court.

Nonetheless, the three most celebrated attorneys in Egypt were appointed by the state to defend them. Bet Zouri met with one, Hassan Djeddaoui, a plump, bespectacled little man, most eloquent pleader in the country. Whether they liked it or not, he informed Bet Zouri, they were to be tried before an Egyptian court and he wanted to help them.

"What is the use of your making a defense of us," Bet Zouri demanded. "We will be hanged and we are ready to be hanged. Your country belongs to the English and surely they want us hanged."

Djeddaoui remonstrated with him. "We lawyers believe in the law. We will do all that is possible. Beside, we are as adverse to the English as you are."

Bet Zouri shrugged. If they could not appear before an international court, they would make the best of it. But he and his companion would prepare their own case, their own defense. They still wanted no attorneys. Would their jailors be good enough to provide them with a Bible, the Egyptian Penal Code and a good modern history of Egypt?

Busily they set to writing.

CHAPTER

3

Explaining the nature of individual terrorism, Itzhak Yizernitsky, who as Shamir, the operations commander of the Stern group, planned the death of Moyne, once said: "A man who goes forth to take the life of another whom he does not know must believe one thing only—that by his act he will change the course of history."

This is the fundamental fact to be remembered about the two Eliahus.

But there are other fascinating facts about the two. They belonged to the same small band of conspirators, had even participated in the same terrorist acts, yet did not meet until they came to Cairo on the eve of the deed. Each was uniquely suited for his role. Both were skilled marksmen, Hakim the most expert shot in the Stern group, Bet Zouri the best grounded and most articulate exponent of Sternist views. Thus, the one assigned to fire at Moyne would not be likely to miss; and if they were caught, the other would prepare an eloquent defense before the world.

Both boys were products of their time. Like highly sensitive instruments, they reflected with extraordinary fidelity what life could do to young people living under an alien government at a time when national freedom became the one cause in their lives, the sum of all their dreams. They had few private dreams. The struggle in which they were involved took up their future as far as they could see. Convinced that there must be a free and independent Israel, they hoped that it would come in their time. To this end they subordinated every personal desire. They were not alone. Virtually every boy, every girl, in the Jewish community of Palestine took part in one movement or another. Only the mean and the simple kept to the bars and cafés.

The two Eliahus joined, as it turned out, the tiniest, the most dangerous and the most extreme movement because they thought its analysis the most realistic, its approach the most effective.

Although their backgrounds were different and their personalities quite opposite, we find interesting parallels in their lives. Their impressionable years coincided with some of the most violent chapters of Palestine history. Eliahu Bet Zouri was born in Tel Aviv in the wake of the Arab riots of 1921; Eliahu Hakim was brought to Haifa from neighboring Beirut at the age of six, a few months before the Arab demonstrations of 1933. Each made his way by different roads to the same conclusion: that Britain would not give up Palestine unless forced to; that freedom would be won only by fighting for it and that if it was to be won, Jewish zealots patterned after those who twenty centuries ago rose up against the might of Rome must now rise up against the might of Britain. Of all the movements which attracted Jewish youth—the semiofficial Haganah, the underground Irgun and the even more secretive Stern, it was the last—single-minded, fanatic and sacrificial—to which the two Eliahus finally gravitated.

So clandestine was this group that parents of members did not know they belonged. That the Jewish community itself considered the Sternists outlaws, their activities treason to the Zionist cause, their philosophy of terrorism counter to every Jewish ethic, did not matter. Indeed, this seemed only to enhance the element of martyrdom that made them feel one with Bar Kochba, Judas Maccabeus, the Hasmonaeans—the heroes of Biblical Israel and Judea, each a David pitted against an army of Goliaths.

Thus the deed in Cairo was a long time in the making, and the plight of the Children of Israel through the centuries was part and parcel of it.

What kind of boys were these?

Eliahu Bet Zouri, the older, was a scholar—and a skilled maker of bombs. He fainted at the sight of blood—yet threw himself into the most dangerous assignments. He read avidly in three languages and enthusiastically translated into Hebrew such disparate writers as Kipling, Stephen Leacock and William Saroyan—the first for his poetry of action, the second for his inspired nonsense, the third for his originality, his freshness of style and humor. Eliahu Bet Zouri was, by every evidence, a good son and friend, respected for his integrity, intelligence and judgment—and with all this he took human life.

As to Eliahu Hakim, dapper, darkly handsome, some of his friends thought of him as a playboy. He was called "Roxy," after a popular Haifa dance hall. But he felt himself an heir to the kingdom of David and wrote fervently of his namesake, the prophet Eliahu, and the Galilean hills upon which he walked. He belonged to one of Palestine's wealthiest families—yet once in the underground, he lived in near starvation, giving his pocket money, his clothes, all he possessed to the movement. He could be as steel in terrorist attacks requiring extraordinary self-control—yet he melted before his mother's tears. He bitterly denounced as "men without conscience" those who dined and wined in Tel Aviv cafés while a shipload of refugees foundered on the Palestine shore—yet he, too, killed.

Thus, the two Eliahus.

To his family, Eliahu Bet Zouri was a *Wunderkind*—an exceptional child. He was born February 12, 1922, of a family which on his mother's side was rooted in the Sephardic Jewish community of Palestine for generations. His father, born Moshe Steinhaus, in

Minsk, Russia, had been brought to Palestine shortly after the turn of the century. Steinhaus in German means "stone house." Once in Palestine the name was Hebraized to Bet Zouri, meaning a man from "Bet Zour"—House of Rock. Bet Zour was also the name of the last fortress held by Hebrew patriots under Judas Maccabeus when they revolted against Syria in 168 B.C. Eliahu's very name reinforced his sense of identification with the heroic past.

In the early 1900's Palestine was just another backward district in the vast, somnolent Ottoman empire. Education was not compulsory. But Moshe Bet Zouri, with the family thirst for knowledge, enrolled at the Alliance Israelite Universelle, a school system operated by a French-Jewish educational society. He was a brilliant student; entering at fourteen he completed the eight-year course in four, and was offered a teaching scholarship in Paris. He refused: Palestine was his home. Fluent in French, German, Turkish, Hebrew and English now, he nevertheless took a job in a local winery, and within a few years was its manager.

With Britain's defeat of Turkey in World War I, and her acceptance of the League of Nations mandate over Palestine, based on her promise in the Balfour Declaration to establish a Jewish National Home, the Holy Land emerged from Ottoman rule. Under the new British regime Moshe Bet Zouri, now thirty-one, was appointed a clerk in the Jaffa post office, where he could make good use of his linguistic abilities. A year before, he had married Rachel Baruch, a delicate girl whose family had fled Spain in the fourteenth century when Jews were burned at the stake unless they renounced their faith. The Bet Zouris and their infant daughter Deborah moved to Tel Aviv, the new, all-Jewish suburb of Jaffa. Here, two years later Eliahu was born.

Small, plump, uncomplaining, he was remembered for his blond curls and the unchildlike gravity with which he surveyed the world about him.

One day when he was seven he jumped from a high wall, apparently because no other youngster dared try it. The fall stunned him; he was hospitalized for several months. Precisely how he was

38

injured, no one knew. One diagnosis was that his heart had been "jarred out of place." So his family believed. His mother spent hours at his bedside, lavishing all her attention on him. When he was brought home, family life centered about him. He was to be ailing most of his youth. His second sister, Aviva, two years younger, remembers that if an especially succulent piece of meat was on the dinner table, she felt guilty asking for it. Everyone knew it was for Eliahu.

But compared to this, the world outside was vastly different. For Eliahu, violence, or tales of violence, were part of his growing up. He heard his parents speak of it and read the horror of it in their faces; of the riots of 1921, the year before his birth, when Arabs attacked Jewish immigrants in Haifa; of his father's escape from harm because friendly Arabs in the post office warned him not to come to work—rioters would roam the streets assaulting Jews that day.

Now, in 1929, came a new outburst of Arab terror. The screams of rioters running amok resounded through the narrow streets. Eliahu could tell of being carried by his father through a window to the safety of the synagogue next door. His playmates could tell of being ordered to lie under the bed, listening, terrified, until the wild shooting outside subsided. Word came that a whole family down the street had been massacred. Then every family bolted its doors and waited, scarcely daring to breathe. "The family Unger has been wiped out. . . ." Rioters had slaughtered them and then committed unspeakable indignities on their bodies.

History, even to a small boy, seemed forever repeating itself. For the children of Eliahu's generation were the children and grandchildren of men and women who had similarly bolted their doors against pogroms in Poland and Russia.

In 1931, when Eliahu was nine, his father was made postmaster of the half-Jewish, half-Arab city of Tiberias. Here Eliahu began to blossom out. He became a gay, teasing, not always manageable youth. Though forbidden physical training in school because of his health, he insisted upon taking part in the most strenuous games after school, challenging his friends to running and wrestling matches—and usually winning. It was as though he had to prove his courage and strength.

Eliahu loved Tiberias. Here he perfected his Arabic, and began to display his own linguistic ability. With Palestine under British rule, he knew English well. Hebrew was his first language; from his mother and his widowed grandmother, a tiny, beshawled old lady who lived in Jerusalem, he learned Ladino, the medieval Castilian dialect used by Sephardic Jews. Later he would take up French and Italian. He began reading every book he could find.

From the first he devoured the history of his country. In the Galilee ancient Israel was laid out before him: every hill, every stream, bore the name it bore in the Bible, given it by his ancestors. Israel had been in bondage to the Romans, the Syrians, the Greeks. It had rebelled; it had won its freedom only to be defeated and dispersed again. It had had to fight time and again to exist. That it should once again be doing so did not seem strange.

By the time Eliahu and his friends were ten and eleven in the early 1930's, they were running between guardposts with food and illegal ammunition for members of the Haganah, the secret volunteer homeguard defending the area against Arab raids. The British, insisting that law and order was their concern, refused to allow a Jewish defense militia; therefore, what arms and ammunition the Haganah could obtain were "illegal"; anyone caught with them was sent to prison. The British treated Arabs and Jews, the raiders and the defenders, as equally guilty before the law.

By the time he was twelve, Eliahu hated the British.

The atmosphere of crisis was intensified with the arrival in Palestine of the first Jewish refugees from Nazi Germany. Newspaper headlines alternated between Arab attacks at home—THREE JEWS KILLED IN RAID . . . SETTLEMENT BURNED IN NORTH—and the latest European dispatches reporting Hitler's campaign against the Jews.

Eliahu had just marked his thirteenth birthday when Moshe Bet Zouri was reassigned and the family moved back to Tel Aviv. Eliahu's father was never to earn a great deal: the Bet Zouris lived frugally in a tiny flat. There was a third daughter, Lea, now five; and a year later, a second son, Uri. None of the five children had his own room. Eliahu, like the others, had a corner for his books, possessions and clothes, which no one disturbed. His father was a rather remote, methodical man who rarely showed emotion; his main interests outside his job were chess and his Masonic lodge. Because of the conflicts rising from the difference in communal backgrounds of mother and father, it was not always a happy household.

At Balfour Grammar School Eliahu was, his father remembered, a "turbulent" boy. He had little respect for the pompous; he was something of a practical joker and more than once his father was summoned to school to smooth over matters. But there were compensatory qualities. "When I want the class to do something, to do it well," the principal told the elder Bet Zouri, "I have only to refer to your son to influence them." His grades were excellent; he was quick on his feet; once called upon to read his homework assignment—an essay on Jack London, whom he admired—Eliahu rose and read aloud from his notebook for several minutes. "Very good," his teacher commented. Would he hand over the theme? It would be put on the bulletin board.

Eliahu turned crimson and began to stammer. He had written nothing. "I just made it up as I went along," he confessed.

In his last year at school he met a boy named Adi Landau. This relationship, begun in school and enduring the remainder of Eliahu's life, was to play an important part in his thinking. Adi, small, slight, emaciated, with huge brown eyes in a narrow face, was a scholar and a dreamer, a nonconformist to whom any kind of coercion was galling. Like others in his family, he refused to follow dietary laws or observe the Sabbath. He was capable of fiery enthusiasms—and like Eliahu, he was a patriot from his knee-pants days.

To Eliahu's memories of waiting with his family for Arab rioters to attack, Adi could add stories told by his mother of her revolutionary days in Russia. A member of the Social Democrats, the anti-

Czarist underground, she had been jailed at eighteen by the secret police. She had escaped and fled to Switzerland. Later she migrated to Palestine.

Here, at twenty-three, she married Isaac Landau, a writer and educator of astonishing single-mindedness. Born in Odessa, he had come to Palestine in World War I with a group of Zionist teachers who felt that Hebrew education was doomed under the Bolsheviks. He was so passionately devoted to the idea of a Hebrew renaissance that he would speak no other language at home, neither Russian while he was still in Russia, nor Yiddish when he migrated. To Landau, Yiddish, the *lingua franca* of Eastern European Jewry, was the language of despair, of defeat, of the humiliation of the ghetto.

Not surprisingly, his son Adi was a Hebrew nationalist from birth.

He and Eliahu became close companions. Together they read about the Dreyfus case, catapulted to their attention by his death. As though anti-Semitism in Dreyfus' time were not enough, the papers were full of the anti-Semitic slurs hurled at French Premier Leon Blum, and of Hitler's appalling measures against the Jews. Eliahu wrote bitterly in his exercise book of a Germany "squatting in a lake of Jewish blood." And underscoring all this was the beginning of new Arab disturbances in Palestine.

The troubles of 1921 and 1929 had been only a foretaste. For the next three and a half years—1936 until September, 1939, when World War II broke out—the Arabs were to loot, terrorize, shoot, rape, attack Jewish settlements and lay waste to farms. The Mufti of Jerusalem, encouraged by Axis successes in Abyssinia and Central Europe, had seized power among the Palestine Arabs. What began as a six-month strike against increased Jewish immigration turned into a guerrilla war in which Arab extremists did not hesitate to attack their own moderates and even the British.

The British Administration, hoping to appease the Arabs, met this challenge halfheartedly. It became unsafe for Jews to venture outside the Jewish quarters of the cities, or to travel in the country without armed guard. Passing an Arab shop one might hear a record chanting in Arabic, "Slaughter the Jews!" Photographs of Hitler began to spring up in Arab barber shops and cafés, side by side with those of the Mufti. Youngsters in Arab villages marched about waving small swastika flags.

In school Eliahu, Adi and their friends held furious debates. What was to be done? British forces in Palestine, now numbering 15,000 troops, seemed unable to cope with the bombs thrown into open Jewish markets, the almost daily ambush of Jewish buses on the main Tel Aviv-Jerusalem road, the shooting and mutilation of Jewish travelers. At the same time they regularly raided Jewish farms and settlements to seek out the guns and ammunition which the Haganah had stored there for defense. And the British in such instances clung stubbornly to the letter of the law. When Jews were found with arms, the sentences were staggering—up to seven years in prison for possession of a pistol. Arabs, however, were usually let off far more leniently. There was no question where the mandatory's favor, now pro-Jewish, now pro-Arab, lay at this juncture of Palestine history.

In the midst of this turmoil the two boys graduated from grammar school. Eliahu won a four-year scholarship to Balfour High School. Recommending him, his principal, Mrs. Hararit, wrote, "The pupil Eliahu Bet Zouri is honest, industrious, intelligent. We find him a responsible youth of high character."

But Eliahu had other matters on his mind than the plaudits of his teachers. In Adi's memory book, on their graduation day, June 16, 1936, there is an entry in ink:

> *Adi:*
> *Flourish*
> *For your people*
> *And yourself!*
> —ELIAHU

In Eliahu's book, Adi had written:

43

Eliahu:
Never forget the responsibility
For the future of your people.
—Adi

Such sentiments, exchanged between fourteen-year-old boys, did not go unnoticed. Both received invitations that summer to join the National Cells, a discussion group of students selected for their intelligence and qualities of leadership.

The invitation came in a little note the two boys found in their books when they returned from recess one day.

"Eliahu—you have been chosen," the note to Eliahu Bet Zouri read.

It was the beginning of the road that was to lead to Cairo.

In Haifa, two hours' drive northward along the Mediterranean coast, Simon Hakim, importer of fine silks, that summer of 1936 moved his family into a spacious house on Panorama Road, on Mount Carmel, high above Haifa Bay. Three years had passed since he had brought his wife, his four sons and his daughter with him from Beirut, Lebanon, and transferred his business to Haifa. It had been a risk but from the first his trade prospered. Simon, born in Damascus of a Jewish community reaching back 2,500 years, had always hoped to live in Palestine.

Simon Hakim had no idea that for his fourth and youngest son, nine-year-old Eliahu—the other Eliahu—his move was also the beginning of the road leading to Cairo.

CHAPTER

4

AT THIS POINT one must see the structure of Jewish Palestine—this extraordinary community in which the two Eliahus were growing up. Only a few decades before it had been a closed and antique world, more like a Biblical engraving come to life than a modern society, peopled by pious Jews who had come to die in the Holy Land in the belief that thus they would be first to be judged by God on Judgment Day. They lived principally in the four ancient and blessed cities of the Bible, Jerusalem, Tiberias, Safad and Hebron, on contributions from co-religionists throughout the world.

Now, however, Jewish Palestine, with its population of more than 450,000, was in a ferment of growth and development. It was no longer a museum piece. It was peopled by pioneers who had come to build and redeem a forgotten land, and in the doing, build new lives for themselves—men and women who brought with them dreams of Jewish independence and dignity.

They had "come up" to Palestine in successive waves of immigration. The first *Aliya,* or coming-up, had taken place in 1881 in the wake of pogroms after the assassination of Czar Alexander II of Russia. Another wave had come in 1904—among them Bet Zouri's grandfather—again at the end of World War I, again in the mid-twenties, and now, again, in the early thirties.

This influx increasingly reflected the dictum of Theodor Herzl and the First Zionist Congress which he convened in Switzerland in 1897: the Jewish problem, however it may be described, stemmed from Jewish homelessness, and Zionism would answer that homelessness by providing the Jews with a "publicly-assured, legally secured home" in Palestine. Through the political leadership of Dr. Chaim Weizmann and his colleagues, the Balfour Declaration had been obtained from Britain in 1917 pledging her to facilitate the establishment of a Jewish National Home in Palestine.

There were difficulties, to be sure, for the British had made promises to the Arabs as well. But the Zionists hoped that the world would see the justice of their claim. They pointed out that the same world war that had produced the Balfour Declaration had, thanks to Allied victory, given the Arabs sovereignty over 99 percent of the Middle East, with new, independent Arab states in Transjordan, Iraq, Syria, Lebanon, Saudi Arabia; they had been given this vast area with the understanding that Palestine, representing the remaining 1 percent, would be set aside for the Jews.

The Zionists had formed the Jewish Agency as an official body to cooperate with the British in all matters related to the goal of a Jewish National Home. But within the Zionist ranks there were differences as to the way to reach that goal.

The leaders of the World Zionist Movement, headed by Dr. Weizmann, and in Palestine the largest political party, the Labor Mapai, headed by David Ben-Gurion, believed in building up the country immigrant by immigrant, settlement by settlement. This meant the establishment of a world-wide complex in which thousands of youngsters in Eastern and Central Europe were trained in agriculture and basic skills to become *haluzim* (pioneers) in Palestine. When they obtained immigration certificates from the British they would emigrate to Palestine, to turn swamp and desert into farm and garden, to build kibbutzim, or collective settlements, to create a new society based on their own labor and to normalize the lives of a people who for centuries had been forced into nonproductive, entrepreneur roles. It meant the collection of vast sums—some of it in nickels and dimes—from Jews throughout the world to buy land in Palestine on which to settle the colonizers, land that would be owned in perpetuity by the Jewish people so there would be no opportunity for exploitation and speculation.

Gradually the population and the country would be built up, and in the end, a Jewish majority achieved and a Jewish state proclaimed. As Dr. Weizmann the statesman-scientist pointed out, a Jewish commonwealth had to be built carefully, painstakingly, scientifically—especially in so backward an area as Palestine—or the whole experiment might fall of its own weight.

But though gradualism was supported by the vast Zionist majority, it was attacked by Vladimir Jabotinsky, a fiery Russian-born writer, orator and political leader, one of the most controversial figures in Zionist history. A man of tremendous personal magnetism, denounced by many as a dangerous adventurer, even a fascist, praised by others as a prophetic statesman, Jabotinsky demanded an immediate independent Jewish state with the historic boundaries of Palestine—Transjordan as well as Palestine. He opposed Mapai's emphasis on trained agricultural pioneers, collective and cooperative development of the land. He preached military preparedness. "It is necessary to plant and to plow, yes," he said, "but it is also necessary to shoot." He admired the British; he felt that Jewish statehood would be won with their help, but in the end, he insisted, Jewish independence would have to be achieved by force of Jewish arms.

To carry out his program—his revision of what he considered was the too moderate Zionist blueprint—he founded his own movement, the Revisionist Zionist party, in the early 1920's.

During World War I Jabotinsky had helped found the Jewish Legion, which fought with the British against the Turks; later, he had been one of the founders of the Haganah. About the time he organized his Revisionist party, he also created a military youth movement, called Betar, with almost mystical overtones. As with so many Hebrew titles, the word has a double meaning. It honored

Captain Joseph Trumpledor, a World War I hero who died in 1920 defending a Jewish settlement from Arab attack; it was also the name of Bar Kochba's fortress in his revolt against the Romans. Thus to its members it symbolized heroism and revolt. Betar boys drilled in black-shirt uniforms after Garibaldi's Freedom Fighters; they marched with flags and trumpets, and saluted with split-second precision, and so idolized their leader, Jabotinsky, that his photograph hung in their homes as an object of veneration.

Jabotinsky's emphasis on militarism and the leadership principle was anathema to the majority of Jewish Palestine. They argued that Jews had suffered too much from such phenomena to tolerate them in the new society they were building. But the cleavage between the Revisionists and the Zionist majority was nowhere more bitter than in their reactions to the problem of growing Arab violence. The Revisionists demanded immediate revenge for each attack; the great majority, however, preached self-restraint—or, in Hebrew, *havlagah*. The moral structure of Zionism would be undermined, they insisted, by any bloodshed save in absolute self-defense. Instead of retaliation, far better was "constructive resistance"—not an eye for an eye, not a dead Arab for a dead Jew, but for every Jewish comrade who fell, a new kibbutz built, another swamp reclaimed, another village founded.

Finally in April, 1937, the split over self-restraint broke into the open in the Haganah, which was made up of a majority of liberal labor members and a minority of Revisionist members. The Revisionist minority broke into two groups: the more extreme emerged as the Irgun Zvai Leumi—or National Military Organization—led by one of Jabotinsky's devoted disciples, David Raziel. Among Raziel's chief colleagues was Abraham Stern, a thirty-year-old poet-revolutionist, who was later himself to break away from the Irgun and form an even more extremist group.

The Irgun proclaimed that it would not accept the authority of the Jewish Agency; it would return blow for blow with the Arabs; it would consider itself the nucleus of the army of the Jewish state-to-be. It began to arm itself with rifles, bombs, machine guns, hand grenades. It set up a military table of organization and established military discipline. It would issue communiqués after each action; its members, if arrested, would demand treatment as prisoners of war.

It threw down the gauntlet to the Arabs—and to the world.

As in a mirror the young people of Jewish Palestine reflected this political *sturm und drang*. They were a breed apart. Native-born, knowing no other country, they were determined not to live furtive and fearful in a world which seemed made for everyone but themselves. In any event, they would not duplicate the lives their parents had led in the old country.

It is impossible in Palestine to grow up without joining a youth movement stemming from one party or another. In school, classwork and politics—the humanities and the problems facing the Jews—were almost indistinguishable. What was their future in Palestine? In the lands of the dispersal, the Diaspora? What kind of society should be created in Palestine? People strode about the streets of Jerusalem talking of the first Jewish state in two thousand years. Was this possible or was it utter fantasy? Was this turning back the clock or an advance toward Utopia so daring, so breathless in its conception, that most of the world could not comprehend it? And in the building of this society or state, what should be their attitude toward the Arabs who contested ownership of the country with them? Toward Great Britain?

The youth movements were as varied as the approaches to the problem.

There was the Hapoel Hatzair, affiliated with the Labor Party. There was the Maccabees, a sports and physical culture group, affiliated with the liberal right, or General Zionist party, which believed in a free enterprise system.

There was the left-wing socialist Hashomer Hatzair, which believed in a bi-national Arab-Jewish State in which both cultures would fuse into an independent Palestine.

There was Betar, the militant youth movement of the Revisionist party—"Jabotinsky's boys playing at soldiers," as it was called by the Laborites.

49

The National Cells, the youth movement to which Eliahu Bet Zouri and his friend Adi received so melodramatic an invitation, was a very special organization. Ostensibly a discussion group, actually it was a reservoir from which the Irgun Zvai Leumi planned to draw its leaders of the future—superior youngsters to whom it would "first give ideas—then guns." Their Tel Aviv cell, made up of ten boys and two girls, each as carefully selected as Eliahu and Adi, was led by a twenty-two-year-old girl, Esther Raziel, sister of David Raziel, commander of the Irgun. It is worth knowing something about Esther for she had a great influence on young Bet Zouri.

Esther had been brought to Palestine from Russia as a child. She had been "born a Zionist." Her father told her he had been a Zionist since the age of four when he woke one night to see *his* father sitting on the floor, his clothes rent, his hair disheveled, rocking back and forth and weeping for the fall of Jerusalem nearly nineteen centuries before.

This was an ancient custom. Biblical Jerusalem had been besieged for three frightful weeks by Roman legions in 70 A.D. They had destroyed the Temple, razed Jerusalem, slaughtered the men by the thousands and taken the women and children into slavery. Ever since, on the anniversary, religious Jews would awake at midnight and sit on the floor lamenting the loss of Jerusalem as one would mourn the death of a loved one. They mourned it not only as a city but as a symbol of their dignity as a people. All over the world their prayers rose. "If I forget thee, O Jerusalem—" Esther's father had seen his father weeping, and had been deeply moved. His father told him why he wept; and he knew, then, that he was in the Diaspora, in the galuth, in *exile*—and he became a Zionist, one who dreamt of the day when he could go forth from exile and into the land of his people.

Esther and her brother David, like Adi had been reared exclusively in Hebrew. Their parents refused to let them attend Russian schools lest their Hebrew culture be tainted. For Esther, as for her brother, "our" meant Palestine—not the Russia into which they had been born, in which they lived on sufferance, within a Pale of

Settlement, their rights intolerably restricted, sorry subjects of a government that periodically used anti-Semitic pogroms to siphon off public discontent.

This was the young woman, sturdy, dark-eyed and impassioned, who now taught Eliahu Bet Zouri and his friends.

Her group met with her after school, usually in her apartment, three times a week. Sometimes they packed picnic lunches and, avoiding the Arab areas, hiked to the plain of Sharon. Sitting under the trees, they read stenciled pamphlets of Israel in the days of her greatness. It was Esther's duty to guide these discussions and especially to find parallels between past and present. She lectured them on Jewish history and gave them pamphlets dealing with the heroic revolts of other nations: the Irish against Britain (the IRA in Dublin sent a plentiful supply of its literature); the Greeks against the Turks; the Americans against George III; Robert Emmet, Michael Collins, Garibaldi and Mazzini, Lord Byron, Washington and Nathan Hale, were names held up to them. They read Josephus' *History of the Jewish War,* and analyzed the failure of the Jewish rebellion in 70 A.D. They studied the story of Spartacus: why did that revolt against Rome fail in the first century B.C.?

Often their meetings would end with dancing of the hora, and then exhilarated and exhausted, still disputing, still debating, they would walk in little groups through Tel Aviv's dark, narrow streets until they came to the Oriental quarter on the edge of Arab Jaffa. There they crowded into a tiny café and with kerosene lanterns flickering on their faces sat over midnight snacks of *pitah* and *felafel,* and talked and talked.

They were a happy group. They knew they had been chosen and they felt they were preparing for lives of significance.

Eliahu was one of Esther's favorites. At this stage he was a rather frail-appearing boy, somewhat short for his age, with the beginnings of a yellow mustache. Usually he wore a washed-out blue shirt with open collar, and khaki shorts and sandals. One rarely saw him when his eyes were not twinkling, or his fair skin was not sunburnt, his nose peeling, his hair recalcitrant no matter how much he tried to brush it down. Though he made friends easily, he never confided: he maintained a certain reserve no one dared encroach upon. He was a strange combination of toughness and sensitivity. Once, with two schoolmates, Amihai Paglin and David Danon, he visited a friend in a hospital. In an adjoining bed lay a man who had just been bled, as was the custom, for high blood pressure.

David said casually, "Look—on the floor."

Eliahu looked, saw a few drops of blood, and promptly fainted. He had to be taken home and put to bed for a day. It was a weakness he fought all through adolescence and which he finally conquered. It did not prevent him from throwing himself into any duty, the more dangerous the better, which Esther assigned. Among these duties were to patrol the streets to watch for Arab trouble-makers—in the alleys of Jaffa, Arabs hidden in doorways could suddenly leap out and attack a lone passer-by—to warn householders, to keep vigil on roofs. Esther preached resistance and retaliation. "Your elders tell you to wait and see. They say, Don't be hasty; never take weapons. I say to you, You'll have to take them before it's too late. You can depend only upon yourselves."

Although one of the youngest in the group, Eliahu was one of the leaders, always ready to debate, hotly, the content of a book, a speech or a newspaper editorial; he contributed essays and poems to the cells's publication, a three-sheet newspaper. One was a translation of Kipling's "If"; others were original verse to which he never signed his name. "I will sign my writings when they are good enough," he told friends.

He was the first to discover Franz Werfel's *The Forty Days of Musa Dagh,* and bring it excitedly before a meeting. He was enthusiastic about *Northwest Passage,* by Kenneth Roberts, and Jack London's *The Sea Wolf*—books that dealt with great acts of heroism. He and his fellow members wrote detailed critiques of the books. They had moments of high emotion. They read the stirring poetry of Chaim Nachman Bialik, who inveighed against the Jewish will to martyrdom through the centuries. Pogrom and massacre had been their history, Bialik thundered: why, why, why?

They read the fiery words of another contemporary poet, Saul

Tchernichovsky, who glorified the ancient rebels of Israel, attacked what he called the "sick spirituality" that had sapped the strength of the Jews, and exhorted Eliahu and his generation to noble deeds worthy of their ancestors. They were almost moved to cry out when Esther Raziel, in her eloquent voice, read from Tchernichovsky's *Pagan Sonnets:*

> *I kneel to life, to beauty and to strength,*
> *I kneel to all the passionate desires*
> *Which they, the dead-in-life, the bloodless ones,*
> *The sick have stifled in the living God,*
> *The God of wonders of the wilderness,*
> *The God of gods who took Canaan with storm,*
> *Before they bound Him in phylacteries.*

And sitting cross-legged on the floor of Esther's apartment— Eliahu never entered by the door if he could help it but came leaping through the open window—they chanted the verses of another poet, Uri Zvi Greenberg:

> *Whatever will be the future, already was in the past,*
> *And whatever was not, will never be.*
> *Therefore I trust in the future, because I have kept before me*
> *The image of the past: This is vision and song.*

And in a crescendo of emotion, Bialik's:

> *Warriors are we!*
> *Last in the era of bondage,*
> *The first to be free!*

Eliahu and Adi, outstanding in the National Cells, were to have chances soon enough to be warriors.

Shortly after their fifteenth birthday, in the early winter of 1937, they were ritually inducted into the secret underground, the conspiratorial military organization known as the Irgun Zvai Leumi.

As Eliahu was about to leave a National Cell meeting, carrying under his arm Voynich's *The Gadfly,* a novel of the struggle for Italian freedom, Esther Raziel came up to him and with a smile warm and all-enveloping took his hand in hers. She spoke softly. She whispered an hour, a place and a password.

CHAPTER

5

Eliahu stood, the beam of a flashlight blinding him, before a table.

Moments earlier, as he was led into the ancient Arab stone villa, he had been able to make out, as in a quick, dreamlike flash, that he was entering an enormous room, obviously the main living room. The small barred windows high in the walls had been covered with blankets so no light showed outside. Now he stood, blinking, and out of the darkness before him a deep voice spoke.

"Why do you wish to join us?"

"To fight for freedom," he replied.

"What do you know about us?"

He tried to answer as best he could. They were dedicated warriors fighting for the dignity of the Jewish people against Arab attacks; they would fight for the liberation of their people when the time came.

"What do you think you will have to do?"

"I don't know," he said lamely. "Fight. Make bombs. Throw grenades. Fight the Arabs so they will let us alone."

There was a rasping noise. A chair had been moved. He heard whispers. He waited.

He had carefully followed the directions on the note Esther Raziel gave him. At the appointed hour he had come to the place—the sidegate of the villa on the outskirts of Tel Aviv. In the darkness someone whose face he could not see approached him. He uttered the password: the other swung open the gate, told him to enter the building and mount the stairs to the second floor. There, in the darkness, another dimly-seen figure led him to a bench in a hall, and whispered, "Sit here and wait." As he waited, other boys arrived, one by one, every few minutes, to take their places in the darkness on the bench. Twenty minutes passed in complete silence save for the sound of breathing and moving of the others on the bench. Then someone touched his arm, under the elbow: he rose and was led through cool corridors until he came into the main room. He found himself standing in front of a table, before a black curtain. On the table stood a lone, flickering candle. Near it he could make out a heavy book—and resting on the book, a revolver, gleaming dull yellow in the candlelight.

Then, suddenly, the dazzling beam of the flashlight, and the questions.

"You understand," the voice began again. "You are here of your own free will?" It was an impersonal, unemotional voice. "You are yourself responsible when you join us. No one has forced you."

"I understand."

"You will carry out without question any order given you?"

"Yes."

The voice went on. "Suppose you are arrested. Will you know how to keep silent—no matter what they do to you?"

"Yes."

"You are not afraid of pain?"

He thought, It is a fighter's duty to stand pain, but said only, "They will get nothing from me."

There was silence for a moment. Then he found himself gently propelled forward until his body grazed the table. The voice behind the curtain said, "Place your left hand on the gun that is on the Bible, raise your right hand and repeat after me:

"I, Eliahu Bet Zouri, do solemnly swear full allegiance to the Irgun Zvai Leumi and to its commander—"

He repeated the words, his hand resting on the cold steel of the gun, his voice trembling despite himself:

"I, Eliahu Bet Zouri, do solemnly swear full allegiance to the Irgun Zvai Leumi and its commander—"

"To its goals and its aims—"

"To its goals and its aims—"

"And I am ready to make every sacrifice, even of my life—"

"And I am ready to make every sacrifice, even of my life—"

"Giving first preference at all times to the Irgun above my parents, my brothers, my sisters, my family—"

"Giving first preference at all times to the Irgun above my parents, my brothers, my sisters, my family—"

"Until we achieve a sovereign Israel—"

"Until we achieve a sovereign Israel—"

"Or death separates me from our ranks—"

"Or death separates me from our ranks—"

"So help me God."

"So help me God."

From behind the curtain a man appeared and shook hands firmly with him. Suddenly Adi was there, hugging him. Then others— Eliahu was astonished to see classmates from Balfour High School.

Once in the organization, like the rest he had no way of knowing its elaborate scope, nor its full membership. There was a five-man High Command that maintained authority over some 800 members, nearly all of high-school age. The remainder were men in their twenties and thirties who worked in the movement full-time. Eliahu never knew their true identity. They bore names like Gad or Issacha, out of the Bible. One man would have several aliases, and be known to each group by a different name, so that it would be almost impossible to trace him. When Eliahu joined, the organization was in the process of developing eight groups.

These were *Manpower,* or recruiting; *Planning,* reprisals against Arabs, raids on British arms depots and paymasters; *Training,* all the techniques of underground warfare; *Supplies,* warehouses for arms, stenciling machines for propaganda, Arab and British uniforms; *Maintenance,* manufacture of explosives, gun repair, forgery of identity cards, auto licenses; *Transportation,* organizing sympathetic cab drivers, auto and motorcycle owners; *Medical,* organizing sympathetic physicians, nurses and private hospitals; and *Actions,* those who took part in actual raids, bomb throwing and seizure of money or arms.

To this last group Eliahu and Adi were appointed. In Tel Aviv it was commanded by a dour young man of twenty-four named Arieh Yitzhaki. Yitzhaki, a plumber and electrician born in Russia, was a fighter who lived for action. He went off on operations himself, armed with grenades, dashing from roof to roof in an Arab attack, single-handedly repulsing a score of the enemy. To their intense pride, Eliahu and Adi became his assistants.

For the first six months they were on trial. Many of their assignments were boring, given them to see if they would carry them out however trivial they appeared to be. They counted trucks parked outside an arms depot; observed every visitor to the house of a suspected informer; kept notes on the coming and going of an Arab merchant.

Meanwhile, they met three nights a week, either in a schoolhouse for what purported to be a dance, boys and girls wearing their best for the occasion, or at someone's apartment for what purported to be a party. Guards and lookouts were carefully posted. At these meetings they learned sabotage (how much explosive to destroy objectives made of concrete, iron, brick); secret communication (writing with an invisible ink made of starch and water which turns brown when exposed to heat) and other underground techniques.

They also had to familiarize themselves with the geography of Tel Aviv and Jaffa, climb in and out, in daylight and darkness, of every house, every back yard, every cellar passageway, every roof, so that they could escape from any given location by half a dozen routes.

They had to march and drill in secret, usually on roofs or in lonely ravines, using broomsticks for rifles. They studied every make of pistol, gun and rifle—Czech, British, Italian, Belgian, French, Polish—so that blindfolded they could take apart and reassemble every weapon available in Palestine. None had ever seen an American Colt, but they memorized blueprints so they could use it if one fell into their hands.

Their instructors tried to instill in them a discipline far removed from the informal way of life of the collective and cooperative settlements. This reflected the philosophy of Jabotinsky, who sought to imbue his followers with *hadar* (dignity) to combat what he considered was the slackness permitted by a liberal Jewish tradition. The boys were given stenciled sheets with instructions for their behavior:

"When you sit before your commander, sit properly. Don't sprawl, don't lean against the back of the chair. Sit erect, your feet together, your arms folded or on your thighs.

"When your commander calls your name, leap to your feet and stand at attention until he tells you 'at ease.' When he gives you an instruction, salute him and say, *'Kidvarecka'* (As you say!)." Bet Zouri learned that this replaced "Yes, sir," which the organization, dissident even in its discipline, considered too much an inferior's response to a superior.

The boys were ordered to obtain a uniform made up of a khaki shirt, khaki shorts, knee-length khaki stockings, with epaulets for the shoulders. Each shirt was to have two pockets; the uniform had to fit neatly and a wide leather belt was to be worn. Actually, without epaulets and belt, the "uniform" was the usual garb of many non-Arabs in Palestine. Epaulets and belt, therefore, were never in evidence save at meetings.

They were also given a special adjuration: never to roll their shorts up on their thighs. This, again, was in protest against the casual life of the kibbutzim, where youngsters rolled up their shorts as high as they wished and flouted any attempt at regimentation.

Finally, the young Irgunists were told: "When you enter a meeting place, or leave, you must stand at attention even if no one is there: this, simply to honor the place. You are not to smoke, to whistle, to hum; you are to speak in a low voice, to serve without noise, to be serious and respectful toward your commander at all times. He is your instructor, educator and leader. He trains your hands for battle and your heart to be brave and heroic. He guides you in peacetime and he will stride before you in battle. Under his command you live and under his command you may die for your homeland.

"Give honor to him, therefore, salute him on duty and at all times in the street or elsewhere show respect for him."

They were to memorize these instructions, then destroy them.

After several months Yitzhaki sent Eliahu out to witness his first offensive action, a retaliation against the Arab owner of a leather shop who had thrown a bomb into a crowded Jewish market, killing and wounding a score of persons. Watching, Eliahu was astonished. It was like a basketball game. Half a dozen boys congregated about the shop. At a signal one boy, carrying the revolver, tossed it to a second, and ran; the second aimed, fired and ran in an opposite direction, as he did so tossing the gun to a third, who made off in still another direction. The others scattered. In a moment one saw only boys dashing off in all directions as though they were playing a game, a wounded Arab staggering out of his shop, and no weapon, no assailant anywhere to be seen.

Eliahu himself was proving resourceful and self-reliant. He was carefully observed by his company commander, a silent, nerveless, powerfully built youth named Itzhak Yizernitsky, who a few years later was to become the mysterious "Rabbi" Shamir, operations commander of the Stern group. Yizernitsky had lectured frequently at the National Cells. He noted Eliahu as a remarkable combination—a boy with a "warm heart and sharp mind."

Eliahu's alertness was brought forcibly to Yizernitsky's attention one summer evening in his room at 34 Balfour Street, in Tel Aviv. In an adjoining room Arieh Yitzhaki, assisted by Eliahu, was preparing a mine to be used the following night in a reprisal action in Jaffa.

Suddenly the door between the two rooms was flung open and Yitzhaki stood in the doorway, all flushed, and said excitedly, "Look at what this little one did here now! He saved you, me and all of us!" Yitzhaki, it turned out, had begun to wind the mechanism in the wrong direction. Eliahu had caught his hand just in time. The explosion would have blown up the entire house.

A few weeks later Yizernitsky took Eliahu to help burn down a street booth used to collect money for the defense fund of the Jewish community. Every bus and taxi passenger going out of town was assessed a few cents for protection against Arab attack. The Irgun opposed taxation for defense on the ground that Palestinian taxpayers were already paying the British to maintain law and order and if the British could not, then they should allow the Jews arms with which to protect themselves.

The two took gunpowder and a fuse. By error, a short, quick-burning fuse was used. Eliahu lit it—and before they were out of the booth, it exploded. Yizernitsky was scorched about the face. Eliahu, wearing a leather jacket and shorts, was badly burned on the thighs. Both managed to escape and though Eliahu was in agony, he uttered no word until they reached a friend's room. A sympathetic nurse was called and the two were taken by car to a friendly physician. Eliahu, exhausted and in great pain, still controlled himself. Later he was moved to the home of friends where he remained for nearly two weeks. His stoicism was remarkable. The boy never spoke about his pain. He did worry about his family, and a note was sent to them that he was well but unable to come home for a little while.

When, years later, a surgeon suggested removal of Eliahu's scars, he refused, saying, "No, scars befit a warrior."

It was not child's play. As the Arab troubles intensified, as the underground stepped up its reprisals, as the British seized and arrested, Eliahu knew the experience of comrades killed, jailed, tortured.

Some of his most effective companions were boys born in Iraq, Iran and Yemen. Among them was Zimri Aba, a silent, liquid-eyed youth from Bagdad who easily passed for an Arab and was often sent on missions into the heart of Arab areas.

One afternoon Zimri was assigned to avenge a savage raid on a Jewish bus. He brilliantined his hair, donned black and white striped trousers, blue jacket, red necktie, big handkerchief, red fez, tucked a leather briefcase under his arm and stepped out—the perfect figure of an effendi, or Arab gentleman. In the briefcase was one of Arieh Yitzhaki's time bombs.

Zimri strolled to an Arab bus waiting for passengers. He boarded it, placed his briefcase under his seat and sat back sleepily. When the bus was full and just before it was to leave, he hurried off as if remembering an errand, leaving the briefcase. The bus started: five minutes later, the bomb exploded. Three persons were killed, five wounded.

Next morning as newspapers carried the story to the horrified Jewish community, the latest Irgun communiqué was found under doors, pasted on walls and telephone poles. "On the night of May 15, in answer to an assault on the Natanya bus on May 10, one of our soldiers carried out an action on the bus to Kalkilieh—"

Two weeks later another of Eliahu's comrades, Yaacov Roz from Afghanistan, was sent on a mission to Jerusalem. Disguised as an Arab porter, wearing wide black pantaloons and white blouse, a small black skull cap on his close-cropped black hair, he prepared to take a huge wicker basket of vegetables, carried on his back and held in place by a rope across his forehead, to the Arab market at the Damascus gate of the walled Old City. Buried under the vegetables was a time bomb.

As he started off a passer-by stopped him. "Why do you go to market—"

Yaacov only smiled agreeably and continued on. He could not know a strike had been called that morning.

When he arrived at the market to find the shops dark, their iron shutters drawn, he stood for a moment, puzzled. It was long enough for a crowd of porters to descend on him, muttering, "Traitor . . . Scab!" He began to stammer explanations. Two men seized his basket and dumped its contents into the gutter. Amid the rolling cucumbers lay the bomb.

They set upon him with knives. He was stabbed a dozen times in the chest and face. Police rushed him to a hospital where he lay in critical condition. Agents of the CID—the Criminal Investigation Department of the British Palestine Police—sat at his bedside, day and night. To all questions he pointed to his tongue—it had been slashed—and used the pretext to remain silent. On the third night, fearing that in his delirium he might speak, he waited till his guard dozed, dug his fingernails into his wounds, tearing them open, and died of loss of blood that night. He died revealing nothing.

Their assignments involved not only retaliation against the Arabs: sometimes it meant punishment of informers among their own people. For this one had doubly to steel oneself—

Their commander would lecture them. "Your elders preach self-restraint. They say, 'Unless you are absolutely sure that only a guilty Arab will be punished, you cannot place a bomb.'

"We say, no. This is a war. The innocent must suffer with the guilty."

Their anonymous leader would look at his young listeners. "You think this is a terrible ethic, a terrible rationale, a terrible thing? I agree with you. It is terrible. But terrible things are being done to us."

To endanger one's own life, he would go on, was not too difficult. What was difficult was the inner voice that said, *It is wrong to take human life.* The powerful admonition in the Ten Commandments, *Thou shalt not kill,* was deeply ingrained in them as the People of the Book. He knew the conflict.

"Do you not think I feel this?" he would ask. "When you place a bomb, you see later what it does. Before it explodes, you walk among the people. You see them talking, gossiping, going about their work, harming no one. When you beat up a man who is an informer, you know you are beating up flesh and blood. You will hear him groan. You may even remember him as he was a moment before, or see him in your mind's eye sitting at his table with his family, eating, laughing, alert, a human being in full life and dignity.

"Yet this is the man you must beat. This is the man you must punish. This is the man to whom you can show no mercy—because he is your enemy."

His audience would listen in utter silence, only a sigh passing through them now and then—

Next their commander would discuss the action to be taken and lay down the rules. "When an action is over, no discussion. No mistakes. No post-mortems. To discuss it afterward is to demoralize yourself. You were ordered to do it, you did it, it was right."

And he would ask again and again:

"What is our cause? Our cause is to stop the Arabs from attacking us. To make them respect us. To make them let us alone so that we can build and create and go about our work."

Eliahu had just marked his sixteenth birthday when a shattering blow fell—his mother died of cancer of the throat. She had never been a happy woman, and what satisfaction she seemed to find derived mainly from Eliahu, her favorite. Now death came slowly, and after much suffering. Toward the end, she was unable to speak, and wanted only Eliahu at her bedside. For months afterward it was a subdued Eliahu who went about his duties. His father, busy at the post office from 8 A.M. to 6 P.M. six days a week, had little time for five children. He was almost helpless because of the tragedy, and Eliahu's grandmother came from Jerusalem for a while to cook and help care for the children. But it was Eliahu more than anyone else who took over management of the household, aided by his closest sister, fourteen-year-old Aviva. Somehow, too, he found time to be with the two youngest children, Lea, eight, and three-year-old Uri. He became their idol. He saw to it that Uri ate well and was properly dressed; he spanked Lea if she ran about too much in the sun. He spent every Saturday with them, either taking them boating on the Yarkon River, or picnicking on the nearby Mount Napoleon. Lea was panic-stricken at the idea of going in a rowboat but she had implicit confidence in Eliahu. With Eliahu, she thought, how could one be frightened? You were safe from all harm for Eliahu was strong and Eliahu knew everything.

He would take them to the river; they would watch as he carefully looked over the boats and chose the lightest and best; he would place them in it and start rowing. As he rowed, he sang, and they listened blissfully to him. Lea, years later, told how proud and high above everyone else she felt because only her brother Eliahu, she knew, could sing and row like that.

In the middle of the river he would stop his song and say, "Lea, come and take my place. Now it's your turn to row."

"But Eliahu, I can't move," she would cry, terrified, clinging to her seat. "The boat will tip over! Besides, I never in my life rowed a boat. I don't know how."

"Don't be frightened," he would say to her gently. "The boat won't tip over. Here, give me your hand."

She would stretch forth her hand to him, and while little Uri clung to his seat, trying not to show fear, Eliahu would help Lea to sit next to him, show her how to hold the oars, and after a few moments, like magic, she would be rowing with both hands. He never said much, nor did he compliment her. He would only say, "Very nice. Move toward me. Take the oars from my hand. Look deep in my eyes." And a little smile would show from under his mustache, and she would see the glint of humor in his eyes. Then she would smile at him despite herself as she bit her lips and lowered her eyes bashfully, her heart bursting with pride because she knew that she had pleased her brother Eliahu, her big brother who knew everything.

Indeed, a fascinating facet of Eliahu's personality was the ease with which he led his dual life. Among his closest school friends was Ada Ron, a petite, dark-eyed girl who was later to become a well-known actress. Eliahu visited her often; she was bright, witty and

65

level-headed. Sometimes he brought his classmate, David Danon. Frequently the three became involved in loud arguments, especially on the subject of self-restraint. Ada and David were both members of Haganah. "All right, you and your *havlagah*," Eliahu would say scornfully. "Child's play. The Haganah wants us to be quiet even if the Arabs provoke us."

"Yes, exactly," Ada would say hotly. "The Arabs are trying to get us into trouble. We'd play right into their hands."

Eliahu would shake his head. "No, no, you must fight back. Otherwise they take it as cowardice. They only respect force."

Sometimes Eliahu got involved in discussions with Ada's father on the rights of man. The elder Ron was a member of Mapai, and a life-long socialist. He enjoyed trying to draw the boy out. "You are young," he would say, after a long argument. "You can't force things. History has its own pace."

"No, it's not true," Eliahu would insist. "We must take steps to do things by ourselves, or history passes us by."

Once Ada entered a theme in a school contest: "How to Live in Peace with the Arabs." She won first prize. Proudly she showed her paper to Eliahu. He read it, his face a mask. "I wouldn't have given you a prize for this," he said.

"Why?"

"Because your thinking is not right. It's the thinking of the European Jews—wait, hope, everything will turn out all right if you wait and hope long enough."

Often he read poetry to her—as he was to do with all the girls he met—usually the stirring, patriotic verses of poets as different as Bialik and Byron. At one period he was deeply taken by Poe. Jabotinsky's Hebrew translation of "The Raven" and "Annabel Lee" were classics in Palestine because of the skill with which they approximated the haunting musical refrains of the original. Eliahu repeated, "Quoth the Raven, 'Nevermore,' " until Ada cried, "Stop! Stop!"

At another time he dashed in, all enthusiasm.

"I want to read something to you," he said, pulling out his notebook. "But if you say it's no good, I'm finished with you—you're not my friend any more!"

He read it to her. It was a delightful short story, charmingly told in Hebrew, of a boy whose uncle had his hair cut.

"Eli, that's excellent," she exclaimed. "Did you write it?"

"No, no," he said. "I wish I had." He had only translated it. It was the work of an Armenian writer in the United States named William Saroyan, he explained. "This man has something new—sparkling and honest. This is a fresh kind of literature, full of spirit."

He was so impressed that for days he went about reading it to friends. He even consulted a publisher about printing his translation.

Once he brought Ada a book of comic verse by Stephen Leacock. "It's a pity you don't understand English," he told her. "I'll translate it." And he did. He also read *Gone with the Wind* in English and insisted that she read it when it appeared in Hebrew.

They saw the film together when it came to Palestine. He was enchanted. He loved the characters, the costumes, the period. And Melanie—"Ah," he sighed. "This is the woman I love."

Ada adored him and so did her mother. Sometimes he would bring a nosegay to the older woman, present it to her, sniff and say, "What are you cooking in the kitchen? Is it good? Let me see." He would walk in and come back, grinning, to report that he had found everything fine.

Mother and daughter admired his good humor, his way of keeping them entertained, his refusal ever to turn the conversation upon himself. What they knew of him they knew in barest detail: that he was poor, that money was always a problem, that he had been sickly, that his mother had died recently and he missed her desperately, that he hoped to make a career as a writer, a critic or a teacher, and the university seemed far distant.

They knew, too, that he was full of odd, endearing impulses. At 10 P.M. he might suddenly say to Ada, "Let's take a walk." They would ramble through downtown Tel Aviv while he went on a nonsense penny shopping spree—loading her down with Eskimo pies, hard candies, toys, lollipops. She never found him a bore. He would say, a moment before anyone realized the need for it, "Well, I think it's enough. I think I'll go home."

Ada admired him because she found him genuine. If he said anything, he meant it. He was as clear as glass.

Yet in these years and the years to come she never knew of anything he did, was involved in, was wounded for, suffered for, in the underground life he had chosen.

CHAPTER

6

In JUNE, 1938, when Eliahu Bet Zouri was sixteen and Eliahu Hakim only eleven, an event occurred which vitally affected the future course taken by both boys. Shlomo Ben Josef, a nineteen-year-old youth, was hanged by the British— the first Jew to be executed in Palestine since the destruction of the Temple nearly nineteen hundred years before.

Ben Josef and two friends, Abraham Shein, seventeen, and Shalom Zurabin, eighteen, all members of the Revisionist youth movement Betar, decided to revenge an act of Arab terrorism. A Jewish taxi carrying five men and an eighteen-year-old girl had been ambushed on the Safad-Rosh Pinna road. The Arabs had shot the men dead, hacked their bodies to pieces before the girl's eyes, then had taken turns raping her.

The three boys armed themselves with guns and grenades and one afternoon waited for an Arab bus carrying passengers from Djouni, the village from which the raiders were known to have come. As the bus passed, they hurled a grenade at it. The grenade failed to explode, the bus raced on, no one was hurt.

On the way home a police patrol seized them. The British Administration, determined to make an example, indicted the three for murder. A military court found all guilty, but Zurabin was ordered to a mental institution and Shein's sentence commuted to life imprisonment because of his youth. Ben Josef was sentenced to hang.

The news shook the entire country.

Shops were closed, hundreds marched in demonstrations, the synagogues were crowded with other hundreds praying. In turn the British military commander in Palestine declared all demonstrations illegal and ordered curfews in the three cities of largest Jewish population—Tel Aviv, Jerusalem and Haifa.

Ben Josef's story fired the imagination—and sympathy—of many people. He had been born in Poland of a poor family and worked from childhood to support his parents. In 1936 he read of the Arab attacks on the Jews in Palestine; outraged, he had left his home and without passport, visa or money smuggled himself across the borders of Europe, somehow managing to reach Lebanon. He was taken aboard a small Greek fishing vessel, bound for Palestine. Halfway there the captain demanded money. When he learned the boy had none, Ben Josef was thrown overboard.

He swam to shore and after days of walking finally reached Rosh Pinna, a tobacco colony, where a Betar group took him in. When there was not enough work there, he hitchhiked to Haifa and found employment at the port, sending what money he made back to his group in the village.

His bearing in prison only intensified popular reaction on his behalf. The night before he was to be hanged in the ancient fortress jail of Acre, three friends were permitted to call on him. They found him smiling and confident. He had written on the wall of his cell, "You cannot conquer the top of the mountain unless you leave graves behind you."

It was in this climate that Eliahu Bet Zouri, Adi, Esther Raziel and others marched through the streets of Tel Aviv chanting, "Save Ben Josef!" The police fell upon them and laid about unmercifully with their truncheons. One scene always remained with Eliahu: the sight of an enormous English officer beating an unconscious man while Adi and the others tried vainly to stop him. Then Esther Raziel, herself so tiny that she scarcely reached the policeman's chest, marched up to him and calmly started to unbuckle his belt. He immediately grabbed his trousers; this gave Eliahu a chance to drag off the victim. He and Adi went home vowing vengeance against the tyrant.

In Jerusalem feelings were so intense that women demonstrators broke through police lines to march upon the residence of the new High Commissioner, Sir Harold MacMichael. Sir Harold, until a few months ago Governor of Tanganyika, was a lean, austere man known for his completely impersonal adherence to the letter of the law. He kept remote from the Jewish community and was, from the very first, one of the least liked officials in the country.

Although appeals had come from all parts of the world, Ben Josef was hanged. The accounts of how he went to his death swept the country. A Jewish officer in Acre prison, Reuven Hazan, who guarded the boy on his last night, wrote later:

I went to Haifa for a rabbi but couldn't find one to perform the last rites. I returned to Acre at 7 in the morning, an hour before the execution. At 6 A.M. they had dressed him in his civilian clothes—shorts and shirt, socks and work shoes. He was already awake and greeted me with a smile. There was no sign of excitement on his face. He had written his mother in Poland, "Beloved Mother, don't feel sorry for me. Try to forget me. Other sons of the Jewish nation finished their lives in far more despicable and tragic fashion." When I told him the rabbi had refused to come, he said he would resist being taken to execution unless he could make his confession to a rabbi. I said the British and the Arabs would not understand his resistance, but interpret it as fear. I suggested that he read with me some of the Psalms and this might take the place of confession. He agreed. So during the hour that remained I read chapters of the Bible and he repeated each sentence after me.

Then he insisted upon being hanged in his Betar uniform. "I won't die as a civilian—I acted as a soldier and I will die as a soldier." I told him this was impossible—he would be dragged to the gallows by force.

"Very well," he said. "Then I will go." But I had to promise to tell his friends that he wanted to wear his uniform.

A second eyewitness account, given by Sergeant Colt of the Acre Prison Detachment:

What impressed me most was the fact that until the last moment Ben Josef did not give up what we call "ceremony." I have seen men go to their deaths with their heads held high. But all of them during the last hours of their lives, when their hope for life was gone, forgot "ceremony"—after all, what mattered now how they stood or acted, since the end was here. This young man never forgot ceremony. He thought of what he had to say and what to wear. At seven o'clock in the morning, a few minutes before his execution, he brushed his teeth. This I have never seen in my life.

On the day of Ben Josef's funeral, Eliahu Bet Zouri was one of those who pinned a black ribbon to his shirt and marched in silence with other students through the streets of Tel Aviv.

In Haifa, among those who also marched in mourning, a black ribbon on his shirt, was young Eliahu Hakim. He had yet to reach his twelfth birthday; but the execution left its mark on him. Years later in Cairo, on the eve of the Moyne assassination, he was to confide to a friend that Ben Josef's hanging "by the foreign ruler" was one of the two or three events that helped convince him there could be no peace for him until his people were free in their own land.

For the older Eliahu and his comrades, the name of Ben Josef became a cry to action. They took to chanting a poem, "The Unknown Soldier," written by Abraham Stern, the poet-revolutionary of the Irgun:

> *We are the men without name, without kin,*
> *Who forever face terror and death,*
> *Who serve our cause for the length of our lives—*
> *A service that ends with our breath.*
> *In the days that are red with the flow of our blood,*
> *In the nights of blackest despair,*
> *Through the length and breadth of our land*
> *We shall raise our banner of strength without fear—*
> *Not driven like slaves at the master's command,*
> *Forced to die at the stranger's behest,*
> *We dream of the time when our people and land*
> *By freedom and peace will be blessed.*

In the months that followed the hanging, high-school life for Eliahu was completely disrupted, his class completely disorganized.

After preparing a bomb or planning a mission of reprisal, school-books palled. Everyone was restless. Eliahu and Adi used to fill paper bags with water, and drop them from the window of the third-floor homeroom, just to hear the sound. Eliahu became trouble-some to his teachers: he, Adi, David and some of their friends disturbed study hours by talking, laughing, even mocking their in-structors; now and then they locked doors between classrooms to frustrate their teachers, or, of an evening, passing the school, for no reason at all tossed stones through the windows, listening to the shattering glass with a curious kind of satisfaction. They were wrathful without knowing why, and it seemed to them they directed their wrath at the school, at their teachers, at every other student who followed the proprieties.

Eliahu's grades began to suffer: he seemed to respond only to lectures on the epic periods in Jewish history. One afternoon his his-tory teacher, Martin Frank, held his class spellbound relating a he-roic chapter of the Hasmonian revolt against the Syrians. When he finished, there was a silence: then, suddenly, a loud handclapping. It was Eliahu. He had leaped up in his seat in the last row and was applauding excitedly, his face red, so carried away that it was some moments before he realized the entire class had turned to stare at him. It was unheard of, a student applauding a teacher.

More and more Eliahu and his friends were involved on the out-side. Sometimes they were not at school two and three days in a row. Their principal asked, "Where are you going, what is happen-ing to you—you of the seventh class?" And then, sadly, "There is no seventh class in my school." He punished them for their repeated absences by ordering the entire class to take examinations each Sunday through the summer.

Suddenly, early in February, 1939, after a series of Arab attacks on Jewish settlements, the Irgun launched its first major terrorist reprisal: its bombs exploded simultaneously in Arab markets in half a dozen towns. Scores of guiltless men, women and children were killed and injured. Haganah leaflets appeared everywhere de-nouncing the act and quoting the Bible: "Thou shalt not kill." The

Irgun responded with its own Biblical admonition: "Thou shalt give life for life, eye for eye . . . burning for burning—"

In this turmoil Eliahu tried to recruit close friends into the organization. One of his schoolmates, Dan Koor, a Haganah member, lived on Herzl Street, near the border of Jaffa. For days Dan dared not cross to the other side of the street lest he come within the telescopic gunsights of a sniper stationed on the roof of an Arab house some two hundred yards away on the Jaffa side. One morning he arrived in class pale and shaken. On the way he had seen a man carrying in his outstretched arms the battered body of a young Hadassah nurse beaten to death by Arabs while on her rounds in Jaffa.

"So?" demanded Eliahu at recess. "Do you reply? How do you feel about *havlagah* now?"

He spoke with great bitterness. A few days earlier his cousin, thirty-year-old Ephraim Chelouch, had been fatally shot by Arabs while driving from Tel Aviv to Jerusalem to visit his fiancée. Ephraim, whose family was one of the most prominent Sephardic families in Palestine, had been a gifted architect and had just come back from studies abroad. As soon as his death was known, Eliahu and his sister Aviva had hurried to the home of their great-aunt, Ephraim's mother. A dignified, graceful old lady, they found her crying, nearly out of her mind with grief, and they had stood there, shocked and stricken, not knowing what to say or do, until someone took them out of the room.

Now Eliahu stood before Dan, challenging him.

Dan was troubled. "It still can't be right, what you do," he said. "We have to think in larger perspective than only revenge. Yet—" He would not be blindly stubborn. "I am ready to meet your people. If they can convince me, I will join."

"Now you speak sense," said Eliahu. Dan was told to be on the roof of his apartment house at six o'clock the next evening. At that hour he found a tall young man of about twenty-five who carried himself with a crisp, military bearing, waiting. They began to talk. After a few minutes, it was obvious that the two were poles apart. A silence ensued. The stranger said curtly, "You may feel free now to leave."

Dan, stung, retorted, "I *always* feel free."

He spoke with some emotion to Eliahu the next day. "When I talked to your friend, I felt my freedom actually slipping away," he said. "I cannot stand that military approach. Something in me revolts—I'm sorry, Eliahu, you've achieved just the opposite of what you wanted. Your group is not for me."

Eliahu looked at him. "Tell me," he said. "How can you have personal freedom when your people are not free? You are free only if you free yourself."

They argued. "We will never see alike," Dan said finally. "When we build a kibbutz in a corner of the desert, so it is ours, and when we defend only if we are attacked, we combine life and death. But your people concentrate only on death."

Eliahu shook his head. "You build—for whom? For the Arabs to take away in the end? For the British to sign away in the end? I tell you it is death for all of us anyway if we do not fight."

"If we do not fight . . ." But why was it necessary for them to fight at all? What was it that drove Eliahu and his young comrades, and the older men who led them, to take to the extremity of violent action? Why should they oppose the established official policy of the Jewish community not to engage in aggressive reprisals against Arabs and offensive attacks upon the British?

It was a situation that bristled with complications and confused issues. Regional politics were having international repercussions. Palestine had been turned into a cockpit for many contending powers—Britain, Russia, Germany, Italy, the Middle East kingdoms and republics. It was Palestine's historic role through the ages to be an arena in the power struggle, but this time the contestants came from farther afield.

And the spark that set off the small brush fire in these ominous spring months of 1939, with their harbingers of the larger world conflagration that would blaze up later that year, was the White Paper issued by Neville Chamberlain's government.

Earlier, in February, 1939, the British government had tried to bring Arabs and Jews together at a round-table conference in St. James's Palace in London. The conference failed to produce any reconciliation between the two; the Arabs had refused to sit with the Jewish representatives.

To Chamberlain and his advisers, it seemed evident that to appease the Arabs was a preferable political course than to favor Zionist demands. Hitler's seizure of Czechoslovakia in March, 1939, Mussolini's parallel march into Albania, were deciding factors. The Middle East must be kept quiescent at the cost of moral commitments toward the Zionists.

In May, then, the British government issued its White Paper on policy in Palestine. The White Paper barred further land purchases by Jews in 95 percent of Palestine, except with Arab approval. It barred further Jewish immigration into Palestine after a five-year interim in which 75,000 people would be permitted—then no more unless the Arabs approved—thus making the Jews a permanent and ever decreasing minority. It proclaimed that in ten years Palestine would become an independent Arab state.

The White Paper, in essence, reversed the promise of the Balfour Declaration.

The reaction was instantaneous. This was appeasement at its most dreadful, appeasement by the same government that only months earlier yielded Czechoslovakia to Hitler. The extremists suddenly found themselves accorded new respect. Was this not proof that violence paid off? The White Paper was the reward given the Arabs for their rioting and terrorism, the reward given the Jews for their high-minded policy of self-restraint. Even more galling was the fact that this limitation should come at a time when European concentration camps were full of Jewish victims of Nazism, when refugee ships were trying frantically to reach the shores of Palestine, when no other country was willing to take Jewish refugees, when immigration into the Jewish National Home meant life or death for thousands.

Winston Churchill denounced the White Paper as a "second Munich." The Permanent Mandates Commission of the League of Nations declared it contrary to the intent of the mandate. The Jewish Agency swore it would never recognize its legality. There were demonstrations such as Palestine, a land accustomed to demonstrations, had never seen. Thousands crowded into synagogues, theaters, every public hall, to take a solemn oath never to accept the restrictions. Dr. Herzog, the Chief Rabbi of Palestine, stood in the pulpit of the great Jeshurun Synagogue of Jerusalem and before the weeping congregation tore a copy of the White Paper to pieces.

In the United States, in England, throughout the world, mass meetings were held; people fasted; strikes were called; denunciation followed denunciation.

But the White Paper stood.

In Palestine on May 17, 1939—the official day of its announcement—the extremists bombed the Palestine Broadcasting Studios. The document was never read over the air in Palestine. The next day demonstrations took place in Jerusalem, Tel Aviv and Haifa, crowds smashing their way into immigration offices and burning every document of "illegal" entry they could find.

Overnight the British Administration in Palestine—rather than the Arabs—became the target of the extremist underground.

Eliahu, Adi and their classmates surged through Tel Aviv streets carrying the blue-and-white Zionist banner. They had no permit for a parade; furthermore, display of the Zionist flag was illegal. The police descended upon them. The boys and girls scattered, ran through side streets and gathered again. Eliahu jumped on an empty barrel and began a fiery speech. "We, the youth of Tel Aviv, denounce the British for this breach of faith," he cried. "We, the youth—"

From around the corner rumbled an armored car filled with police. Eliahu leaped from the barrel. He and Adi ran until they reached the square at the end of Allenby Road. Here the students remassed their ranks and began to march again, three boys carrying the Zionist banner at the head.

Two policemen tore the flag from their hands. Seeing this, Adi lost all caution. He threw himself at the men and ripped the flag away. One struck him over the head with his club; Eliahu and four others came to his aid; in the free-for-all, the flag was lost, the two officers fell, the boys kicked and beat them. Someone pulled Adi away. He heard the cry, "Run!" He was suddenly aware that his shirt was covered with blood. He had not felt the blow nor the blood streaming down his face. A friend came by on a motorcycle, scooped him up onto the handlebars and rushed him to a private hospital. Eliahu sat pale at his side—the sight of blood was still an ordeal—while a doctor stitched Adi's scalp.

In Haifa, the other Eliahu, too, was caught up in that day of rioting against the White Paper. School had shut down for the day and he was at his favorite spot: on the terrace of his home high on Mount Carmel, above the harbor, binoculars to his eyes, watching the excitement spread through the city, the crowds up and down Kingsway, Haifa's great thoroughfare that runs parallel to the sea. At twelve still too young to join any resistance movement, what Eliahu Hakim read and heard in these days—even more, what he saw—was building up a resentment in him that sooner or later would explode.

The riots of the general population on May 18, on the heels of the bombing of the broadcasting station the day before, brought swift retaliation from the British. They could not imprison the population itself, but they could launch a manhunt for the extremists who had attacked the station. In a matter of hours they had rounded up virtually all the high command of the Irgun save two: Commander David Raziel, Esther's brother, and his colleague, Abraham Stern. Raziel was seized by the British on May 22, but Stern escaped the net only because he was in Poland on a mission for Jabotinsky.

For several years the Revisionist leader had warned that the Jews of Poland were "living on a volcano." Anti-Semitism was so deeply ingrained there, he declared, that mass evacuation to Palestine was their only hope. The Polish government agreed to aid such a plan. World Jewish leaders were horrified and denounced the scheme as a shameless collaboration with anti-Semitism and one that could set a dangerous precedent.

Stern, a man with a Messianic complex who had one obsession —Jewish independence in Palestine—had gone to Poland to arrange with government circles there for the delivery of arms to his organization and the military training of Irgun commanders and instructors. But he was also on a mission of his own. He told Polish leaders that the Irgun would train 40,000 Jewish youths, gathered throughout Europe, for a one-day invasion of Palestine, to be launched from Italian ports sometime in October, 1939. They would seize the government from the British, raise the Zionist flag over Jerusalem and proclaim an independent Jewish state. "We will decide the fate of Palestine in one action," he promised. The Italians, who had their own colonial differences with the British, were ready to go along. Whether the Poles took Stern's invasion plan seriously, we do not know: but at any event, they did supply the arms and did help establish an officers' training school for the Irgun. It was in the mountains of Zakofna in southwest Poland—a huge, three-story farmhouse with living and training accommodations for a large number.

To this farmhouse in the spring of 1939, traveling from Palestine in utmost secrecy, had come a score of young Irgun instructors all under thirty, moving in separate groups by separate routes, many with forged passports. Here Polish army officers lectured them on military tactics and strategy, trained them in partisan fighting, in sabotage, in all the arts of guerilla warfare, as well as in regulation army skills. Stern spoke at the first graduation exercises in early May. Other groups would follow, he promised, both at this training school and others which would open in the months to come.

As fantastic as this invasion scheme, was a corollary of it which involved Jabotinsky himself, then in Switzerland. The Revisionist leader, incognito, would join a group of illegal immigrants in a secret night landing at Tel Aviv. The Irgun would stage an uprising, seize Government House—the residence of the High Commissioner —raise the Zionist flag over it and proclaim the establishment of the Provisional Government of the new Jewish state, headed by Jabotinsky. Sooner or later, of course, the British would seize him, whereupon his colleagues in Europe and the United States would constitute themselves a Jewish government-in-exile.

In late May with the British roundup of Irgun leaders in Palestine, all hope for this grandiose plan vanished. After Raziel's arrest, Stern hurried back to Palestine to help take over command of the organization.

He learned that some of his imprisoned colleagues were being tortured by assistant superintendent of police Ralph Cairns, head of the Jewish section of the CID. Cairns, who spoke fluent Hebrew, was infamous for mistreating Jewish prisoners. The Irgun, which by now had acquired a secret radio transmitter, broadcast a warning to Cairns. When he disregarded it, torturing a Yemenite Jewish girl found carrying a bomb in her basket of vegetables, they pronounced sentence of death on him.

The Irgun launched full-scale warfare, now attacking Arabs, now the British. On May 28, a week after Raziel's arrest, Irgunists mined the Rex Cinema in Jerusalem. Five Arabs were killed, eighteen wounded. Forty-eight hours later, they attacked the village of Bir Adas, from where many raiders had come. Five more Arabs were killed. Four days later, in a concerted attack on British installations, they destroyed mail and telephone boxes, slashed telephone wires between Jerusalem and Jaffa, destroyed railway tracks and blew up part of the main post office in Jerusalem.

How much of a role Eliahu and Adi played in all this is not known. We do know that many of the bombs were made by their weapons commander, Arieh Yitzhaki, to whom they had originally been assigned as assistants and whose life Eliahu had saved by quick thinking.

On the night of August 5, Yitzhaki was working on a bomb with Adi assisting him. Eliahu was not there. Suddenly it exploded in Yitzhaki's hands. As once before, he must have become confused and wound the clockwork in the wrong direction. His right hand was blown off at the wrist, his left was in shreds. Adi's neck and face were cruelly ripped by shrapnel. When the police burst in minutes later, Yitzhaki sat there blinded, bleeding, in agony.

He heard them and tried to look about him with his sightless eyes. "Adi, is that you?" he asked. But Adi, despite his own wounds, had managed to escape. For the next five years the police were to search for a slight, emaciated, scholarly youth named Adi, but he had vanished under a new name, Jacob.

The police clutched Yitzhaki by the shoulder. "What is your name?"

Yitzhaki said, "My name is Death-to-you—" and lost consciousness.

At Hadassah Hospital in Tel Aviv he underwent incessant grilling by CID agents. They had come upon a major arms cache—mines, grenades, dynamite—in his apartment. He was obviously a key terrorist. In the attempt to make him talk, it was later reported, he was tortured. To all questions he would say, "Let me die, you dogs. It's useless to try to get anything from me. Go away and let me die."

He died the next day.

And Adi? Adi had rushed out of the building and stumbled through back alleys until he saw an open window: framed in it was a woman, seated reading under a lamp. He stood, shaking, at the window. "Excuse me, lady, I need help—" he began. She looked up from her book to see a wild, bleeding apparition: a terrible scream burst from her. He fled again until he reeled into a corner pharmacy. The druggist took him to the Magen David—Jewish first-aid post. They suspected that the name he gave them was false. The doctor said paternally, "Look, my boy, it's for your own safety. Tell us where you live and we'll send someone over to clean out any incriminating papers." Half mad with pain, Adi told them. The police were promptly notified.

Almost instantly the Irgun grapevine alerted friends, who stole into Adi's hospital room, wrapped him in a blanket and carried him away. When a police squad roared up twenty minutes later, he was gone.

At the home of David Raziel—considered safe from the police since Raziel had already been seized—Adi slowly recovered. He underwent extensive plastic surgery. Then he dropped from sight. When friends asked Eliahu about Adi's absence—unaware of his involvement in the Yitzhaki explosion—Eliahu would only say, "He went to Jerusalem to study." Those who knew Eliahu at the time remembered him wandering about almost dazed, such was his closeness to Adi.

The police redoubled their hunt for Abraham Stern. Two days later, August 7, on an informer's tip, they surrounded a house in Tel Aviv and seized Stern and three of his colleagues.

On September 1, 1939, when Hitler marched into Poland and World War II began, forever dooming the Jabotinsky-Stern *coup d'état* and Polish Jewry as well, the entire top leadership of the Irgun was behind barbed wire in detention camp.

But a week before that date, one more Irgun act of violence rocked Palestine. Police Inspector Cairns, despite all his precautions, was killed by a land mine. The sentence of death had been carried out.

CHAPTER

7

THE WAR CHANGED everything.

The war—and Hitler's growing strength and slowly succeeding campaign against the Jews—acted like a strange and distorting magic. Some events it speeded up, telescoped, jammed together, so that what might have taken decades was achieved in months; other events it slowed down, expanded, stretched apart, so that what might have been achieved in months took decades.

No individual, no group, no institution, no nation escaped this bewildering anarchy in cause and effect.

The outbreak of World War II in September, 1939, clearly changed the course of history in the Middle East. The two Eliahus, their families, their friends, felt it in their personal lives. The majority and minority elements in Zionism felt it. The Jewish community of Palestine felt it. Coloring all else for them was the fact that Great Britain now fought the common enemy, Germany; but tinged with this was the bitter knowledge that had not Britain shut the doors of Palestine, countless Jews might have been free who were otherwise doomed to Hitler's mercies.

In an attempt to placate the Arabs, the British had been steadily cutting down on the permits allowed for Jewish immigration into Palestine. From 1936 to 1939 refugees from Nazi persecution had entered the country in large numbers, assisted unofficially by various Central European governments who saw Palestine as the only hope for these people. Now it was inevitable that thousands would attempt to find haven in the Jewish National Home without certificates—in British eyes, "illegally."

Until the White Paper the Irgun as well as the Haganah played a role in this movement. After the White Paper, the Jewish Agency developed this into the "Aliya Bet"—a vast, underground immigration movement which brought hundreds of small ships filled with refugees to run the British blockade of the Palestine coast. With the outbreak of war, the Aliya Bet increased in tempo, although it was to dwindle sharply at the height of the hostilities. The war would be won, the immigrants brought in, the land colonized, no matter what. Surely in the end world opinion, the conscience of humanity —above all, the inherent British sense of fair play—would reverse that evil document and the Zionist vision would be achieved.

David Ben-Gurion, chairman of the Jewish Agency, summed it up with: "We shall fight the war as if there were no White Paper, and fight the White Paper as if there were no war."

The war was only hours old when the *S. S. Tigerhill,* packed with more than fourteen hundred refugees fleeing certain death in Poland, attempted to land off Tel Aviv. A British naval patrol opened fire on it. Several people were killed.

These deaths, the first to result from overt British action of this kind, climaxed months of anguished Zionist appeals to London. Weeks before, when hostilities were imminent, the Jewish Agency had asked for immediate admission of twenty thousand children from Poland and ten thousand young people from the Balkans. The British Administration refused. Earlier, in March and April, three ships bearing German and Polish Jews had reached Palestine but were not permitted to land. The protests had been universal; the government had been questioned in the House of Commons.

Captain Noel-Baker had inquired of Colonial Secretary Malcolm

MacDonald as to the fate of the passengers. "They have been sent back where they came from," was the reply.

Noel-Baker: "Does that mean to concentration camps?"

MacDonald: "The responsibility rests with those responsible for organizing illegal immigration."

Cold words, brutally impersonal, a virtual death sentence—

Now, with the affair of the *Tigerhill,* there were again protests, and again word from London: "To authorize the indiscriminate landing of refugees in Palestine would worsen rather than improve the security position there." How the admission of fourteen hundred men and women would affect the security of the country was not explained. But the news discouraged thousands of others still in Europe who might have tried to escape. They, too, were left to die.

Now come a series of attempts on the part of the Jewish community of Palestine to aid the war effort, and a series of galling rebuffs on the part of the British Administration. Within weeks of the outbreak of war, under the aegis of the Jewish Agency, more than 130,000 Jewish men and women registered for service in the British forces. The Haganah placed itself at the disposal of the British military authorities in the Middle East.

But none of the 130,000 were called into service. Nor would official censorship allow any reference in the press to the Agency's recruiting centers; nor to Ben-Gurion's proposal—and the British refusal—to create a 60,000-man Jewish brigade to fight in the front lines, as the Jewish Legion had fought with the British against the Turks in World War I. Indeed, the censors banned all mention in print of the Jewish war effort; at the same time, they banned all mention of the pro-Axis activities of the Mufti of Jerusalem, who had fled to neighboring Lebanon and was later to take refuge in Berlin. Clearly, the British were doing all they could not to antagonize the Arabs lest they be driven into the Axis camp.

In the first month of the war forty-three Haganah officers were arrested for "illegal training in arms." Each was sentenced to five to ten years in prison. What outraged the Jewish community was the fact that all forty-three had been originally armed and trained by the British themselves: they had conscientiously observed *havlagah,* self-restraint: they had trained for self-defense only.

As the war continued, the Haganah was to perform an increasingly important role. To understand precisely what its activities were, it is necessary to go into the nature of this unique organization which ultimately was to emerge as the Army of Israel and fight off seven invading Arab armies.

Haganah (defense) had its roots in the turn of the century when Jewish settlers, to protect themselves against Bedouin raiders sweeping in from the desert to loot farms and settlements, established the Hashomer, or "Watchmen"—armed volunteers who rode their rounds with rifles across their saddles and built up a tradition of fearsome valor.

After General Allenby's victory in Palestine in 1917, the Jews turned in their arms to the British occupation forces who henceforth would maintain law and order. In the Arab riots of 1920-1921 this protection proved negligible and the Jews suffered great loss of life. The British then armed villages with a limited number of shotguns, but kept them locked in steel cases, with the key held by the muktar or headman of the village. In case of attack, one had to find the muktar to unlock the case. By that time the damage had been done. Haganah members had no alternative but to build up their own secret arsenal. It was fortunate they did so for in 1929, without explanation, the British withdrew the few rifles they had issued.

In the new outbreak of Arab rioting in August of that year, Jewish settlements possessing Haganah arms repelled every raid. Where they had none the Arabs slaughtered almost at will. Manifestly, without weapons—"illegal" or otherwise—Jewish lives were forfeit. From 1929, therefore, the Haganah began to collect guns and ammunition with almost religious determination. It imported them from every country in Europe, even bought large quantities from the Arabs themselves. The British had armed the Arabs heavily in World War I and had never collected the rifles supplied them by T. E. Lawrence—Lawrence of Arabia—and these ancient weapons, too, found their way into Haganah armories.

After 1930 the British again allowed the Jews a measure of self-defense. The Haganah was permitted to create a small Settlement Police Force, but they were not allowed to pursue raiders beyond the boundaries of the settlement. A year later, however, when Arab mercenaries attacked the oil pipelines from Iraq to Haifa, the Haganah received a major impetus: a blue-eyed, red-bearded jungle fighter named Captain Orde Wingate was dispatched by the British to Palestine to meet this challenge. Wingate, a highly unorthodox soldier who spoke fluent Hebrew, a non-Jewish Zionist burning with an almost mystical fervor, made brilliant use of the Haganah: he handpicked members to form his famous "Special Night Squads," taught them his own brand of guerrilla warfare and led them into the hills at night to ambush the Arabs with spectacular success. Some of his night fighters later became top officers of the Army of Israel.

Not until late 1940, when Suez was threatened, did the British Army accept Jewish volunteers—and then only in supply and auxiliary units. But the Haganah was busy on its own, in a hundred different forms of activity. It sent its agents through Europe to guide refugees into Palestine; at home it trained civilians, parents and children for the day when they might have to fight off invasion. It enlisted virtually every able-bodied man and woman in a Jewish population of 475,000—almost everyone except the ultrareligious who maintained that God, not man, would protect them in the Holy Land, and the Irgunists, who, as we shall see, had their own approach to the war effort.

The first real use of the Haganah by the British was to come in 1942 when Rommel's breakthrough at Tobruk threatened the entire Middle East. Haganah units underwent commando training in preparation for guerrilla resistance against the German Afrika Korps. Hundreds of members volunteered to parachute into German-occupied Balkan countries—countries where many of them had originated, and whose language and geography they knew as well as the palms of their hands—to carry out missions for British intelligence, to rescue not only Jewish underground agents but British and American pilots. One out of two of these volunteers perished.

But if the British availed themselves of some of the Haganah's strength and skill, they were reluctant to draw on all of it. The guns given to Haganah fighters this day might be turned against His Majesty's Forces another day. As a result, ambivalence ran like a major thread through the fabric of Anglo-Jewish relations.

Perhaps the most ironic example of this blowing both hot and cold had taken place in the fall of 1940. Even as the British, concerned over Suez, for the first time accepted Palestinian Jewish volunteers into the army, they intensified their efforts to prevent Jewish refugees from reaching a haven in Palestine.

The battle of illegal immigration had been growing in intensity as desperation grew in Europe. The struggle reached a climax that November of 1940 when two tramp steamers, the *Pacific* and the *Milos,* carrying 1,800 passengers, were intercepted by British patrol vessels and brought into Haifa harbor under guard. Many of the 1,800 had no sooner set foot on Palestine soil, kneeling and kissing the earth, when they were led into internment camps, held a few days behind barbed wire and then ordered aboard a British freighter, the *S. S. Patria,* to be deported to the island of Mauritius in the Indian Ocean.

The deportation order came from Sir Harold MacMichael, High Commissioner for Palestine.

The Jewish Agency protested vehemently to Sir Harold that most of the passengers were *halutzim,* agricultural workers who had trained all their lives for Palestine; if war had not broken out, they would now be in the country. Nonetheless, MacMichael announced that not only would the refugees not be allowed to remain, but as punishment they would never—at no time, not even *after* the war—be permitted to enter Palestine. He added, as a warning to those who might still nurse hope of fleeing Europe, "Similar action will be taken in the case of any further parties who may succeed in reaching Palestine with a view to illegal entry."

Forced aboard the *Patria,* the refugees could take no more. The ship was just preparing to leave port when they blew themselves up. The explosion shook all Haifa. More than 250 men, women and children drowned as the ship went down.

Despite the catastrophe, MacMichael informed Moshe Sharett, who as chief of the Jewish Agency's political department had been laboring ceaselessly on behalf of the refugees, that the deportation order still stood. Those who survived the sinking of the *Patria* would be exiled to Mauritius as soon as another ship became available. Only when MacMichael was overruled by London, after Dr. Weizmann carried the appeal to Whitehall itself, were the hapless survivors allowed to remain. Without revealing what had happened, Sir Harold announced that this decision had been made "as an exceptional act of mercy." *

The week of the *Patria* tragedy another appalling blow came. Some 1,700 refugees from Danzig, Austria and Czechoslovakia arrived aboard a typhoid-ridden freighter, the *Atlantic.* They were put behind barbed wire at the Haifa detention camp, then ordered deported. They fought not to go; in the end, soldiers dragged men and women by the hair, the arms and legs, beat them with batons, literally drove them aboard the ship. Two days later, another freighter, the *Salvatore,* unable to land its passengers because they lacked British visas for Palestine, sank in the Sea of Marmora with a death toll of 231 men, women and children.

Throughout his formative years, as he stood on the family terrace high above Haifa Bay, young Eliahu Hakim was eyewitness to all this.

Despite all the frustration of the refugee ships, the Haganah cooperated with the British when called upon to do so, went its own way when not. In the latter role it grew into a people's defense militia, complete with officers and men. It built up the appurte-

* The survivors were counted and that precise number was deducted from the next allotment of certificates granted.

nances of a true army: home-fitted armored cars, gun carriers, machine guns, mortars, rifles, automatics, hand grenades, bombs and ammunition, all strategically distributed about the country. Much of this was hidden in the kibbutzim, which were to be the heart of the resistance in case of invasion. Guns were secreted in hollow fence posts, ammunition buried in orchards. Teen-age girls transported small weapons in their blouses. Repeatedly there were British searches of buses. A man carrying a weapon would immediately pass it to the nearest woman who without a word would hide it on her person, knowing that British soldiers at that time did not subjugate women to physical search.

The Haganah's curriculum was comprehensive. Housewives rolled bandages and studied first aid. Husbands and sons went on thirty-hour forced marches, carrying heavy packs. There were intricate maneuvers between Blue and White armies in the field. Some were held along the desolate Mediterranean coast or in the endless valleys and plains between the deserts.

But most took place in the settlements. There were more than four hundred of these, many quite isolated. Search though the British might—as they alternated between ignoring what was happening and vigorously raiding and confiscating arms—it was impossible to know that five or six hundred troops were engaged in maneuvers in the fields of a remote mountaintop kibbutz.

Thus the Haganah steered its difficult course: on the one hand, full cooperation with the British war effort; on the other, stubborn resistance to the British White Paper policy.

Meanwhile, the outbreak of war posed a problem, too, to the dissidents—the Irgun High Command.

Their strategy was to have a direct effect on Eliahu Bet Zouri. Meeting behind barbed wire at Sarafend Detention Camp, they decided that since the British were fighting the Germans, they would call a truce against the mandatory administration in Palestine, and resume their revolt only at the end of the war.

On this rock—cooperation with the British—the organization

split wide open into two factions, one led by David Raziel, the other by Abraham Stern.

Stern flatly opposed the truce. He would not cooperate with the British Administration when, he declared, the British, by refusing to save Jewish refugees, were in fact collaborating with Hitler in their destruction. The argument boiled over two months later, in January 1940, when Raziel was unexpectedly released from internment and Stern and his followers were not. Stern charged that Raziel had made a secret deal with the British.

Five months later, in June, Stern and the others were released.* Raziel confronted them in a dramatic meeting, denied he had made any deal, denounced Stern for "flinging mud" at him and resigned as commander of the Irgun. Stern took over. An appeal to settle the dispute was made to Jabotinsky, who as head of the Revisionist party was spiritual leader of the Irgun. Jabotinsky, then in the United States on a lecture tour, had always distrusted Stern's fanatic Anglophobia. In August he cabled Raziel to resume command and Stern to step down and cooperate.

Stern refused; the situation remained tense for another eight days. Then news came that Jabotinsky had suddenly died of a heart attack in a Betar camp in upstate New York.

At this major blow the movement all but disintegrated. In September Stern walked out of the Irgun and set up his own group. He served notice he would fight not only the British in Palestine but British imperialism everywhere. He severed all ties with the Revisionist party; he rejected all authority but himself; his group would go forward on its own.

The split demoralized Bet Zouri and his friends. As Irgunists they were already members of a tiny minority, ostracized by the Jewish community. They had been able to endure this only because they believed in the rightness of their cause. That their commanders could quarrel over aims and methods, even attack each

* There has always been a question as to the timing of these releases. Some have charged that the British played Raziel against Stern, in the hope that their rivalry would immobilize the Irgun.

other, dismayed them. Even more shattering was the manner in which they were pulled by their various leaders, first this way, then that.

One memorable Saturday night Eliahu and David Danon, who had left the Haganah and joined the Irgun because he had become convinced that self-restraint was not an effective policy, were summoned to a remote schoolhouse. Irgun guards silently directed them to a classroom where to their astonishment they found nearly fifty other youths aged fifteen to twenty—obviously, like themselves, members of the Irgun. This was unheard of, to meet in so large a group, to allow so many to recognize each other. The faces about them were solemn: this disregard of all rules of conspiracy could only mean disaster. They soon learned why they had been called together: they were to be addressed by a representative of each faction.

First, their twenty-two-year-old group commander spoke. He was obviously laboring under great emotion. Undoubtedly most of them, he began, had heard of the "difficulties" within the organization following the "disagreement at headquarters." He, personally, did not feel he could advise them—he dared not take the responsibility —where their duty lay; to remain with Raziel or leave with Stern. "Let each of you make your own decision in such a matter of conscience—" He wanted to say more but his voice began to betray him, his eyes grew moist, and he turned and ran from the room.

He was followed by the Irgun commander in Tel Aviv. Far more controlled, he made a brief speech. "If you are ready to follow our great leader, Jabotinsky, then accept his judgment and be loyal to the man he named." He read Jabotinsky's cable to Raziel: "I reappoint you to functions heretofore held with full power to appoint and remove any colleagues," and the one sent to Stern: "Reappointing R and formally ordering you to comply with these directives." He concluded: "Long live Jabotinsky!"

David leaned toward Eliahu and whispered, "I cannot understand such blind devotion to any man." No matter how wise, how could another decide a question of one's own conscience?

92

Eliahu nodded but said nothing.

Now the entire group of fifty were ordered to proceed in utter silence to another classroom. Here a short, square-shouldered, square-faced, muscular man awaited them—Itzhak Yizernitsky, who had once taken Eliahu with him to burn down the tax booths in Tel Aviv.

He stood, stolid as an oak, as if he had grown where he stood, waiting for them to file in and stand at attention. Then he spoke tersely, summing up the reasons behind Stern's decision to walk out of the Irgun. "I tell you no fairy tales," he said. "If you join us, you must bring money to buy arms and ammunition—we have no organization behind us, no political party, no one to help us, no one to back us but ourselves. We will demand painful sacrifices from you."

He paused, and looked at them from under his heavy black brows.

"Men!" His deep voice rumbled. "If you want to smell fire and powder, come with us!"

He turned on his heel and left the room.

Silently the two boys walked home from the meeting. David spoke first. "Fire and powder! Is that an aim in life?"

He remembered later Eliahu's slow reply. "If only we could do without it—"

In the course of their walk, they agreed they could not go with either group.

Discouraged and disheartened, in a mood bordering on a plague on both your houses, Eliahu turned his attention to his own future. He had not returned to school with his class—now the eighth class; he had refused to take the weekly examinations imposed as punishment; he clashed with several of his teachers; when he was informed that because of his attitude his scholarship was revoked for the final year and he would be required to pay full tuition—which he knew his father could not afford—he simply dropped out. He enrolled in night school to obtain a diploma, and began to think of an academic career. He rarely saw Adi: secreted in a small basement room in Tel Aviv, Adi was allowed no visitors—not even his mother—lest they lead police to him, and was permitted to go out only at night for an hour's fresh air.

That autumn Eliahu enrolled in the Hebrew University. He would become an Orientalist and instructor in Semitic languages. He spoke of branching out into drama criticism, newspaper writing, book translation. His father, delighted that his son seemed to have found himself, did his best to help him financially. Eliahu moved to Jerusalem, the seat of the university, and lived with his grandmother.

With him went a slight, heavily bearded young man who had had considerable plastic surgery done on his face. This was Adi. Tel Aviv had become too dangerous for him, and in Eliahu's grandmother's house he had a perfect hideout. In addition, his brother Avigad also lived in Jerusalem. Avigad, twenty-six, was an older edition of Adi. A nonconformist, a scholar in ancient Semitic literature, he was at this time head of the Irgun in Jerusalem and a member of Raziel's High Command. Because of the truce the organization was marking time, but Avigad convened its meetings regularly with full military discipline, recruited new members, lectured them on political ideology and prepared them for the day they would resume their struggle.

Eliahu's grandmother, a diminutive, black-eyed old lady full of superstitions, lived on Jaffa Road in a one-story stone house built in Moorish fashion. It had a rolling stone floor, thick iron doors, barred windows and a cobblestone courtyard with its own exit. In the courtyard a small brick blockhouse had been built. Eliahu's grandfather, as senility came upon him, went through phases of great belligerency. The old lady had been forced to keep her husband locked in the blockhouse, sometimes for hours, to prevent him from berating his neighbors. In this one-room cell with iron bars on its windows, Adi was to live for nearly six months. Later he moved out and lived with Avigad and his wife, Miriam, a schoolteacher.

For Eliahu these were months of self-analysis. He spent most of his time at the university, where he browsed through the immense stacks of its library. He borrowed books by the score: *Martin Eden,* by Jack London; Dostoevsky's *The Brothers Karamazov, Crime and Punishment* and *The Idiot*. To add to the small sums he received from home, he marked papers, tutored and worked on translations. Money problems constantly harassed him. In a letter home on January 21, 1941, he wrote that he needed another forty-five piastres—roughly, two dollars. Could his father send the money? He went on: "If you could make a further effort and send me still another fifty piastres for shoes, I'd appreciate it. My shoes are coming apart and have already reached a ripe old age."

He grew dissatisfied as the months wore on. A diary he began in mid-1941 reveals his state of mind.

Now that I have time to think and consider my behavior, I look with horror on these last two years or so. I haven't done anything—I haven't written anything—nothing of value. I see that I have been attacked by such idleness as I never experienced before. Apathy and clumsiness surrounded me on all sides. Routine mastered every bit of my will power. I have decided that I will be strengthened and overcome them. First, I shall have to begin a diary. Last night I thought about it and discovered I really don't know how to begin. I decided I would start by giving a summary of my life as far as I can remember it. So today I skipped the lecture and tried beginning my life story. . . .

The militant nationalism that found its outlet in underground activity, had been stifled by the truce, and though he attended Irgun meetings called by Avigad, something had to fill this vacuum. He and Adi took long walks at night; Eliahu, seeking an understanding of himself and his background, became absorbed in a theory which had completely obsessed Adi during his hideout in Tel Aviv.

This theory was that their generation, born in Palestine, was evolving a new nation that had no connection with Jewish communities anywhere else. Adi asserted that Eliahu and he were not so much Jews as Israelites, or, more popularly, Canaanites—literally, descended from the ancient inhabitants of Palestine.

"Elsewhere the Jews are religious communities," Adi would explain in his quiet, insistent way, as they sat together in the little blockhouse. While he talked, his fingers skillfully wired a tiny time bomb: he was so in love with his work that he had rewired his bedroom clock so that when the hands showed seven, they triggered a contact with the time-bomb mechanism. But instead of setting off a charge, it set off the alarm.

"Here in Palestine," Adi would go on, "we are a nation, emerging with every sign of a nation: a common language, a common culture, a common ancestry stemming from a common soil. Our cultural patterns, our heritage, are those of ancient Israel. We have nothing to do with the Jews in Poland, England, America. Their language, their cultural patterns, their citizenship, are those of the country in which they live. They are Poles, Englishmen, Americans. We are Canaanites, living in the land of our ancestors. The Bible is our history book. We are Canaanites, or Israelites, or Hebrews —one and the same thing—but not Jews."

A Canaanite group had been formed and met regularly. It had begun issuing a monthly newspaper called *Aleph*—the Hebrew letter A—signifying starting from the very beginning. "Our language is our best proof," Adi would say heatedly. "It doesn't connect us with the Jews of the Diaspora—actually, it separates us." All belonged to the new nation who spoke Hebrew. Whether they practiced Judaism or not did not matter. Indeed, what had they, the proud, natural sons of Israel, in common with the ritual-haunted, ultrareligious, caftan-wearing, compliant Jews of the ghettos of Russia, Poland and Rumania?

Eliahu was doubtful about much of this, but he toyed with the idea of joining the group. Here was truly a form of nonviolent nationalism. The Canaanites, a handful in all, sat in cafés at night excitedly arguing their point. Eliahu spoke to his friends about it— one, in particular, Tamar Vered, a slim, quiet girl who had been at Balfour High School. Tamar, who suffered from a heart ailment, had come to Jerusalem to stay in a convalescent home and Eliahu dropped in almost every afternoon to read to her.

Sometimes his other schoolmates—Amihai Paglin and David Danon—on weekend visits to Jerusalem joined in these afternoon calls and debated the wisdom of becoming Canaanites. They enjoyed Tamar, who was direct, logical and unsentimental. When she felt equal to it, they would take her to see the latest Laurel and Hardy comedy. These were favorites with the foursome, and the silly little bouncing melody that introduced each one intrigued them. It became their private theme song. They whistled it when they saw each other. They would wait for Tamar outside the convalescent home, whistling the tune under her window. If she could come out she whistled a few bars in return. Then they walked together, arms linked, to the cinema, whistling their melody in concert and giggling at the passers-by who stared at them.

Tamar had small patience with the Canaanites. "How can I forget my aunts and uncles in Europe?" she would demand. "Besides, not all of you came here on your own—you were brought by your parents and grandparents. We are all Jews—I don't see that any of us can put on airs and say we are Canaanites." She would direct most of her scorn at Adi, when he joined them of an evening.

"No, no," Adi would protest. "What we're talking about has nothing to do with biological origin or religious views. This is true modern nationalism—Israeli nationalism, not Jewish nationalism; nationhood, not peoplehood; the unity of those in the same territory, not the unity of those of the same blood." He would argue: "The Irish brought their children to America. But are those children now Irish or Americans? The Spaniards brought their children to Argentina: are they growing up to be Spaniards or are they Argentinians? On this Canaanite soil we are Canaanites—not Jews."

Eliahu's imagination was not really fired until the late summer of 1941 when he met a friend of Adi's, a thirty-three-year-old Polish-born poet who had taken the name Jonathan Ratosh and was the spiritual leader of the Canaanites. The two stayed up all of one night, talking; and by dawn Eliahu was almost convinced. Adi was delighted. He wrote Eliahu a letter saying, "I bless you," composing it in the ancient Hebrew calligraphy of the first millennium, the time of the Canaanites. Eliahu did his best to reply in similar fashion—and had to give up after three lines. But he saw Ratosh again and listened more.

Ratosh, at nineteen, had gone to Paris to study. This was in 1928, the Paris between the wars, the Paris of the Café Dome and the

Rotunda, of Joyce, Hemingway and Pound: a time of ferment in art, writing and philosophy. A thin, intense, burning youth—the name he chose is the Hebrew verb, "to rend"—Ratosh had met a number of French Orientalists, among them one Adolf Gourevitch, who preached that the Biblical story of the Exodus was a vast exaggeration. To be sure, there had been *an* exodus—a thin trickle of Hebrews who had gone into bondage in Egypt and had found their way back to Palestine, the ancient land of Canaan. But these few refugees, Gourevitch maintained, never formed the nucleus of the Hebrew nation. Rather, when they returned to Canaan, they found their own kinfolk there—Hebrew-speaking, resembling them in physical characteristics—their own people. In short, the Hebrews and Canaanites were one; the majority of the Canaanites had never left the land of Canaan; the Hebrew religion evolved among them; the Hebrew language was, in fact, actually a Canaanite dialect.

Ratosh, deeply influenced by Gourevitch, returned to Palestine and developed the Canaanite thesis, emphasizing the identification of the people with the land. In later years he was to demand, "Why did the Jews of Europe walk to the death ovens like sheep, and why did the Jews of Israel revolt and fight like men inspired against the seven Arab armies surrounding them? Why, for two thousand years in all the lands of exile, was there no struggle for Jewish independence, but in our time independence was won in Israel? It is the land that did it, the land that made the difference."

Adi caught fire from Ratosh, and he in turn influenced Eliahu, who at one point wrote a friend, "We are not Zionists. We are the natural sons of the soil of Israel. Our war against the British is the natural war every patriot wages against one who will not let him be free. We suffer with the Jews of Europe as brothers in humanity —but we are a free nation, formed and created on this soil through generations of time."

But even though Eliahu luxuriated in the glory of the ancient Hebrews, he did not lose touch with the present: when Avigad announced an advanced Irgun course in underground techniques,

Eliahu immediately enrolled. He and Avigad took pains to see every American Western and gangster film that came to Jerusalem and unashamedly copied the techniques blueprinted for them by Hollywood. These included how to draw two guns and use them simultaneously; how to take command of a roomful of people by leaping on a table and firing three times into the air; how to disarm and search a man; how to open a locked door with a submachine gun by firing a circle of bullets around the lock; how to capture a moving truckload of goods by pulling alongside in a car, leaping onto the top of the cab and leaning down to hold a pistol at the driver's head.

When the course ended, appropriate graduation exercises were held. Eliahu was promoted to platoon commander, and chosen to speak on behalf of the new officers. At the party celebrating the graduation, never one for liquor, he drank too much. Avigad himself helped him, half-staggering through the blacked-out streets, to his grandmother's house, calmed her alarm and put Platoon Commander Bet Zouri to bed.

Unexpectedly, his university career ended. A combination of war, politics and economic necessity forced him to drop out as the spring, 1942, semester began. The Germans were advancing in North Africa; Rommel had reached Tobruk. The Jewish Agency, already training special Haganah commandos to defend strategic areas in case of a German invasion, pressed university students to volunteer in the British Army. Bet Zouri refused, on principle. He would not join an army which treated Jews as natives, barred them from combat units and relegated them to Palestinian regiments detailed to clerical and supply duties. When the time came, he would fight the enemy his own way. With Avigad he spent days exploring the Judean hills around Jerusalem, looking for caves, marking where water and food could be stored. If Rommel invaded Palestine, Avigad, Eliahu and their comrades would hole up in the caves and from there launch their own guerrilla warfare against the Germans—if necessary, turning their last bullet upon themselves rather than surrendering.

Because of his refusal to volunteer, Eliahu found his position at the university more and more difficult. Then, from home, his father wrote that he could not afford to pay the coming semester's tuition. The money Eliahu earned by tutoring would not make up for this loss. In addition, Adi was no longer in Jerusalem: he had fallen in love with a girl from Tel Aviv and moved back there.

In early 1942 Eliahu left the university, went back to Tel Aviv and began to look for a job.

CHAPTER

8

Even as Eliahu returned to Tel Aviv, time was running out for Abraham Stern, the man whose philosophical legacy was to send Eliahu on his fatal mission to Cairo.

Stern, the dissident among dissidents, had made his movement anathema in Palestine in the brief time since he had walked out of the Irgun. To his enemies, he was a fanatic; to his tiny band of followers, he was a selfless leader who inspired near adoration.

This man, whose name was to become synonymous with the bomb and the gun—and with whom the two Eliahus were to be forever identified—was one of the most unlikely persons to be cast in the role he played. Now, in the year of his death, he was thirty-five, slender, strikingly handsome, with jet-black hair; his face, narrow and aquiline, the nose and brow forming one straight line, the eyes dark and brooding, might have come from an El Greco canvas. He had a soft voice and tremendous charm. He was an excellent poet; he spoke perfect Russian and Polish, he had read Homer in the original, he knew Italian well and his Hebrew was out of the ordinary. A stranger meeting him would never dream that he was a terrorist. He did not indulge in fiery speeches; he seemed invariably calm, almost preoccupied; his manners were exquisite. But those who knew him recognized that for all his gentleness, there was a decision in his tone which cut through all opposing argument: that under the velvet, the man was steel.

Born in Poland in 1907 he had come to Palestine at fifteen after an adventurous trek through half a dozen countries in the aftermath of the Russian Revolution. In Palestine he joined the Revisionist movement; later, he enrolled in the Hebrew University, tutoring fellow students to support himself. He was an outstanding scholar in Greek and Latin. He became a favorite of Dr. Judah L. Magnes, president of the university, who described him as a "pure, enlightened soul" and predicted a brilliant academic future for him. At twenty-one he received his degree and won a year's scholarship to Italy. He went to Florence to study and here came under the revolutionary tradition of Garibaldi.

Italy was in ferment. Mussolini had taken over the stage, the dynamic socialist leader who had captured the imagination even of the democracies. Stern was impressed. In Italy he developed a growing distrust of the Great Powers and especially of Britain. In 1929 he returned to Palestine in time to take part in the defense against Arab rioters.

By 1933 he had abandoned his academic studies and was deeply involved in underground activity. There was then a cleavage in the national wing of the Haganah between the two rival groups—the Liberals and the Revisionists. Stern became active in the latter group (from which he was later to walk out), but his approach to Jewish statehood was now far more extreme that that of the Revisionist leader, Jabotinsky.

Stern wanted a vast Hebrew empire with the original boundaries promised Abraham in the Bible—that is, stretching from the Euphrates to the Nile. As he saw it, the Jewish state would come about as a result of two powerful forces. One was what he termed the Hebrew Liberation Movement of Palestine, designed to free the country from foreign rule; the other was the more traditional Zionism. Both, he believed, were roads to the same goal, one external, the other internal. Zionism dealt with the Jewish problem outside Palestine; liberation dealt with the yearning for freedom of the young Hebrew nation developing in its homeland. Zionism was a movement of Jews in exile who sought a Jewish state as a haven, an answer to anti-Semitism. The Hebrew nation's yearning for freedom was not a search for a solution to a problem but the natural aspiration of every living entity for self-determination in its own environment. For the Hebrew Liberation Movement—which he sought to crystallize, to strengthen and to lead—freedom was not to be a means to an end but the end itself.

Stern argued that he was not denigrating traditional Zionism by making this distinction. As he saw it, the liberation movement, stemming from different sources, might use different means to achieve its goal; and to this movement any foreign rule, whether British or Russian, American or French, whether benevolent or tyrannical, was intolerable.

This difference between what Stern called the interior and exterior aspects of the drive to Jewish statehood was crucial to his philosophy. Ultimately it was to find its way into Bet Zouri's thinking and reflect itself in his defense at the trial in Cairo. It fell in with his thinking about the theories of the Canaanites.

As Stern's beliefs crystallized, they underlay his every action: his part in the formation of the Irgun in 1937, his mission to Poland in 1938 to plan an invasion of Palestine. Although he went to Poland as Jabotinsky's emissary, he was independent, even hostile to the Revisionist leader. Jabotinsky believed that world-wide diplomatic action, with Britain in the forefront, would bring about Jewish independence; he saw the Irgun as the armed force needed to protect the Jews while they created a majority in Palestine. If the Irgun revolted against the British, Jabotinsky insisted, they must not do so indiscriminately: they must damage British civil institutions, the machinery of colonial government only—post offices, police stations and the like—but not military installations; and they must warn the British beforehand so that all personnel could be evacuated and no lives lost.

Stern regarded all this as dangerous romanticism.

His convictions remained firm when he returned to Palestine from Poland just before the war to help take over command of the Irgun on Raziel's arrest; they remained firm with his own seizure by the British thereafter, and with his release, some months after Raziel's, in the summer of 1940.

As we have seen, the two men broke apart even in detention camp on the issue of cooperation with the British, and the rupture worsened when Stern charged that Raziel's release was part of a British deal. In May, 1941, word came of Raziel's death in Iraq while on a secret British mission. The Mufti of Jerusalem was in Bagdad, spurring an Iraqi revolt against the Allies. At the request of British military authorities in Palestine, Raziel and several of his lieutenants disguised as Arabs flew into Iraq to blow up oil installations. Raziel secretly intended to use this opportunity to kidnap the Mufti. Before he could succeed in either plan, he was killed in a German air raid.

Bitterness between the Stern and Raziel factions overflowed.* Stern's anti-British phobia deepened. He began writing industriously, disseminating his views in stenciled pamphlets and in poetry. His poetry was violent, impassioned, full of phrases such as "We are struck with the madness for kingdom," and "Yes, we shall pray for freedom—we shall pray with the revolver, the machine gun and the mine!" He hammered home the theme of freedom: he would walk with Satan himself if it meant the freedom of his people. "It does not matter who the enemy is," he preached: the enemy could be known by one fact only—that he prevented Jewish freedom. "God, our Lord of Hosts, strengthen our hand: we are the freedom fighters for Israel!" his verse proclaimed.

He had now taken an underground name—Yair—which was to

---

* The degree of hostility was sometimes hard to believe. During a critical period Raziel learned that one of his trusted aides was secretly a Sternist and had been stealing Irgun weapons and taking them to the Stern side. When the man, bound to a chair in an adjoining room, confessed after a hearing, Raziel ordered Avigad to give the traitor a tablet of cyanide. Avigad refused. "It's a question of relative morality," he argued. "Had he done for you what he did for Stern, you would have given him a medal." After nearly an hour's debate, Raziel said, "All right. Have him beaten up and thrown into the street."

become almost legendary among his followers, as it was legendary in Jewish history. Eliezer ben Yair was the hero of Masada. After Jerusalem fell to Titus in 70 A.D., Yair led one thousand patriots to the nearby mountain fortress of Masada, on the edge of the Dead Sea, and there swore them to a solemn oath never to let themselves become servants of the foreign ruler. For three years they withstood a terrible siege by Titus' legionnaires. In the end, knowing they would be captured, Yair called upon his men to kill themselves and their families rather than fall into the hands of the Romans. By lot they chose ten men to kill all the rest; and when this was done, the ten chose one by lot to kill the other nine and then himself.

Stern saw himself—as did his followers—as a modern Yair, unshakable even to the point of death in his resolve never to bow to the foreign ruler.

Working closely with him at this time was a huge, barrelchested man of thirty with the thin, high voice so often associated with men of great physique. This was Nathan Friedman-Yellin, a Polish-born civil engineer and tutor in mathematics, who had come to Palestine a few months earlier from Warsaw, where he had edited a fiery Revisionist newspaper, *The Act*.

Friedman-Yellin, who was to succeed Stern as leader of the group, was a curious combination, a man of precise mind and enormous ingenuity. He grew up in a small Polish town which during World War I was successively occupied by the White Russians, the Germans, the Poles, the Lithuanians, the Communists and then the Poles again. The realization came to him that though all these peoples were struggling for freedom, their struggle seemed to have nothing to do with him: no matter who occupied Poland, he and his fellow Jews would be a minority subject to cruel or benevolent rulers, as the case might be. He inured himself to the anti-Semitism about him, now by using his fists, now by losing himself in the pages of Hebrew periodicals from Palestine and the heroic literature of Henryk Sienkiewicz and other Polish writers. At thirteen, he joined Betar and became one of its leaders. Later he won a government scholarship to the Warsaw Institute of Technology—a considerable feat, since only three Jews to every hundred students were permitted to enter—which enabled him to receive his engineering degree. In 1936 he met Stern in Warsaw, was immediately taken with him and joined the Irgun as an organizer. In 1940 he escaped to Palestine from Poland, one step ahead of the NKVD, the Communist secret police, to whom Zionists, as Jewish nationalists, were considered counterrevolutionaries.

Now, as Stern's lieutenant, he worked secretly with him in Tel Aviv, coming to Stern's hideout before dawn each day and leaving after dark. Stern, unable to show himself publicly and therefore unable to work to support himself, received the equivalent of ten dollars a month from his group, which in turn obtained its funds by periodic robberies of various branches of the Anglo-Palestine Bank. His wife, Roni, a kindergarten music teacher, lived apart from him for her own safety, but visited him once a week with food and supplies.

Friedman-Yellin tried to dissuade Stern at this point from taking any anti-British action. Public opinion was not ready for it, he warned; the Jewish community would not understand Stern's motives; they would look on him at best as insane, at worst as a fifth columnist. Stern's stenciled leaflets were on a poor quality of paper, the ink spread, hardly a word was legible—and even when legible, his highly involved prose, sprinkled with Biblical and classical allusions, was hard reading.

Stern refused to heed Friedman-Yellin's warning.

At this point the Nazi plan for the total annihilation of the Jews was not known; the talk was merely of exiling them to Madagascar. Stern said, "Let's persuade them to make it Palestine." He decided to try to make contact with the Axis so that if it captured the Middle East, his group would be recognized as leader of the Jewish community. The idea would have seemed suicidal to anyone less fanatic than Stern in his distrust of Britain, his obsession with the cause of liberation; where this policy might lead was apparently of no consideration.

In late 1941, he sent Friedman-Yellin to the Balkans to persuade Axis authorities there to allow fleeing Jews to use the Balkans as their escape route to Palestine. He declared, "The British are fighting for British independence, the French for French independence, the Czechs for Czech independence, the Poles, the Yugoslavs—all for their own freedom. But the Jews are fighting for British freedom. When they fight for their own independence, they find Germany and Britain arrayed against them—the one crushing them where they are, the other preventing them from reaching refuge. Why should we not turn for help where we can get it? Why should we cooperate in our own enslavement? Is it I who am insane, or the others?"

Even the Irgun printed pamphlets warning all resistance groups to avoid him.

Two months later Stern was dead. The beginning of the end came when he sought to avenge the torture of several of his men by a Captain Geoffrey Morton of the CID. He sent Morton an anonymous tip that a Tel Aviv apartment was a Sternist hideout, then booby-trapped the apartment so that anyone forcing the door would be blown up. Morton, guided by some second sense, did not lead the raiding party himself. Instead, he sent two Jewish policemen. They were killed instantly.

The Jewish community reacted violently. This man Stern—or Yair—or whatever he called himself, not only preached treason, not only tried to persuade their young people to turn against their leaders, but now had begun murdering his own people. Overnight Stern's photograph appeared in all newspapers; it was placarded on walls and telephone poles with the British offer of $5,000 for information leading to his capture. He moved about like a wraith in the blacked-out streets of Tel Aviv, carrying a small suitcase containing a Bible, a Hebrew dictionary and a prayer book, and on his back, a folding cot. He never knew where he would find shelter for the night.

On the morning of February 12, 1942, as he hid in the fourth-floor apartment of a follower, Moshe Svorai, at No. 8 Mizrachi B. Street, there was a knock at the door. Svorai himself had been wounded and captured by the British two weeks before. Mrs.

Svorai, hearing the knock, knew it was not the signal agreed upon by the few who knew the identity of her guest. Stern, who had been writing at the kitchen table, working on the text of a leaflet, gathered up his material and, as usual, slipped into a large wooden wardrobe. Mrs. Svorai locked him in and opened the front door.

Captain Morton stood there with half a dozen armed police.

They brushed by her, searched the apartment, broke down the wardrobe door and dragged Stern out.

Morton signaled to two of his men. They led Mrs. Svorai, protesting, from the apartment. She caught a glimpse of Stern surrounded by policemen manacling his wrists behind his back. She was escorted down the stairs into the street, where a police patrol waited. An enormous crowd had gathered. For nearly two hours the neighborhood had stirred with unusual activity. Men who were obviously police but in civilian clothes had been strolling about watchfully. Half an hour earlier a police tender had come by, six men had jumped off and scattered into nearby streets. A grocer had called his customers' attention to the fact that virtually every roof in the vicinity of No. 8 seemed to have a man posted on it. Then, just moments ago, the police patrol had silently drawn up and Captain Morton himself with a squad of men had hurried out and up the steps.

Now Mrs. Svorai, a plain-clothes man on either side, found herself on the sidewalk amid the crowd.

Suddenly three shots sounded from her apartment.

She began screaming to the people, "Brethren, brethren, they are killing Yair. They are killing Yair! Help him, help him!"

The plain-clothes men were still trying to control her when, minutes later, the body of Stern, wrapped in a bloody blanket, rolled down the front steps of the house, propelled by the kicks of two policemen.

In the Svorai apartment, his captors had ordered the handcuffed man to walk before them. He had taken a few steps when he was shot. The official records would say, "Shot while attempting to escape." They had wrapped his body in the blanket and rolled it down the four flights of stairs to the street.

Mrs. Svorai saw them load it on the patrol wagon and drive away.

They took the body to a morgue at a hospital in Jaffa, the same in which Moshe Svorai, Stern's host, was held prisoner while recovering from his wounds. The next morning Constable Ewer of the CID walked in on Svorai and began, for perhaps the twentieth time, to question him.

"Don't waste your breath," Svorai told him, as he had time and again.

Ewer seemed more confident than usual. "You'd better tell us, my boy," he said. And when Svorai simply looked at him, Ewer said, smiling, "You're finished, all of you, anyway. Your Yair is dead."

Svorai said, "I don't believe it."

"No?" Ewer seized him by the arm and dragged him into another room. A body lay under a sheet. Ewer tore the sheet off, lifted up Stern's head by the hair. "See? Here's your chief. Do you believe me now?"

With Stern's death, the backbone of his movement was broken. At most, there had been 200 followers. Within days the British, with the help of the Jewish community, rounded up all but twenty-five of them. Friedman-Yellin, who had gone on to Syria to find ship smugglers willing to transport refugees, received a note Stern had written him a week before his death. It asked him to return to Palestine to take over a newly organized Sternist department of information. On February 7, en route home, Friedman-Yellin was seized by the British in neutral Aleppo, brought back to Palestine and interned in Mazra Detention Camp. What few Sternists escaped the dragnet vanished completely.

Twelve days after Stern's death there occurred one of those events in history which rouse endless speculation. Had the tragedy of the S.S. *Struma* taken place a fortnight sooner, Stern, his disciples later asserted, would have been honored rather than hunted down. For the *Struma* gave evidence that the White Paper policy would continue, whatever the cost; it served as a chilling reminder that though there was the Britain of Balfour and Churchill—understanding, sympathetic—there was also the Britain of the Foreign Office—unyielding, implacable. The *Struma* gave a tremendous impetus to those who asserted, ever more vehemently, that the Balfour Declaration was a dead letter, that independence was no longer to be won across a council table but, as Stern preached, with the bomb and the gun.

The *Struma*, an ancient tramp steamer built eighty years earlier to transport cattle up and down the Danube River, limped into Istanbul harbor the day after Christmas, 1941. Designed to carry at most 200 persons, it was jammed with nearly four times that number of Rumanian Jews fleeing a Nazi nightmare—wholesale massacres, the herding of people into freight trains dispatched to unknown destinations—indeed, the first inkling of what was later the incredible revelation that Hitler had begun the mass extermination of the Jews. The *Struma* was a shocking sight as it wheezed into port; it listed far to one side, its engine labored, its hull leaked; the passengers, too many to be accommodated in the hold, overflowed onto the small deck where they were packed in giant wire cages to prevent them from falling overboard. Threatened with suffocation below, they fought for a chance to get air on deck. Some were half insane. Food and water were perilously low, one toilet had to serve all 800 passengers and crew, there were neither lifeboats nor life belts. The captain warned harbor authorities that his ship was completely unseaworthy; if his passengers were not removed at once, he refused all responsibility.

Instead, the ship and all those aboard had to remain at the dock for nearly eight weeks while the Jewish Agency and the Turkish government negotiated with the British to allow the refugees to land as transients. The Turks would accept them only if the British permitted them later to continue on to Palestine. At least, the British were asked, grant entry to the children under sixteen.

The Agency worked frantically. Again in Jerusalem Moshe Sharett engaged in endless conferences with High Commissioner MacMichael and his political adviser, Chief Secretary Sir John

Shaw. Because of the war, Sharett pleaded, the 1942 immigration quota even under the White Paper was not filled. Surely these desperate people could be admitted and 800 certificates deducted by the British from the next quota allotted.

MacMichael said no. He was not prepared to feed 800 persons. Moreover, he told friends, some of the refugees might be Gestapo agents, since they came from enemy-occupied Rumania.

Sharett redoubled his appeals. The Jewish community in Palestine would take over the feeding. They were ready to accept cuts in their own food rations to help the newcomers. The American Joint Distribution Committee was ready to aid; and if the High Commissioner seriously feared that some of the Jewish refugees were Hitler spies, the entire 800 could be interned for the remainder of the war.

MacMichael remained adamant. He would not allow them to enter Palestine.

The Turkish government thereupon sent the *Struma* and its despairing human cargo off to sea.

Then word came from Jerusalem that the British Administration would grant certificates to children under eleven who were aboard. Sharett immediately wrote Chief Secretary Shaw asking that the *Struma* be halted at the nearest Turkish port so the children could be taken off, but it was already too late.

On February 24, 1942, buffeted in the Black Sea, the *Struma* virtually disintegrated: it broke apart and sank within minutes. Save for a sole survivor, all on board—746 passengers, including 240 women and children—drowned.

In Palestine the Jewish community mourned as one. All public events were canceled. A nationwide strike was called by the Jewish National Council; a voluntary curfew was observed, with every Jewish citizen remaining in his home from 1 to 7 P.M., grieving over the dead.

It was then that the placards appeared.

111

CHAPTER

9

THAT MARCH MORNING they seemed to spring up everywhere. In Tel Aviv, in Haifa, in Jerusalem, in Safad and Hebron and the towns of the Galilee.

Sometime between midnight and dawn, fourteen- and fifteen-year-old youngsters had spread through each city and, avoiding British patrols, had tacked the placards on telephone poles, newspaper kiosks, even on the walls of police stations. People on the way to work paused to read them, glanced about fearfully and hurried on. Then came the police, thin-lipped as they ripped the posters down.

They bore the photograph of the High Commissioner and read, in Hebrew and English:

WANTED FOR MURDER!

Sir Harold MacMichael, known as the High Commissioner of Palestine, WANTED FOR MURDER by drowning of 800 refugees aboard the S.S. *Struma*.

In his massive and austere Government House, high on the Hill of Evil Counsel outside Jerusalem, Sir Harold blockaded himself behind tanks, troops and barbed wire.

From the very beginning of his term in Palestine, Sir Harold had been out of his depth. Son of a clergyman, married at thirty-seven to the daughter of a clergyman, he was a dry and meticulous man. Before coming from his post as Governor of Tanganyika, he had spent thirty-three years in the Sudan. He had gone there immediately upon graduation from Cambridge, determined to make the Sudan and its surrounding area his life work. His book, *The Anglo-Egyptian Sudan,* published in 1934, was accepted as the definitive study of the subject. But in 1937 the Foreign Office, appointing him High Commissioner and Commander in Chief, Palestine and Transjordan, plucked him out of the idyllic simplicity of Central Africa and dropped him into the extremely complex world of the Middle East, with its intricate involvements of British colonial policy, conflicting Jewish and Arab aspirations, its endlessly tangled skeins of French and Syrian political rivalries. He was constantly in difficulty; and nowhere did this show itself more vividly than in his handling of the problems rising from illegal immigration into Palestine.

As that sorry story unfolded, as Hitler's advancing armies trapped more and more Jews who fled what was at first personal and economic humiliation and then later became brutality and death itself, as ship after ship attempted to run the blockade and land refugees in Palestine, it seemed that Sir Harold grew steadily more obdurate. Whatever the humane considerations involved as each new shipload tried to reach harbor, Sir Harold had insisted upon holding to the absolute letter of the law. Now, in the wake of the culminating tragedy of the *Struma,* he was reaping the harvest of that policy.

In Haifa, young Eliahu Hakim stood, arms akimbo, reading one of the notices. He made no attempt to hide the fact.

113

A policeman brushed roughly by him, ripped it down, eyed the boy coldly and walked on.

Hakim stared after him. He permitted himself the ghost of a smile.

He had been one of the boys who had put up the posters before dawn that morning.

The separate paths of the two Eliahus were beginning to converge.

One day that spring of 1942, Bet Zouri and his friends from high school—Amihai and David—sat on the steps leading to Amihai's home. It was late afternoon. Their conversation touched on many things. Their lives were moving in aimless circles; a great impatience had seized them.

For Bet Zouri, everything seemed to have reached a dead end. His university education had been halted; he had enrolled in a course given by the Government Department of Surveying because he did not know what else to do and had to have a trade. He would become a surveyor, but it did not excite him. There was nothing to capture his imagination in the rods and maps, plumb lines and measuring tapes.

He and his friends sat, becalmed.

There were many such days. One of them would spring to his feet and cry out. "Let's walk—let's go somewhere—anything but sitting here." They would walk, then, to the seashore. Dusk came, the moon rose and they walked for hours, or sat in the moonlight, talking. What could they do? The refugees, the British, their own idleness, their helplessness, drove them frantic.

"Let's think," Amihai said. "We are young, we owe no allegiance to anyone, we can think clearly—what shall we do?"

The situation came to a head with the latest of many demonstrations in memory of the *Struma* dead. Almost the entire population of Tel Aviv marched in the streets. Not only they, but the world itself, had been outraged. Everyone had heard of the Parliamentary debates on the *Struma,* for though British censorship kept the full story out of the Palestine press, it was impossible to halt word of mouth. People spoke of Sir Josiah Wedgwood's charge in the House of Commons: "A sabotage of Jewish freedom and British interests has taken place because crypto-fascism rules in the Near East and lurks in Whitehall. They don't like Jews, won't use Jews, won't accept the Balfour Declaration and are determined to break it. . . . They would sooner the Jews drowned in the *Struma* than that they landed in Palestine. That is the measure of their hate."

And in a mighty peroration that echoed through the country he added:

"I hope to see the day when those who sent the *Struma* back to the Nazis will hang, as Haman did, side by side with their prototype and leader, Adolf Hitler."

Strong words these! And by an Englishman!

In the midst of the demonstration a small red sports car bore down on the marchers. It was driven by Major John Fforde, Tel Aviv Chief of Police; he would show that he could break up a protest march singlehanded.

The three boys watched. Amihai said, "Look, it's only a small car. When it comes by, let's lift it up—"

The car, hemmed in by the crowd, stopped for a moment. The three boys got behind it; Amihai and David actually lifted it a few inches by the rear bumper. The crowd suddenly parted; Fforde jammed down his accelerator; the back wheels began to spin. Eliahu pulled out his penknife and held its point against the spinning tire, as if he were working at a lathe. The sight of Eliahu, his tongue clenched between his teeth, so seriously intent on his work, was too much for David and Amihai: they began to laugh and let the car fall. It spurted forward. The three began running after it.

When Fforde reached the head of the procession, he saw an elderly man carrying the Zionist banner. He vaulted out of his car and seized the flag. "The demonstration is over," he shouted. "Back to your homes, everyone!"

He was re-entering his car, flag in hand, when Eliahu, his face red with fury, snatched at it. Fforde clamped his wrist with a vise-like grip. "All right," he said. "You'll come with me—"

At this, the crowd literally mobbed Fforde. He found himself

115

pressed back, trying to maintain his grip on Eliahu. In the crush, Eliahu suddenly twisted free and ran. Around the corner, the three met again.

They walked home, tense and disturbed. Amihai spoke up. "Look, we've been in a stupid demonstration—" He paused. "We risk ourselves whether we want to or not. So if we do risk ourselves, let's do so for a real aim. Something really worth while."

The people wore black armbands. The streets were full of lamentation. Raziel dead, Stern dead, the Irgun immobilized by the truce, the Sternists by imprisonment . . . what to do?

It was Eliahu who said firmly, "We must act on our own." They would form a three-man cell. They would practice with weapons and so prepare themselves for a major action. When the time came. No resistance movement now appealed to them. If, later, one of the groups seemed right for them, they might join it. Otherwise, they would go it alone.

Eliahu managed to obtain a pistol. David had a Nagan, a Polish revolver, one of the most efficient ever made, which Polish partisans used against the Nazis. Amihai stole a bayonet from a dozing British soldier.

Whenever the three had a chance they practiced with their weapons in a nearby orange grove. David and Amihai were interested in tactics: Eliahu in the spirit motivating the action they would agree upon.

"It must be a historic event," said Eliahu. "Something that will shock people, move them, make them see what's going on—"

It was Amihai who said, "All right then. Let's get rid of Mac-Michael."

The two looked at him. Why not MacMichael? He was the most hated man in Palestine and had been so almost from his arrival in 1938. His record in office—the *Tigerhill,* the *Patria,* the *Salvator,* the *Struma,* and all the others . . .

"Yes," said Amihai. "If we are going to take risks, let's take them for something worth while. Let's begin with killing the High Commissioner."

Amihai spoke bitterly. His brother Neriel had given his life on a secret mission for the British. He had been one of twenty-three specially trained Haganah volunteers assigned to blow up the Vichy oil refineries at Tripoli. They had slipped out of Haifa in a motorboat under command of a British officer. An Axis patrol launch surprised them off the coast and all twenty-three had died.

Amihai was so full of the MacMichael scheme that he even confided in Tamar Vered. "But what will you gain?" she asked, after her first shock. "You get rid of one High Commissioner and they'll only send another."

Amihai drew himself up. His black eyes flashed. "Woe to him!" he cried. "And woe to the one who comes after him!"

For days the boys discussed ways and means. One Sunday they took a bus to Jerusalem and carefully studied Government House and the area around it. The three spent all that night huddled in a nearby ditch watching the changing of the guard. They returned to Tel Aviv disheartened: their plan appeared impossible.

A few days later Eliahu excitedly met the others. He had discovered that one of the policemen on duty was a former classmate at the university. Eliahu's surveying duties would soon have him transferred to Jerusalem; he would cultivate the man and manage to learn what there was to learn about MacMichael's protection.

In time Eliahu gathered the information that MacMichael's bedroom was on the second floor. A heavy rain pipe led from the roof to the ground, passing within a foot of a window. One of the three, chosen by lot, would climb the pipe to the second floor, push open the window—in the summer's heat it would be partly ajar—cut the mosquito screening and climb inside. He would carry a small hatchet tucked into his belt, after the fashion of the American Indians. And he would kill the tyrant as he lay sleeping in his bed.

Their act would have to wait the propitious moment: when they knew precisely at what hour the High Commissioner retired, what night he would be alone, what instant to strike, when best to elude the guards, how to retreat. . . .

Yet, now that it was planned, they began to have second thoughts.

"Are we ready to do the final act?" Eliahu asked one night as they walked along the Tel Aviv seashore. "Suppose we have Mac-

Michael here this moment. All we have to do is kill him. Can we do it? Can we kill a man cold-bloodedly? Suppose we have a knife. Can we push it into his body? Or if we used a gun—can we pull the trigger as he stands before us? And if he falls wounded—can we then fire again?"

The three fell silent. They admitted that they could not. It was one matter for Eliahu to make bombs, to burn down tax booths, to organize a raid on an arms depot . . . but deliberately to kill another human being? If they had to face this horrible thing—to kill a man—how could they train themselves to be capable of it?

"I'd never be able to use a knife," Amihai confessed—Amihai who had first suggested the act. "But if I had an ax, maybe I'd have enough courage to lift it up and then by power of will I'd order my muscles to let it fall of its own weight—perhaps that would do the job. Because if I touched his skin, I'd recoil. I could not touch the living flesh of a man and then kill him."

They came to a solution. Each must develop split personalities.

One side would be technical: it executed the deed. The other would be intellectual: it ordered the deed. The first would follow the command of the second automatically, as if by conditioned reflex. Once you pulled the trigger of the pistol, you automatically pulled it again and again—at least three times. You must destroy the target. If you fired just once and only wounded the man, your instinct would be to drop the gun and run to his help, to give him first aid. How could one kill a helpless, wounded man? "No, we must finish it at once," said Eliahu.

They began their training. Lest they be seen they hiked each afternoon to the sand dunes and wadis outside Tel Aviv. Here they could shoot without being heard. Each taught himself never to mix his "two personalities." One was the everyday man of thought and sensitivity who would go out of his way not to harm a fellow man, an animal, an insect; the other was the emotionless, unthinking technician—the man of action who carried out the deed, who, having to do it, did it properly and to the end.

Logic must dominate. Once logic dictated the act, conditioned reflex carried it out.

Eliahu practiced his marksmanship on empty petrol tins. "I'd go without the cinema for a year if I could find a place to buy enough ammunition so I'd know that when I shoot, I shoot well." When he had no ammunition, he practiced with a stick. He would strike the tin once, then again and again, mechanically, without thinking, doing his best to be first one personality, then the other: the mind that ordered, the body that acted.

So the three boys taught themselves, night and day, to think: *concentrate, do it without thought as if it is not you but someone else: remember, do it—one, two and three! Never one only, for you may miss, you may only wound, then you will stop, you will not carry through, it will be a double tragedy. Do it—one, and two, and three!*

David was later to say, "When I read how Eliahu fired three times at the driver of Lord Moyne's car, I knew how he must have shot as in our practice—one and two and three!"

Eliahu was writing a letter home. He had been sent out into the field, to Jenin, an Arab town, to work with Arab student surveyors on the road. He lived with them in pitched tents, perfecting his colloquial Arabic, reading the latest news to those who were all but illiterate, learning his trade as a surveyor. The letter was nostalgic, lonely—

[March 16, 1942] Dear Father. How are the children? When I saw them last they were not in the best of health, nor was Grandmother. I am well, as always. I'm advancing very nicely in this work and feel I'm halfway in the direction I've set for myself. Are there many air raids?

[A few days later] Father, I would like you to be more specific in your letters as to how everyone is at home. Just to write, "Regards from everyone," or "Everyone is fine" is not enough. I want to hear news of the family.

[March 20] It's a little hard to describe the feeling of spending one's first Sabbath eve in a completely strange place. But in general I can say I'm not depressed. True, the special atmosphere of a Sabbath is lacking, as when we speak among the family, or as when one sits and feels the peace and quiet of the ancient Jewish sacrament upon him. In spite of this we celebrated Sabbath eve as it should be, and the relationship between ourselves and our neighbors is fine.

Now, for the first time, he had enough money to send some to his grandmother, who was living in Jerusalem again after her brief stay in Tel Aviv after his mother's death. He also sent money home, keeping just enough for bare essentials. When he had leave from work he went back to Tel Aviv to visit his family. Deborah, twenty-two, worked in the post office; Aviva, eighteen, was at a farm school; and the two smallest, Lea, now twelve, and Uri, seven, had been sent because of the danger of air raids to live on a farm not far from Tel Aviv.

Eliahu's visits there were exciting events for the children. Even the neighbor's youngsters trailed after him as Lea and Uri took him on a tour of the place. Eliahu would be full of questions. "What's new at the barn? Is there a new cow? What's her name? How much milk is she giving? Has the goat had her kids? Yes? Congratulations!" He would fire questions at Uri, who did his best to answer them at the same rapid pace. Eliahu would turn to Mosi, one of the neighbor's children. "And Mosi, what's new at your place?" Six-year-old Mosi would answer, and Eliahu would listen attentively, making remarks here and there and offering his considered opinion to Mosi.

Lea would look on adoringly. When her brother passed the goat, who was eating grass, patted her on the side and the goat stopped eating, looked at Eliahu, wiggled her short tail and brayed, Lea thought, "Even she is probably blessing Eliahu with a hello. He knows how to speak even with a goat!"

Summer moved into autumn. Eliahu was transferred to Naharia, on the Mediterranean, then to Jerusalem. Soon he would receive his certificate as a licensed surveyor.

When they could, his friends Amihai and David came to Jerusalem to see him.

The work of their cell waited.

120

CHAPTER

10

Now two curious and remarkable men, in the company of the curious and remarkable men who play their role in the story of the two Eliahus, enter the narrative. They were among the handful of Sternists still at large after the massive roundup following Stern's death.

One was a frail, taut little man, hardly over five feet tall, so explosive that he seemed to electrify a room simply by entering it. This was Israel Sheib, a thirty-two-year-old Bible teacher, who was to become one of the three leaders of the Stern group. Born in Poland, the son of a baker, he learned Hebrew when he was six, and at twelve had joined Betar. A brilliant, highly unorthodox student, he graduated from the Rabbinical Seminary in Vienna, then went on to take his Ph.D. degree at the University of Vienna, writing his doctoral thesis on Schopenhauer. When he came to Palestine in 1941 he first took the underground name of Sambation; then, later, adopted the name of Eldad, after an eleventh-century Jewish traveler who according to folklore came from behind the legendary River Sambation.

Sheib, or Sambation, or Eldad—perhaps it is best to use the name

Eldad, by which he was generally known—had been a heretic from the very first. Because of his radical views Eldad was ousted from his position on the staff of the Hebrew Teachers' Seminary in Vilna. He went to Warsaw, where he became an editor on *Der Moment,* a Yiddish daily. Here he further alienated himself by attacking virtually every Zionist leader, the extreme as well as the moderate. Though he was an officer in Betar, Jabotinsky's youth movement, he dared bait the master himself at a Betar conference in Warsaw in 1938. Jabotinsky, by now an oracle to his followers, made a speech eulogizing Ben Josef. "The most impressive thing about him was that before he was hanged, he asked for a comb." He quoted the police guard who had marveled at Ben Josef's bearing, who had seen him brush his teeth moments before he was led to his execution.

Not yet turned thirty, Eldad followed Jabotinsky on the rostrum. He said, "I envy Mr. Jabotinsky his feeling about Ben Josef. But I say that the most impressive fact for us is that the British hanged him!"

Jabotinsky, white-faced, rose and strode from the room.

"The difference between you and me, Mr. Jabotinsky," the irrepressible Eldad shouted after him, "is the difference between the nineteenth and the twentieth centuries." And he went on to declare: "There was a moment when you could have met with Mussolini. You said, 'No. Not with the Italians and not with the Russians.' I say you made a mistake. This had nothing to do with ideology: it had only to do with politics, and only a Don Quixote believes there is any morality in politics. You take as allies those who will help your cause." Later he cited Britain's agreement with Hitler to let him take over Czechoslovakia, and Stalin's pact with Hitler because he thought it would help Russia. Jabotinsky could never have made such a step, Eldad believed: Stern could.

From this time on, the rebellious Eldad was aligned with the rebellious Stern. In March, 1941, he came to Palestine and joined Stern's little group.

Now, after Stern's death, Eldad obtained a job teaching school in Tel Aviv and bided his time.

The other Sternist still at large was sixteen-year-old Joshua Cohen. Joshua was a one-man army. Born in Palestine, son of a farmer, he was skilled in military tactics, expert in sabotage, deadly single-minded in purpose and the swiftest pistol draw in the country. He had escaped months ago from a British detention camp. He now hid in a small orange grove near Tel Aviv, keeping himself alive on oranges, stale bread and water brought by his girl who lived in a neighboring kibbutz.

Tall, lean, with a great mop of black hair, a wild, straggling beard, black eyes blazing out of an emaciated face, he looked like an apparition out of antique Jewish history, one of the ancient Zealots who hid in the caves of Galilee from which they stole out nightly to strike death among the Romans and vanish as swiftly as they came. Despite Joshua's youth, the British had placed a price of $3,000 on his head. He carried his gun day and night; and through the early spring and summer of 1942, hiding in the grove, he collected arms and ammunition, storing them among the roots of the orange trees, waiting for the others—one by one—to find their way to him.

Stern had so ordered it—and Joshua knew it would come true.

Days before his death Stern had written a letter to his colleagues in the detention camps. He knew he had not long to live. Wherever he went he saw his photograph with the caption WANTED and the price the British were prepared to pay anyone who informed on him. Sooner or later the police would catch up with him.

His colleagues read his final letter as a last testament. "If I fall," he had written, "do not avenge me, but see that our movement continues." The language in which it was couched testified to his own sense of his Messianic mission. He charted the one path left for the underground—escape, and then action. He knew that according to tradition, revolutionaries usually languished in prison. This was romantic, but absurd. On the outside, he wrote, were a handful of youngsters who needed leadership. They could do nothing effective by themselves. But they were hardy; the older men, unable to take the universal enmity, the manhunts, had either given themselves up or left the movement. He addressed himself to the leaders still imprisoned. "I call upon you to make a supreme effort to escape so that you can join and strengthen them and reorganize our ranks, bringing in choice souls, fearless and dedicated."

He listed the names of those he wanted to see free.

Among the first of these was Itzhak Yizernitsky—the slow-spoken, nerveless instructor who had lectured Eliahu Bet Zouri in the National Cells, who had noted his "warm heart and sharp mind," who had helped train him in his first months in the underground: Yizernitsky, the man of steel, who had once appealed to Eliahu and his friends: "Men! If you want to smell fire and powder, come with us!"

On the night of September 1, 1942, Yizernitsky carried out the will of Abraham Stern. He and a colleague named Shaoul escaped from Mazra Detention Camp.

It had been carefully planned, with friends inside and outside.

Chief among those inside was Nathan Friedman-Yellin, who had worked so closely with Stern. Friedman-Yellin promised Yizernitsky that after the latter had reorganized their small movement outside so that it "could absorb more members," he would also attempt an escape, and take with him as many Sternists as possible. Meanwhile, they would keep in touch with each other by coded letters smuggled in and out of the camp.

Yizernitsky and Shaoul crawled out from under the third of three barbed wire fences surrounding the camp just after midnight.

Before dawn they had found their way to an apartment in nearby Haifa. Awaiting them there were two youths. One was young Eliahu Hakim; the other, a schoolmate, David Shomron, who just a few months before had brought him into the Irgun.

The apartment belonged to one of Hakim's brothers, Joseph, who had gone on vacation and left him the key. Young Hakim had prepared the place well for his two guests. He and Shomron had brought food, drink, two Polish army uniforms and two pistols for them from an Irgun warehouse. The two men ate, slept a few hours and presently were in a car bound for Tel Aviv. Their disguise was perfect. At the time hundreds of Polish soldiers, who had been released in the East by the advancing Russians, were in Palestine, training in General Wladislaw Anders' brigade. Yizernitsky and Shaoul, both Polish-born, simply melted among them.

A day later, amid the thickets of his orange grove, Joshua greeted the two men. That night the first Sternist meeting outside prison since Stern's death was held under the trees. Six members appeared. There were Joshua, his girl, Yizernitsky, Shaoul and two others. Eldad, in Tel Aviv, had been unable to come.

In the moonlight filtering through the branches that September night, the six shook hands all around, very soberly. They had made a beginning.

Within days a handful of other Sternists appeared. When they gathered, they could not help mocking themselves. Yizernitsky estimated that at most twenty-six Sternists were free. Each time they met, someone would demand ironically, "Are all twenty-six here?"

Yizernitsky hid in the grove for several weeks, letting his hair and beard grow. Like Joshua, he lived on oranges, stale bread and water, faithfully supplied by Joshua's girl. Since both Joshua and Yizernitsky were known escapees, known terrorist leaders, they went armed day and night. The British were thorough when they seized terrorists: they photographed them from every angle, they took motion pictures to record their gait and posture, they measured their features so that no future disguise would be completely foolproof. The photographs were distributed to every CID station, and police were required to carry them on their person. The terrorists, aware that they were marked men, that no colleague dared contact them, that all doors were closed to them, were doubly bitter, doubly desperate. They saw their lives as completely forfeit. It was this attitude which, in the months to come, would give the Sternists the reputation of the most ruthless and dangerous of men.

Joshua began to train the group in guerrilla warfare. The grove was excellent for this purpose. The trees, planted in quadrangles, were only ten feet apart. The foliage, thick and luxuriant, made a perfect blind. A dozen men could be moving about and nothing be visible to police cars patrolling the road fifty yards away. Guns and ammunition were kept in milk cans buried amid the roots of the trees, and only two members knew their location. If one were captured, the other disclosed the hiding place to one more.

Joshua taught his charges marksmanship, using sacks of sand to absorb the bullets; the lightning draw of pistols; the use of silencers; the construction, handling and dismantling of grenades, bombs and mines; the uses of gunpowder and dynamite. Those Sternists unknown to the police drilled without arms in nearby fields. A lookout was posted and a soccer ball was conspicuously in evidence. Should police stumble upon them they would find a group of boys playing soccer.

Meanwhile, Yizernitsky underwent a transformation.

Once clean-shaven, muscular, with a military stride, he became "Rabbi" Shamir—a bent, bearded, wheezing Talmudic scholar, complete to long black caftan, broad-brimmed black hat and luxurious black side curls, muttering Hebrew prayers under his breath as he slowly shuffled about in his shiny boots. The night came when he dared leave the grove and make his way to Tel Aviv, where he took a tiny room. Here he hid, moving about only when dusk fell. It was December, toward the end of the year 1942. In his mind he carefully went over the names of those he could recruit into their small movement. He thought, again and again, of Avigad—and of Eliahu Bet Zouri.

CHAPTER

11

Eᴌɪᴀʜᴜ ɪɴ Tᴇʟ Aᴠɪᴠ for the weekend, stood at a street corner waiting for a bus to take him home. He was thinking, How do we handle MacMichael? How do we carry out our plan?

Moving automatically forward in the queue, he noticed a heavily bearded orthodox rabbi in the broad-brimmed black hat and curly earlocks of the extremely pious approaching him. The bus arrived. Eliahu, about to board it, saw out of the corner of his eye that the rabbi continued to come directly toward him—not attempting to queue behind him. Would so ethical a man seek to push his way into the bus out of turn? But the man was only a foot away from him now, and he heard him say, in a low and mysterious voice, "Eliahu! Eliahu!" For a moment Eliahu was startled, in that moment unaccountably driven back centuries as if to some previous incarnation in Biblical times, when the Angel of the Lord might have called him in his sleep thus urgently, "Eliahu! Eliahu!" As if in a dream, Eliahu stared, feeling the prickling of his scalp; then the spell passed: he realized he was in Tel Aviv in 1943. He stepped out of line and replied, "Yes?"

The other said in the same voice, "Come with me. I wish to talk with you."

Again, almost in a spell, Eliahu followed him through winding streets to a crowded back yard and up half a dozen wooden steps to a wooden landing. As he climbed the steps he became aware that two other men were behind him. On the landing the rabbi stood aside, clutching Eliahu's arm, while the two pushed by them, opened a door and entered a room. They began searching it. They looked under the bed, behind the tiny sink, they carefully checked the walls and peered into the shade of a small bed lamp. Then they turned: "Please—" and beckoned them in.

In the room, with the door closed and bolted, the rabbi removed his hat and with one gesture stripped off his earlocks. They had been pasted on. He grinned at Eliahu. "Don't you know me? It is Yizernitsky."

He told Eliahu he had escaped from Mazra Camp four months ago. He was in deep hiding, waiting for his beard to grow. There was a price upon his head: no precautions could be too great. He explained that he had taken the disguise of an orthodox rabbi —"I am now Rabbi Shamir, if you please," he said, with a smile— who spent his days studying the Talmud and ventured out only rarely, and only at night. Then, as they sat together, he spoke quietly and earnestly. They were reorganizing the Stern group. He wanted Eliahu to join them.

"We are to start everything anew," he said. "I will not fill your head with tall stories or impossible plans, Eliahu. We have no real organization—if we are thirty in all, we are lucky. The others are still sitting in jail. But I say to you only that our business will go on, and we want you with us."

Eliahu told him that he and two friends had been working on their own plan of action. He did not reveal that they had in mind the assassination of MacMichael. "If we can carry it out—it will be an important act. And we will do it ourselves, without any organization."

Shamir did not press him. He knew Eliahu was with them in

heart. In time he would join. Before they parted, Eliahu said, "I suggest that you speak to Avigad. I will bring him to you."

King David Park is a small oasis of loveliness in the heart of Ramat Gan, a garden town near Tel Aviv. It is one of the show places of Israel, and to one wandering amid its green beauty it seems almost incredible that little more than a generation ago it was sand dune and desert. At night King David Park is a place of soft music and gaiety. The flickering lights from the marquee of the Cinema Rama across the road from the park bring the green leaves and rich shrubbery into sharp relief. Young lovers stroll among the oaks and cypresses, and half-hidden by the deep-hanging foliage, embrace each other. In the center of the park is the circle of a goldfish pond, with lilies floating in it, the water reflecting the lamplight all about.

Here Shamir, Avigad and Eliahu met a few nights later. Eliahu and Avigad, who had moved to Tel Aviv, where he now taught school, arrived together. A few minutes after eight o'clock Shamir materialized from the darkness, and the three began to stroll slowly through the park.

As they walked, Shamir explained the reorganization. Avigad, as a former member of Raziel's High Command, could be most valuable. It was an important rebuilding, he emphasized. He, Eldad and Friedman-Yellin—though the latter was still in detention camp, letters were smuggled in and out almost daily—had agreed on the new character of their group and its new name. It was no longer to be a military organization but a secret revolutionary society. No squads, no platoons, but cells, perhaps not more than three men to a cell. No epaulets, no belts, no military bearing, no saluting—not even public *hadar* (dignity). Their members were to be casual and inconspicuous, melting into the general population. All military titles were to be done away with. Instead of "commander," it would be "He-who-is-responsible." Thus, as Friedman-Yellin had explained in his last letter, "our members will overcome all weaknesses of pursuing honors, titles or rank." Only

129

the execution of the task was important. In short, anonymity, dedication, completion.

The new name of their group would be "The Fighters for the Freedom of Israel"—in Hebrew, *Lohmey Heruth Israel*. The initials spelled LEHI—the Hebrew word for "jaw." This was perfect symbolism. Samson had defeated the Philistines with the jaw bone of an ass; so the sons of Israel, using the Lehi, would smite the British. "From now on we shall be Lehi among ourselves, the Fighters for the Freedom of Israel—the FFI—to the outside," said Shamir. In the darkness they heard the dance music floating across the park from the garden cafés on the other side; the gay voices and laughter of children on the swings and seesaws. Shamir spoke slowly and earnestly, and to anyone watching, he might well have been what he appeared to be—a teacher painstakingly explaining a fine point of the Talmud.

"The new organization will express its objectives differently from the Irgun," Shamir said. "We shall publicly assert that we do not recognize the Englishman as the legal ruler who oppresses us: we consider him an illegal ruler who must be driven out. What is our aim? It is to free our nation from foreign rule. This is our fight with England—out, out of Palestine! We do not fight the British Administration to make it better, to force it to give us favors. If Britain gave us every concession, this would not change our determination." And strolling in the darkness, he asked, "Now, how shall we do this? At most we shall be a tiny group—the few against the many. We shall be alone in our fight. The population will be bitterly against us until we can educate them. How do we drive the English out? What can we do?"

A military revolt? No, said Shamir, answering his own question. "We might toy with the idea, it is exciting and romantic, but completely impracticable. We have neither the arms nor the men to maintain ourselves in power."

The answer was guerrilla warfare. This was the only weapon of the weak against the strong. This was the only way to equalize forces when one force was of infinite strength, the other ridiculously inadequate in comparison. Hit—and run. Choose the time, the place, the object, strike hard, without warning—and vanish. Then strike hard again. "Experience teaches us that after every action the authorities will be doubly alert, they will bring out all their forces to find us. But soon things will fall back to their normal pattern, the emergency will be over, they will no longer be on guard all the time—then we choose the moment, the place and the object, to strike again."

But—he asked aloud—what were the hardest blows they could deal the enemy? "None of us has studied in a military school. We are all self-taught. We can only do what will be possible for us. We might attempt sabotage, but large-scale sabotage calls for enormous numbers of men. We shall have a handful. It calls for tons of explosives—we shall have a few kilograms. It calls for machine guns —our deadliest weapons are pistols.

"What operations, then, can we carry out with limited arms, a few men—and yet be effective?"

He answered his own question with an explosive phrase:

Individual terrorism.

That was the answer. Acts of individual terror aimed at important personalities at the head of the administration, at the pinnacle of the pyramid of foreign power.

"Such acts," he said, "will render the government weak and ineffectual. Such acts will have powerful echoes everywhere. Such acts will prove to the authorities that they cannot enforce law and order in Palestine unless they keep vast forces here at the cost of thousands of pounds."

He paused. The strains of dance music across the park played a strange counterpoint to his words, delivered with such earnestness. "We have no illusions that we, the Lehi, by ourselves, will free the country. But I am convinced that if we carry out large acts, they will serve as an example, they will rouse the people, they will draw them to our cause." And he quoted Abraham Stern: "Yair said, *'Actions educate.'* "

Would Avigad undertake to reorganize the Jerusalem branch of the Lehi? Be responsible for recruiting of members, their military and tactical training, their security, the conspiratorial methods to be followed? Would former Platoon Commander Bet Zouri join Avigad in the new organization?

It was just ten o'clock as a car drove up next to the curb where the three men walked and a door opened. "Shalom," said Shamir, and slipped in. The car rolled away.

Why did Eliahu Bet Zouri, who not so long ago had said in effect, "A plague on both your houses," join the Sternists? Years later Shamir put it in these words: "What influenced him were our careful and definite statements that we wanted to free our country from foreign rule. Not because that rule was British, but because it was foreign. Not because of the Jewish problem, or because Zionism was the answer to that problem—but simply and basically because this is our country, our homeland, the land of our ancestors, and in it *we*—not strangers—must rule."

Twenty-four hours after his meeting with Bet Zouri and Avigad, Shamir received a guest in his room in Achad Ha'am Street. It was Sergeant Benjamin Gefner of the Royal Engineers, on leave from Cairo. Sergeant Gefner, a surveyor from Tel Aviv, had enlisted a few months earlier, just after the fall of Tobruk. A tall, strapping man with a high-cheek-boned, Indian-like face, he was to take part in the invasion of Sicily, to volunteer for especially dangerous duty behind the enemy lines and ultimately to be decorated by the British government as a war hero. At this moment, however, other matters were paramount. Shamir spoke to him as a fellow Sternist. Would he organize a small FFI branch in Egypt when he returned to Cairo? The exact nature of its work would be determined later: at the beginning, it would be made up of perhaps half a dozen boys and girls in the various camps. They could make themselves useful, said Shamir, smuggling small arms and ammunition into Palestine when they came home on leave.

"I will go ahead with it," said Sergeant Gefner.

Within a week Shamir had begun the reorganization of the FFI in Jerusalem, Tel Aviv, Haifa and Cairo.

The task of building a secret society was no simple one. Avigad, faced with the problem of establishing methods of communication and meeting, protection and security of members, read everything he could find on the subject. During his Irgun days he had collected an entire library of Irish Resistance Army literature. He used these as a base. He studied the conspiratorial techniques of the Narodnaya Volya, or "Freedom of the People's" party, the Russian terrorist society whose members assassinated Czar Alexander II in 1881. There was no ideological parallel between the Fighters for the Freedom of Israel and the Freedom of the People's party; the Russians were revolutionary terrorists fighting an entire social structure. The FFI was dedicated to only one objective: independence. It had no political line, no ideological unity. The Irgun had been frankly Revisionist, nationalist, militarist. The FFI would reflect every variety of thinking: right-wing antilaborites and left-wing socialists; orthodox Jews who prayed three times a day and confirmed atheists; Polish intellectuals and Yemenite artisans; all brought together by one obsessive conviction—the foreign ruler must be forced out of Palestine. What government would then be set up was no concern of the FFI: their goal was freedom.

Avigad pored over books dealing with the Serbian Black Hand, which had assassinated Archduke Ferdinand at Sarajevo in 1914. Like the FFI it had begun with cells of three to five members, above them district committees and above them a Central Committee. The Irgun called its leadership the High Command; the FFI's would be a three-man Central Committee: Friedman-Yellin, operating from Latrun Detention Camp, Dr. Eldad and Shamir. To what Avigad read he added his considerable ingenuity and his experience in the Irgun. To protect the new group, he set up an intelligence service—a central file of data on CID agents, their descriptions, idiosyncrasies, strengths and weaknesses. As far as techniques to outwit the police, he had already made it his duty to see every gangster and Western film; now he read American magazines carrying stories on Al Capone and the Chicago gangs, the G-men, the battle of wits between bootleggers and prohibition agents. All was grist for him.

133

As a result, FFI security measures were astonishingly effective. In the course of time Avigad and his successors, Bannai and Aviel, invented code names for places and simple ways to disguise time and dates. FFI men used these not only in communications but in conversation to mislead eavesdroppers. In their code, each day meant two days earlier. The hour cited meant two hours earlier.

Avigad taught his men how to write notes in the fewest words, in the tiniest letters, on paper no larger than cigarette paper. These, folded tightly and sealed with adhesive tape, were small enough to be passed between members when they shook hands.

Communication by message was all-important, for FFI men met only when absolutely necessary and even avoided greeting each other on the street. One never knew who was being shadowed.

In Tel Aviv a soft-drink stand on the corner of Nahlat Benjamin and Allenby Road, operated by an FFI couple, became the official communications center. Bet Zouri would order a drink and with the money hand the girl a tiny sealed note. If she had a message for him she passed it along with his change.

A technique was worked out to make possible the meeting of two members in the open. At the appointed hour each was to circle the block, one to his right, the other to his left. To any observer, their meeting would appear to be pure chance. If more than three or four had to meet, each carried lecture notes to use as an alibi: they were bound for night school.

Finances were a major problem. A group of members were assigned to obtain money—often by shop-to-shop solicitation. Merchants contributed small amounts, either because they were intimidated or were in grudging sympathy with the band. Later, when the FFI grew stronger, it robbed neighborhood banks, usually getting away with small sums. Sometimes it was to make daring raids, its men dressed in stolen British uniforms or posing as bank examiners. Once inside the vaults, their guns were drawn: the mere announcement—"We're members of the Lehi—" was enough to terrify their victims.

Other practical matters were taken up. Warehouses—usually a school basement made available to them because the principal was a sympathizer—were used to store not only arms and ammunition but a stenciling machine. The latter was important, for Avigad turned out voluminous instruction sheets with such titles as, "Rules for Those Who Must Hide Out," and "How to Enter and Leave a Place Without Causing Suspicion." These told how to choose the neighborhood in which to hide; the type of room; the private entrance required; the name to assume—a translation into Hebrew of one's first name or father's name was safest; what to tell a curious landlord; how to conceal the fact that one was in his room all day and went out only at night ("Open the door loudly, close it, get into bed, lie there for three hours without a sound, then silently go to the door, open it loudly again, and close it"); precautions to take, such as destroying group photographs, stripping labels from medicine bottles and laundry, erasing names from books. Nothing was left to chance.

Meanwhile, in Latrun Camp, Friedman-Yellin wrote a major article which appeared in the first FFI publication, *In the Underground,* a two-page stenciled leaflet distributed only to members. Later a second publication—*Hazit* (The Front)—would be published for general readership as the principal propaganda medium of the FFI.

In his article, "Let Us Liquidate the Prisons," the FFI chief wrote in essence:

Prisons are the enemy of the underground. They siphon away people from our work with drastic results. Either our people (1) sit in prison, impotent; or (2) they become broken in body and spirit. Therefore, we must eliminate the prisons. From now on we do not allow ourselves to be arrested—no matter what the cost. From this day on, our men must carry arms day and night, asleep or awake. If there is a sudden checkup of civilians in the street, a roundup for questioning and examining of papers, you do not submit: you resist; you sell your life as dearly as possible. Kill—or be killed.

This may seem harsh advice, he added. But we assume that it will have certain constructive results. The police will not be too eager to make a street checkup if they know a bullet awaits them.

135

Friedman-Yellin's declaration, appearing in the February, 1943, issue, opened a new and desperate chapter of the FFI. Unless known to police, Sternists until now had gone unarmed on the theory that possession of a weapon immediately identified them as terrorists. Though many had escaped the police sieve in this fashion, others had been arrested, gun or no gun, and thrown into prison without trial, simply as suspected terrorists. Now Friedman-Yellin had made it clear that every member was precious: no chances of arrest could be taken.

Kill—or be killed.

CHAPTER

12

Walking down Princess Mary Avenue, in Jerusalem Eliahu Bet Zouri, every inch the Englishman: blue-eyed, ruddy-cheeked, a blond mustache, a pipe in his mouth, wearing a blue sports-jacket, gray flannel slacks, rubber-soled suède shoes, in his hand the badge of an Englishman in Palestine —a rolled-up copy of the *Mid-East Mail,* the newspaper published for British personnel in the Middle East.

Eliahu was on his way to meet Avigad, at their usual rendezvous in Jerusalem, the least likely place anyone would look for a terrorist—the YMCA. Where better than this popular gathering place of British civilians and Christian Arabs to discuss the strategy of recruiting new members for the Fighters for the Freedom of Israel? One of the showplaces of Palestine, the YMCA was a magnificent structure built through the bequest of an American, with a tower itself more than ten stories high. Here later were the headquarters of the American Red Cross and various departments of the American Military. Three floors were occupied by permanent residents, nearly all Christian Arabs, with a sprinkling of transient British and American war correspondents. The building boasted a gymnasium, swimming pool, restaurant and snack bar, an auditorium (in which met the commissions of inquiry sent out at intervals to find a solution to the insoluble Palestine problem), club rooms, library and museum. Outside were a soccer field, a baseball diamond, running tracks and tennis courts.

Eliahu was disguised as an Englishman because he and Avigad now virtually commuted weekends between Tel Aviv and Jerusalem in their FFI work, and they had to move with the greatest care. Most Jews used the bus for the hour-and-a-half trip between the two cities or bought a seat in the seven-passenger taxi which plied between them. But buses and taxis were both subject to sudden searches by the British, endlessly hunting illegal immigrants or trying to match the terrorist photographs they carried with them to the right faces. The only other transportation was the train, used almost exclusively by the British and by wealthy Arabs. "Then we shall use the train," Avigad had said; and since both were fair-complected, they went as British civilians, Palestine-style.

At the YMCA they usually met in the little snack bar off the lobby, overlooking the soccer field. Here, over beer dispensed by an ever-smiling Arab counterman, they discussed names and approaches. Eliahu began by calling on former Irgunists, at their houses or places of employment. He drew them out gingerly. Were they interested in resuming action? In renewing the fight? In driving out the British?

Two of the first he approached were the fellow members of his own amateur cell—David and Amihai. He said, "Look. We all agree action is needed. Now that I've met and talked with Yizernitsky again, I'm convinced that if anyone will do anything, it will be the Lehi. These people have destroyed every bridge behind them. They are moving on a one-way road now—they can't turn back, they can only go forward."

The three had discussed for some time the problems faced by their little cell. The MacMichael plan, which seemed so brilliant at the beginning, grew increasingly complex. Suppose they succeeded: what then? Was it logical to kill MacMichael if such an act was not part of a long-range program? They had no such program: even if they could formulate one, they certainly could not carry it out by themselves. What was needed was an apparatus—an organization. Either they must create a new one or join one already existing. Both David and Amihai had already made overtures to re-enter the Irgun. Now Eliahu was asking them, instead, to join the reorganized Stern group—the FFI.

Both David and Amihai had reservations. "I'd have to know these people better," Amihai said. "Especially your Yizernitsky-Shamir. These people are the only bridge between you and the idea for which you must be ready to die. In other words, you're wagering your life on their political judgment." He shook his head. "I have no way of knowing if they are right or wrong, but it doesn't follow that just because they are first-rate fighters their political judgment is also first-rate."

David, for his part, could not forget Yizernitsky's "fire and powder" remark in the days immediately following the Raziel-Stern split. "I hate the smell of both fire and powder," he said with some heat. "I'll live with them if that's the only way to drive the British out—but is it the only way?"

When Eliahu saw how they felt he did not press them. He looked up other former colleagues. Here he worked with infinite caution. Anyone who entered the FFI entered what might well be a suicide corps. Not only would a British policeman turn one in, but a neighbor or a landlady might do it, convinced that the terrorists were as capable of blowing up the Jewish Agency as a British installation. A new candidate had to be recommended by at least two members. Then he was shadowed to see whom he met and whether he made contact with the police. One never knew when a man had become an informer; or—and this posed a difficult problem—had been arrested, then released to be followed in the hope he would lead CID men to his associates. Only when a man passed every test was he sworn in.

The induction was similar to the Irgun's. In the darkened room the candidate heard a man's voice, deep and grave:

"You know if you join us, you will be an outcast from the community?"

"Yes."

"That no one will give you shelter—the kibbutzim will not hide you, your neighbors will not protect you, the community will not defend you—"

"Yes."

"You realize the physical danger? If arrested, the British will kill you. If they do not kill you, they will torture you. Pliers to squeeze your testicles, toothpicks under your nails, lit matches in your armpits, water down your nostrils to suffocate you—are you prepared for that? Can you remain silent?"

"Yes."

"You face, if not death, if not torture, then exile, perhaps for years—"

Yet slowly, man by man, the FFI grew.

When Avigad and Bet Zouri had collected a nucleus of members —about a dozen—Shamir sent Joshua Cohen to Jerusalem to train them.

Shamir informed Eliahu, who did not know Joshua, that an "instructor from Tel Aviv" would call on him. Joshua's directions, in turn, were to go to Jerusalem and meet a young man who would be wearing a gray sweater and sunglasses, strolling near the southeast corner of the Italian Hospital. The hour and password were given both men.

The two met. Joshua was immediately impressed. Eliahu's "rough face, as if hewn out of rock, not round and smooth" struck him as the face of a youth of strong character and power of decision; and when he spoke, the choice of his words, the quality of his thought, as those of an intellectual. On the hospital roof was a bronze replica of the celebrated statue of Romulus and Remus. As they walked away, Eliahu told Joshua the story, which he had never heard, of the she-wolf feeding her cubs, symbol of the founding of imperial Rome. Eliahu took at once to the thin, relentless Joshua, who seemed immune to fear. With a few others they began training in the barren hills outside the city. They found an ideal place—a remote area in the hills, not far from the deep burial caves of the Sanhedrin. The caves were ten feet high and about fifty feet deep. Their walls smothered the sound of gunfire as the boys practiced shooting at petrol tins. They spent hours marching, drilling, perfecting the swiftest kind of firing—that direct from the hip.

One afternoon, in the midst of a grenade drill, a squad of three British policemen suddenly appeared over a wadi about fifty yards away. They had stumbled on the boys.

Eliahu saw them first. He plucked at Joshua's sleeve.

The latter turned and with lightning speed whipped out his pistol and barked in Hebrew, "Hands up!"

Usually the British met with no resistance. The sight of the British uniform, that uniform symbolizing absolute authority in colonies all over the world, was enough to cow a man into submission—no force, not even the quiet words "You are under arrest" were necessary. No terrorist surprised by the British had dared pull a gun on them. Instead, the usual policy was to drop one's arms, prepare to stand trial and deny any connection with the weapons.

But Joshua, almost without thinking, had drawn his gun.

The absolute authority suddenly vanished.

The British did not understand his Hebrew, but at his command, at the sight of his revolver produced with such bewildering speed, they threw up their hands.

"Your pistols!" Joshua demanded. Eliahu, watching the miracle before him, translated the order.

Tremblingly they pulled their service revolvers from their holsters and dropped them.

"On your bellies—fall on your faces, quick!" Joshua snapped. Eliahu's words echoed his. The three men fell prone and lay there, their faces in the yellow dust, their bodies quivering, expecting to be shot at any moment. Eliahu stared, amazed. He had never imagined anything like this. Suddenly he realized, as he told Joshua later, the power of the drawn gun at the right time.

From one of the men came a terrified stammering. "For God's sake, don't kill me—please, I have a Jewish wife, I've done no harm to you, I'm going back to England after the war—"

Eliahu translated for Joshua.

Joshua said: "Search them—then tie them with their own belts."

While the man pleaded again—"Take our guns, take our uniforms, but don't kill us," Eliahu followed orders. Joshua picked up the revolvers, shook out the bullets and tossed back the empty weapons. He spoke rapidly to Eliahu, who interpreted again. "We'll spare your lives this time. Don't move for the next hour. The first man to lift his head will be shot."

With that the group of boys withdrew, turned and in minutes had lost themselves in the winding streets of the Old City.

"The gun, oh the gun!" Eliahu wrote in his diary. "From now on it is my best friend. It equalizes all—the strong and the weak, the oppressor and the oppressed."

It was impossible for his family not to note his absences at all hours. By now his older sister, Deborah, had married a schoolteacher, a man who was a stanch member of Haganah. His younger sister, Aviva, closest to him, also belonged to Haganah. They suspected that Eliahu was involved in the extremist underground, using the cover of his surveying job, but he shed no light on his comings and goings. His little brother, Uri, was to remember how often Eliahu, on a visit home, would send him out to play while he locked himself in a room with his friends. "But it's my house, too." Uri would wail in protest. "Why do you throw me out?" Eliahu's father, playing chess with Aviva of an evening, would watch this tableau. Sometimes he tried to reason with his son. If Eliahu refused to discuss his activities, he made no secret of his violent anti-British stand, and Moshe Bet Zouri, too, suspected that his son was deeply involved in the terrorist underground.

On one of these visits home the old man would begin to talk to Eliahu, speaking in his slow, methodical fashion, choosing his words as carefully as he chose his moves on the chessboard. "What are the arguments against your point of view? One: England is fighting Germany—surely our greatest enemy. This is not the time to trouble her. Second: Churchill is a Zionist. He has pledged his word to our leaders that he will deal honorably with them after the war. Third: the Labor party has a good possibility of coming to

142

power in England in the next elections. They have promised to revoke the White Paper, to open the country to immigration—"

He would look at Eliahu, who would say nothing.

"Notice how the English act when they hold their elections. Though they are rough with each other, though they say strong things and feel deeply, when the elections are over they accept the decision. Why shouldn't you adopt such conduct?"

Again his eyes would search out Eliahu, who would remain silent.

"Do you think you understand more than our people at the top —Dr. Weizmann and Ben-Gurion and the others who have devoted their lives to this subject? Why shouldn't you give a chance to those who understand the ways of government, and are experienced?" He would shake his head. "It is not right, Eliahu; it is anarchy to act against those elected by the majority of the people."

Again, silence.

Moshe Bet Zouri would lose some of his self-control.

"Those in your underground are children, babies! They and their half dozen will drive Britain out of Palestine? Egypt cannot do it, India cannot do it—but those fanatics will, those people who fill your ears with wild—"

Eliahu would stand up, his face flushed. "Father, stop. I won't let you speak this way. I have friends among them."

But his father would go on, shaking his finger at him. "I tell you, you may yet be grateful that it is the English who are here and not the French or the Germans or the Russians! Have you any idea what they would do in this situation? They would answer you by wiping out whole towns and villages if you did to them what you do to the English!"

Eliahu, controlling himself, would turn away. The discussion— no, the monologue, by Moshe Bet Zouri would stop. Eliahu would go out into the night, back to Jerusalem—to conspire, to attack, to do God knew what. . . . His father would turn back to Aviva. "He listens, he sits there with his arms folded and listens, but he will not argue." And with a sad, ironic smile, "Your brother is like rock. One may as well talk to the wall."

143

Father and daughter would rearrange the chessboard and, heavy at heart, lose themselves in the game.

In the spring and summer of 1943 Eliahu in Jerusalem corresponded frequently with Avigad in Tel Aviv, writing in simple code. Books meant guns; library meant warehouse; the librarian, the FFI man in charge; money meant ammunition; a student meant a new recruit.

On February 18, 1943:

Greetings to you, Avigad. Nothing to report. I'm still waiting to be paid the money owed me by the librarian. He's become difficult, especially after I stopped borrowing books from him. After I studied the first volumes, I discovered they are outdated. I told him I had no use for them. I think he was insulted. I told him he still owes me money and he said he will be receiving new funds soon and will pay the debt. I also had a long conversation with our friend Selah. I must say that everything he tells us is fairy tales. I don't put much faith in him. I may come to Tel Aviv this weekend.

A month later:

Warmest greetings, Avigad. The student you sent has arrived. He knows his books but I haven't been able to teach him more, especially as he didn't bring his other books with him. I sent him back to get a letter from his earlier teacher saying just how far his studies have progressed and also to bring more study material. He is a nice fellow who learns quickly—he should be able to pass his examinations without trouble. If you expect work here and want me to remain over the weekend I shall. Otherwise, I will come to Tel Aviv on the 9 A.M. train. Regards to Miriam.

Eliahu's surveying job ended abruptly. He got into a dispute with his superior; both agreed that he should leave, although he was given a letter of recommendation. Eliahu returned to Tel Aviv and in the late summer of 1943 obtained a job with a private surveying firm. And for the first time, he fell in love.

After he had been working several months, a pretty eighteen-year-old girl named Hannah Kushnir was hired as office secretary. Shy, dark-eyed, soft-spoken, with a slow smile that lit up her face, she appealed to Eliahu the moment they met. They found themselves lunching together at a neighboring dairy restaurant. In the course of a few weeks she took him home to meet her family. Presently his entire circle knew that he was spending nearly every free evening with Hannah. Eliahu had always had warm friends among other girls, but these were essentially platonic relationships. He had always spoken disparagingly of himself as a ladies' man. "I know I'm not handsome, I'm no prize for the girls, but I'm not a bad fellow," he would say. And although he was always gallant, he had never been serious about a girl. Hannah was different; he courted her in earnest; when they missed each other during the day because he was out in the field, he left little notes of endearment in her desk, as if to remind her of his presence.

One night, soon after he met Hannah, he telephoned Tamar Vered. She had invited him to a party. "I'm bringing over a girl— tell me what you think of her," he said, and then, half jestingly, "You'd better like her because I think she's going to be the one." Among those waiting to pass judgment were Amihai; Ada Ron and her husband, Harold; Avigad and his wife Miriam; and Adi, now called Jacob, and his wife Shoshanna. Actually, Adi and Shoshanna were not married. Although they lived together, Adi, who was more nonconformist than ever—he now identified himself as a Canaanite and was drafting a credo for the society—had small respect for such religious conventions as marriage. "But Jacob," Tamar had demanded in her typical, no-nonsense manner, "what if a baby comes?" Adi, still insisting that he was compromising his principles, was prevailed upon to go through a wedding ceremony a few weeks later.

Hannah, for her part, was terrified at meeting Eliahu's friends. She knew she was being put to the test. All went smoothly, however, and Tamar later solemnly assured Eliahu that he had made an excellent choice. All the time he talked about Hannah he blushed furiously.

In her wildest imaginings Hannah could not have dreamt that her gay and teasing companion, so busy translating another English writer he had discovered—the latest was Damon Runyon— or so enthusiastically reading aloud a poem that delighted him, or so diligently poring over his blueprints, or so shyly yet proudly

145

showing her off to his friends, was a member of the Stern group. She assumed that like everyone she knew he belonged to the Haganah. Often, when they were out for an evening, he would apologize and suddenly go off, leaving her to make her way home alone. When he saw her at the office the next morning he would give no explanation. She took it for granted that he had been involved in some Haganah activity one didn't talk about. Perhaps he had received a summons to hurry to a lonely stretch of beach for some emergency arms drill; perhaps it was an important assignment dealing with the defense of a kibbutz in a strategic area. . . . Hannah, modest and retiring by nature, would have been the last to question Eliahu on such matters.

But what he was involved in, this autumn of 1943, was an altogether different action. When it occurred, on the night of October 31, it electrified all Palestine. And it signaled the resurgence of terrorism such as the country had never before known.

CHAPTER

13

SHIELDED IN A CLUMP of bushes
outside Latrun Detention Camp, he watched the searchlight sweep
the horizon in a vast, 360-degree circle every thirty seconds. He
could see the dim lights of the watchtowers at each of the four corners of the huge compound; he could hear the German police dogs
barking as they roamed restlessly about. They were let loose every
night as soon as the prisoners were locked in their bunkhouses.
Twenty-five feet away from him, almost invisible under the trees,
stood an empty bus. A driver waited at the wheel.

It was a few minutes before 1 A.M., the morning of November 1,
1943.

Eliahu Bet Zouri was waiting for twenty-one Sternists to break
out of the escape-proof detention camp of Latrun. At this very moment in an audacious, an incredible operation, the twenty-one were
crawling to freedom through a tunnel they had dug—a tunnel
complete to electric light and ventilation, six feet below earth, 135
feet long, some of it through solid rock. It led from the stone floor
of Bunkhouse No. 4 to this point where he stood beyond the ten-
foot-high barbed-wire fence surrounding the camp.

147

The escape took place while Palestine still seethed over the first reports of the liquidation of the Warsaw Ghetto. Full details were yet to come but it was already known that nearly half of Polish Jewry had perished. In this supercharged atmosphere, the feat of the FFI gave the movement a powerful impetus.

All odds were against the escape which Nathan Friedman-Yellin had promised. When the FFI men were rounded up early in 1942 after Stern's death, they had been interned in Mazra Detention Camp near Acre. After the escape of Shamir and Shaoul late that year, the British transferred those prisoners considered most dangerous—and these included Friedman-Yellin and some one hundred other Sternists—to the larger and more secure Latrun Camp, which held several hundred inmates, including Italian prisoners-of-war. The newcomers found themselves distributed in bunkhouses throughout the enormous compound. It took weeks for Friedman-Yellin, working with scientific ingenuity and infinite patience, making use of pretended illnesses and trumped-up personal feuds, to bring about a series of transfers of prisoners so that in the end all twenty-one inmates of Bunkhouse No. 4 were Sternists.

Then the problem arose of obtaining digging tools. Overnight the inmates of No. 4 became gardeners. They surrounded their drab wooden building with elaborate flower and vegetable gardens. They were allowed rakes, hoes and other implements, taking them each morning from the camp supply and returning them each evening. Unaccountably, some of these were lost or mislaid; parts were broken; tines snapped off; and it was these, hammered and slowly shaped on homemade stone anvils, which became their tools.

But where to start a tunnel? It would be impossible to do so outside the bunkhouse: no one could hide the fact. The bunkhouse floor was made of stone paving blocks, neatly cemented together. How dig a tunnel inside the bunkhouse without visible evidence? One man was inspired. If a clothes closet were built in one corner and a curtain hung as a door, they might start digging inside it, down through the floor and into the earth.

In the interests of neatness, camp guards were only too glad to grant permission to construct the closet. When it was finished, clothes were hung inside, and boxes of possessions and suitcases piled on the stone floor. The guards, impressed with the job, called the camp commandant who promptly ordered all other bunkhouse chiefs to visit Bunkhouse No. 4 and see for themselves what initiative could accomplish. He praised the leader of No. 4, a huge man with gold-rimmed spectacles and a high-pitched voice, called Stein. "If the others were as neat as you chaps," the commandant said, "we'd have a model camp." Stein, who was Friedman-Yellin, with a price of $4,000 on his head, smiled modestly and said nothing.

They began to dig their tunnel. So careful were they that not even the Sternists outside No. 4—nearly one hundred—knew what was going on. Friedman-Yellin's first major technical problem was to hide and dispose of the excavated earth. The obvious solution was to enlarge their gardens. Day and night the gardens surrounding the bunkhouse grew. The guards watched, amused to see their prisoners employed in so idyllic a pastime. The men worked throughout the day but mainly after 10 P.M., when the guards locked them in for the night. Four times each day, as inspection hour approached, they labored feverishly to replace the heavy flagging. More than once guards pushed aside the closet curtain to peer inside; several times they moved the suitcases about to examine the floor. Tunnels were not unheard of in Palestine. But the FFI men had even devised a cement to place between the blocks so they would appear not to have been disturbed. Made of flour stolen from the bakery, lime from the pharmacy, cigarette ashes and water, it had the color of old cement and dried almost instantly.

Each prisoner had sewn huge pockets inside his clothes. They took turns; each time one man left the bunkhouse for a stroll, he carried with him excavated earth, which he got rid of by sprinkling it around the roots of the flowers and vegetables. How was anyone to know that the fresh earth showing there was not recently turned up on the spot itself? These diligent gardeners were forever tending their patches.

149

After a while the gardens could take no more. Their level was noticeably higher than the surrounding terrain. The men took to scattering the earth as they walked about the camp.

At one point their tunnel was on the brink of collapse. The rainy season had begun and the water-soaked earth was dangerously heavy. Here Friedman-Yellin's training as an engineer came to his aid. His men stole wooden planks from the latrine and shored up the roof of the tunnel.

At another stage, because of lack of air, an epidemic of fainting attacked the diggers. They met this challenge by fashioning a bellows from a raincoat, benzine tins and a length of garden hose. With this they pumped air into the passageway.

Then came the day they discovered they could advance no further without lighting their way. One of their men, an electrician by trade strung wires a few inches below the surface of the earth to an electrical outlet in the latrine and used this to obtain current for a series of lights in the tunnel. If bulbs seemed to blow out in the latrine with surprising frequency, who was to know that the old ones, still good, were now lighting the way of men burrowing underground?

After twelve weeks of round-the-clock labor they broke through. Their tunnel ended in an embankment just past the outermost fence of Latrun. The hour of escape agreed upon in letters to Shamir was 1 A.M. of November 1, 1943.

Now the occupants of Bunkhouse No. 4 were guilty of a childish thing. At 8 P.M. of the night of October 30, five hours before the hour of escape, they dared throw a farewell party, even inviting several of their guards with the explanation that it was a birthday party. Everyone enjoyed himself. At 10 P.M. the guards took friendly leave, locking the prisoners in with more than cheerful goodnight. The lights were turned out, and in the darkness, they waited.

The hour arrived. The first Sternist, a rope about his waist, descended. Rapidly he crawled through the tunnel until he emerged at the other end. All was well. He tugged three times on his rope

—and in groups of seven, roped together, his companions followed. In the huge pockets which once carried earth, they now carried pepper to strew behind them in case dogs were put on their trail.

When they emerged they slipped aboard the bus. Eliahu and his colleague had commandeered it at gunpoint on the Jerusalem-Tel Aviv road less than an hour before. The bus took the twenty-one men to a hideout in Tel Aviv. As they rode, each was given an identity card carrying his photograph and a new name. The cards had been prepared in the FFI documents laboratory and in every detail—paper, printing, stamping and official signatures—appeared identical with those officially issued by the British Administration of Palestine. Before dawn that morning each man, at three-minute intervals, stole into the blacked-out streets and proceeded to a place specially prepared for him.

One can only imagine the expression on the face of the guard who turned the key in the door of Bunkhouse No. 4 on the morning of November 1, 1943. His frenzied shout is still remembered by those who were in the camp.

"My God!" he screamed. "The whole bunkhouse has vanished!"

The Sternists had left behind a final taunt: conspicuously open on a table near the closet lay a book entitled *Escaping Club*—a collection of first-person accounts by British officers of their escapes from German POW camps during World War I.

For the first time in two years the three-man secretariat of the Fighters for Freedom of Israel—its Central Committee—could meet together. Until now at least one of the three was in prison. For the next few months, until early March when the police caught up with Dr. Eldad, the triumvirate met once a week.

Elaborate precautions were taken, particularly by Friedman-Yellin and Shamir. Though there was also a manhunt for Dr. Eldad, the CID had no idea who he was. His two colleagues moved only at night, in the blackout, and in disguise. Shamir by now bore small resemblance to the Itzhak Yizernitsky who had escaped from Mazra a year before. Friedman-Yellin, light-haired and sandycomplexioned, had dyed his hair, mustache and eyebrows black. The three never met in the same place twice. They exchanged messages by means of seventeen- and eighteen-year-old girl couriers. Each man had a courier assigned to him, who alone knew where he could be found. No courier carried a message direct save to her own man: instead, all brought their notes to a fourth girl who acted as liaison. Thus, even under torture, each girl could reveal the whereabouts only of the man to whom she was assigned.

Each of the three had his responsibilities. Friedman-Yellin handled propaganda, negotiations and contacts with those outside the FFI, which included, on rare occasions, being interviewed by foreign newspaper correspondents who were invariably blindfolded before they were brought to him so they had no inkling where they were. Though Friedman-Yellin had never been officially named as head of the secretariat, he was generally recognized as the FFI chief because he alone appeared as its spokesman. Shamir was in charge of administration and organizational tasks, and the carrying out of Sternist operations. Eldad edited and wrote extensively in the *Hazit,* and lectured in the underground.

In their meetings the Central Committee discussed problems ranging over the entire spectrum of their activity: Eldad's next editorial in *Hazit,* supply and money problems, propaganda needs, how to deal with informers and how to deal with other groups. One example of the last problem was a tense situation which arose when three FFI youths insisted on distributing the *Hazit* in the meeting hall of the Hashomer Hatzair, left-wing socialists who were violently hostile to the FFI. A Hashomer Hatzair boy tried to seize the leaflets; a Sternist fired into the air to frighten him; someone struck his hand at that moment and the bullet wounded a local boy.

Feeling ran high. The FFI feared this might lead to serious trouble between the two groups. The important thing was to maintain the neutrality of the Haganah, the most powerful organization and the conscience of the Jewish community. Friedman-Yellin was authorized by his colleagues to discuss the subject with Eliahu Golomb, commander of the Haganah.

The two men met after much preparation. When they sat down, Friedman-Yellin brought out a small loaded revolver and placed it before him on a little coffee table. Golomb, a man of immense authority and one of the leading figures of the Jewish community, asked dryly, "Why do you bring a gun?"

"Look, Eliahu," said Friedman-Yellin in his high voice. "You have your kibbutzim, you can arrest us and keep us there. We don't have kibbutzim, we can't arrest you. So all we can do is kill you. Frankly, I trust my gun more than I trust you."

Golomb smiled grimly. But they resolved the problem before them. At whatever cost there could be no civil war among the Jews of Palestine. Bitter though the Haganah was toward both the FFI and the Irgun, actual war between any of the groups meant catastrophe. Yet Golomb, before they parted, asked, "Why do you strike such bloody blows?"

Friedman-Yellin said, "If you will make your fight against the foreign ruler more extensive, we will make ours less intensive. If all the Jewish community fights, the extensive struggle will make up for the loss of the intensive struggle."

There was no use trying to reconcile the two points of view. The difference stemmed from deep conflicts in philosophy and political experience. Friedman-Yellin refused to recognize that the Jewish Agency, under the terms of the mandate for Palestine, had to negotiate and cooperate with Britain, who held the mandate, even while it fought the White Paper, the closing of the gates of Palestine, the seizure of "illegal" immigrants, the pro-Arab orientation, the injustices of colonial rule. And Golomb could only dismiss as a combination of irresponsibility and fanaticism—a complete flight from reality—the FFI thesis that regardless of international covenants and League of Nations authority, and in the face of British might and an Arab majority, the only solution was an immediate armed uprising by the entire Jewish community, a major effort to oust the British by gun and bomb.

The discussion ended on a quiet note. The FFI promised it would not distribute the *Hazit* inside the halls of other organizations but only outside, beyond a radius of fifty yards. The Haganah, meanwhile, would maintain a watchful neutrality in such matters. All Golomb could ask was: Temper your actions.

As early spring, 1944, approached, as the tide of war turned against the Axis—Italy had already surrendered, Russia was driving Germany westward, the American Second Front was not too distant—the FFI Central Committee formulated a long-range plan of attack.

This was spurred not only by the FFI's growing strength and the diminishing fear of Axis invasion and victory, but also by the fact that the Irgun had suddenly ended its truce and become active again.

In January, 1944, under the leadership of Menachim Begin, a thirty-year-old lawyer and editor from Warsaw, the Irgun Zvai Leumi issued a call for revolt against the British:

> Four years have passed since the war began, and all the hopes that beat in our heart then have evaporated without a trace. We have not been accorded international status; no Jewish Army has been set up; the gates of the country have not been opened. The British regime has sealed its shameful betrayal of the Jewish people. There is now no moral basis whatever for its presence in the Land of Israel. . . . There is no longer any armistice between the Jewish people and the British Administration which hands our brothers over to Hitler. Our people is at war with this regime—war to the end.

The Irgun, which now boasted a hard core of some 800 members and a few thousand sympathizers, demanded immediate transfer of power to a Provisional Hebrew government and concluded with a passionate, "Enough! The hand that touches our sister, our father, our child—that hand shall be cut off!"

The FFI leaders, ever since Stern, had insisted that their method of warfare was far more effective than the Irgun's. To them the Irgun's emphasis upon military organization, its insistence on attacking only the installations of civil government and not individuals themselves, its policy of warning the British each time they prepared to blow up a building—all this they considered romantic and ineffectual.

Friedman-Yellin would argue each time he met Begin, whom he

had known in Poland, "The British don't mind your blowing up their buildings. They'll simply rebuild them with the money of Palestine taxpayers. And what is the point of your gallant warnings? We are pygmies compared to the British. When a pygmy fights a giant, it is immoral for him to endanger his own life by telling his enemy where and when he strikes. Do the British warn us?"

Whatever the case, the two groups now moved into action, each following its own strategy.

The full FFI Central Committee took up the question of implementing the rough blueprint Shamir had drawn months before: lightning attacks on key personalities in the government. Obviously, the most important target, the head of the dragon, was the High Commissioner himself, the symbol of foreign rule in Palestine.

What could be the most powerful blow they could strike?

The liquidation of Sir Harold MacMichael.

The three men, meeting now in this room, now in that, debated the question over wine and fruit. Sometimes they made notes which they later tore into shreds and burned, scattering the ashes. Since Sir Harold was the most hated man in Palestine, hated by moderates* as well as extremists, might this not be interpreted as revenge? If so, this was both favorable and unfavorable to the FFI. It was favorable because, as they saw it, it was justified: horrified as the Jewish community would be, MacMichael had much to answer for. But so far as educating the Jewish population to the FFI and its aims, the effect would be unfavorable. It would suggest that the FFI was concerned only with punishing individuals rather than with fighting a war of liberation. "We must show the youth that ours *is* a war of independence," Friedman-Yellin said. "They must never think that we react only when an individual harms us. Our enemy is our enemy even when he commits no wrong against us."

* On March 6, 1942, after the *Struma* disaster, Dr. Weizmann wrote Viscount Cranborne, Colonial Secretary: "I have not tried to describe the painful, hopeless task of my colleagues in Palestine who have to deal daily in matters great and small with an Administration so unwilling to cooperate with us, so ready to injure us. . . . For my own part, I repeat what I said to you: that Sir Harold MacMichael has, in my opinion, proved himself unfit for the post he holds."

Months before, in the rage and fury following the *Struma,* a truly demoniac scheme had been proposed. The FFI would assassinate the police chief of Jerusalem. The man deserved it, but his death would also be a means to an end. His funeral would bring out all the high officials of the administration, including MacMichael himself. One bomb thrown into their midst . . . The plan was never put into effect. The two chief rabbis of Palestine, the revered Chief Rabbi Herzog of the Ashkenazim community, the equally revered Chief Rabbi Uziel of the Sephardic community, would certainly appear at the funeral. Could one risk killing the worthy with the unworthy? For a while the FFI considered locking the rabbis in their homes that morning—then abandoned the idea. It was all too impracticable.

Yet something had to be done. Shamir said, "Now is the time. The Allied Powers are on the way to victory. Our people are being massacred in Europe. Refugees from these horrible fires of hatred seek to come here and the British turn them away. The Jewish people are licking their wounds. I say that we must do more. This is our decisive hour. We are growing stronger—we have a national sense—if in this decisive hour we do not act, we shall be finished. Either we begin now to emerge as a nation, or we sit back and allow ourselves to be destroyed."

Friedman-Yellin summarized it:

"Yes, the war will soon end. The problem of Palestine is not on the agenda of the great powers. We must therefore draw the attention of the world to the situation here. This can only be achieved by a grave and decisive and shocking action—something that will shake the world."

The Central Committee of the FFI made its decision.

First, the assassination of Sir Harold MacMichael.

Then, after a decent interval to give the Jewish community time to get over its shock and horror, and to assimilate the reasons (to be cogently stated in *Hazit*), they would consider the next step. Shamir and Eldad, even while Friedman-Yellin was in Latrun, had discussed it—even begun to lay the groundwork. Perhaps it was only a wild dream. The liquidation of MacMichael's superior —Lord Moyne.

MacMichael . . . then Moyne. It was right, it had its own inevitability, they agreed. It would educate the Jews of Palestine and it would educate the Arabs, too. They were victims of imperialism as well. They, too, had suffered from colonial rule. They, too, would see that the FFI fight was not only a struggle for a people's liberation, but had a wider meaning for all the peoples of the Middle East. The FFI, the true anti-imperialists, would strike a massive blow for all.

Avigad was assigned to organize the MacMichael action.

CHAPTER

14

Two years before, Eliahu Bet Zouri, restless and frustrated, had walked with his two high-school friends David and Amihai and dreamed of slaying the tyrant, MacMichael, in his own bed in Government House.

Now, with a kind of curious appropriateness, it was Bet Zouri to whom Avigad broached the subject.

Late one night in March, 1944, when Eliahu returned to Tel Aviv from Jerusalem, where he had taken Hannah to meet his grandmother, he found a messenger from Avigad awaiting him. Eliahu and Hannah had spent a delightful evening at the ancient stone house on Jaffa road, its walls hung with Persian tiles, its kerosene lamps throwing a yellow glow. They had dined with the old lady, dipping their water from a huge earthenware jar in the courtyard where Adi once hid out, and they had eaten Oriental foods prepared as his grandmother's family had prepared them through the centuries. They had spent the rest of the evening at cards, playing for chocolate instead of money, with Eliahu teasing his grandmother—she believed cats were reincarnated demons; she wore innumerable amulets against the evil eye—and they had enjoyed themselves so thoroughly they had nearly missed the last taxi back to Tel Aviv.

Now, humming a tune, Eliahu was approaching his apartment house when an FFI boy stepped out of the darkness. Avigad wanted to see him. The youngster led Eliahu through the blacked-out streets to a sleepy little chess club above a bookshop on Ben-Yehuda Street, a block from the Mediterranean. In the rear of the room, its dark blinds drawn, sat Avigad, studying a chessboard. At his elbow was a glass of steaming tea. Eliahu slipped into the chair opposite, and as the two began to move the pieces, Avigad quietly briefed him.

Dr. Eldad had been caught by the police. That was Avigad's first bit of news. Ever since the first issue of *Hazit,* in July, 1943, the CID had been trying to track down its elusive and infuriating editor. A week ago Avigad's intelligence division had learned that the CID had virtually identified Eldad as the man they wanted. Eldad was warned to leave his teaching job immediately and go underground. He demurred: he was preparing his eighth-grade class for college entrance exams and needed a few more days. Yesterday four Englishmen, dressed in civilian clothes, had called at his high school and politely asked the principal to summon Eldad. The principal had left the four seated in his office and hurried upstairs. Eldad was at his blackboard, analyzing a difficult passage from Job. "Tell them I shall be right down," he said. He took his brief-case, which had the latest *Hazit* in it, and handed it to a student with instructions to drop it at the Eldad apartment. Then he walked out of the room and tiptoed down the stairs, pausing at one landing long enough to look into the principal's office, see the four men—obviously police—then hurry on. Once in the street, he made a strategic mistake. He began to run. Halfway down the block, he ducked into the apartment house of a friend.

The police, meanwhile, had had their fill of waiting. After a moment's investigation, they set off on Eldad's trail. A group of children, playing in the street, had been astonished to see a goateed little man dash by, and when one of the pursuing police demanded, "Which way did the thief go?" they pointed out the house. Eldad,

159

hiding in a third-floor bathroom, heard the doorbell below; he opened the window, wriggled out into a huge drainpipe, began to shinny down it, lost his grip—and fell, breaking his back. Now he lay encased in plaster from knee to neck in Central Prison, Jerusalem. Shamir, said Avigad, had been in touch with him. The irrepressible Eldad was in good spirits; they had wanted to put him in solitary confinement but no solitary cell could accommodate a man lying in a cast, so they had taken him to the infirmary and lashed him, cast and all, to a bed. Fortunately, in the adjoining cot, recuperating from a bullet wound, lay an eighteen-year-old FFI youth named Anshel, and, Avigad reported with a sardonic smile, Eldad was busily dictating to Anshel a steady stream of denunciatory articles for the next issue of *Hazit*. Smuggling them out of prison in the slit cardboard lining of laundry boxes posed no problem at all.

But Avigad had a more urgent matter to discuss. At the last meeting Eldad attended, before his arrest, the Central Committee had unanimously agreed that the time had come to strike their first blow at the head of the dragon. Would Eliahu participate in an action against the High Commissioner?

For Eliahu, the circle thus came full turn. What his own amateur cell had not been able to accomplish was now to be carried out.

"Yes," he told Avigad. "I shall be proud to take part in it. It should have been done long ago."

Who knew how many more souls might have been saved from the Nazis if a less rigorous man had been carrying out British policy in Jerusalem? And there were rumors that MacMichael planned to submit to London a final desperate formula not only to break the back of all resistance, official and unofficial, but to destroy the Jewish National Home altogether—to declare the Jewish Agency illegal and abolish it; to disband and crush the Haganah; to write finis, at last, to the Zionist dream. Even if none of this were true and MacMichael had been the most beloved of high commissioners—he was still the symbol of the intolerable: a foreign rule imposed on free men.

"Very well," said Avigad, sipping his tea. The action would proceed. Eliahu would be informed.

FFI scouts were put on MacMichael's trail. Since the *Struma* he had cut his public appearances to a minimum; no announcement was ever made in advance of his movements. The scouts learned that he frequently attended 10 A.M. services Sunday at St. George's Church in Jerusalem.

To check his protection on such occasions, an FFI boy, pretending to be a painter, set up an easel and canvas diagonally across from the church on the preceding Sunday. He could report to Avigad that MacMichael arrived heavily guarded—motorcycle police before his car, a tender with armed police following, and behind that a red CID car. When the High Commissioner attended a public function, it was in the traditional manner of royalty in unstable countries: he was always the first to leave, and always by a side door; all other persons remained in their seats, all exits remained locked, until he was safely out of the building and on his way.

It was discovered that a sewer pipe ran directly under the stone paving outside the church exit used by MacMichael. The FFI decided to place a mine inside the pipe and detonate it the instant the High Commissioner left the church and set foot on the paving. Thus no worshipers would be hurt.

One moonless night two FFI electricians laid the mine. From it they led a cable, concealed six inches under the earth, a distance of one hundred yards to the entrance of an apartment house around the corner out of sight of the church. Behind the house was a small yard from which it was possible to vanish into an intricate network of alleys.

It would be Bet Zouri's duty to set off the mine.

On the appointed Sunday he disguised himself as an Arab of Jenin. During the time he had worked there as a surveyor, his Arabic had taken on the local accent. His mustache was thick and luxurious, his hair shone with oil and he wore the typical pin-

161

striped jacket of an Arab businessman. Arabs then were on far better terms with the police than Jews; in any event, the presence of an Arab in that non-Jewish quarter would stir no attention.

He sauntered to his place in the entranceway of the apartment house and stood there, idly smoking a cigarette. The cable from the mine led to a detonator switch concealed under a straw mat at his feet. He could not see the church, but he could see another Arab across the street from it, squatting next to his lambskin of water, selling water to passers-by. This was an FFI colleague, appropriately disguised, who would take off his skullcap and scratch his head the moment MacMichael set foot on the paving.

Suddenly Eliahu heard a sharp voice demand in English, "Do you live here?"

He turned, shaken. A policeman stood a foot away from the mat, staring suspiciously at him. Eliahu managed an apologetic smile. "I await my cousin who is to take me back to Jenin," he said in Arabic.

The policeman obviously did not understand the language and repeated his question. Eliahu spread his hands helplessly. "Please, Sair—"

The other took a long, disgusted look at him and moved on.

Minutes passed.

Across the street from the church the water seller lifted his skullcap and lazily scratched his head.

Eliahu stepped on the mat, hard.

Nothing happened. There was no sound. The water seller put his skullcap back, lifted it and vigorously scratched his head again. Eliahu stepped on the mat again. Still nothing happened. He turned and hurried away. Mechanical failure, either in the detonator or in the mine. There was nothing else to be done.

MacMichael got into his car and his entourage was on its way.

The water seller moved on slowly, crying his wares.

Next morning the papers carried a headline: LAND MINE DISCOVERED! A gardener that afternoon had noticed the freshly turned earth and come upon the telltale cable.

Two weeks later a second plan was put into effect. When the

162

High Commissioner drove into the downtown area, he had to pass the David Building, a Jerusalem landmark. The road turned sharply there and all traffic was forced to slow down.

Joshua Cohen was in charge, because Avigad had been assigned to Tel Aviv to train new recruits. At the chosen hour a surveying team was busily at work at this corner—a British major of the Engineers' Corps with two Arab assistants. Nearby, chewing indolently on a blade of grass, sat an Arab boy, guarding the rolls of long blueprints and a basket of food for the men. A hundred yards away another engineer was at his tripod, peering and measuring.

All five were FFI youths. Inside the long tubular rolls of blueprints were submachine guns; hidden under the food were hand grenades. The engineer with his tripod was a lookout who would signal when MacMichael's car came into sight.

A strange coincidence occurs here. The idea of using the surveying team as a cover for the action had been suggested by Bet Zouri. Eliahu had purloined both blueprints and tripod from his office. He took no part in the action; it would be wiser for him to establish an alibi by keeping to his office that day. But the Arab boy chewing on the blade of grass was the other Eliahu—Eliahu Hakim. This close the two came to meeting—and thus closely were they involved in this attempt on MacMichael.

But the High Commissioner did not leave Government House that day, nor for several days thereafter. The plan was abandoned. The surveying team dared not remain too long at any one place.

A third attempt came at the première of the film *Spitfire,* at the Rex Theatre some nights later. MacMichael was expected among the distinguished guests. Two FFI youths waited at a turn of the Jerusalem road to lob grenades into his car as it slowed down. Once more the scheme fell through. Police recognized a lookout as one of the twenty-one who had escaped from Latrun; within seconds everyone had scattered.

On the heels of this a fourth attempt—this time near an empty lot opposite another intersection on the Jerusalem road, near the residential suburb of Talpyot. An Arab boy lay in the grass, engrossed in a book. Hidden in every pocket, inside his shirt, about his waist, were hand grenades. Not far away another Arab young-ster, wearing the white *Kaffiyeh,* the customary Arab headdress bound about his forehead with a double black braid, was munching a piece of Arab bread. This was Hakim. Hidden in the grass lay a third boy, cradling another machine gun.

When MacMichael's car slowed down, the reading youth was to leap up and hurl his grenades. Hakim and the other boy were to cover his escape. If necessary, they were to use tommy guns, hid-den in the grass. Otherwise they were to hurl a barrage of smoke grenades—harmless weapons which made a great noise and threw up a tremendous amount of thick black fumes.

As they waited a military jeep roared by. It came to a halt down the road with a screech of tires, backed up and a British officer hopped out. He advanced upon the boy with the book. "What are you doing here?"

The boy grinned and held up what he was reading. It was a paperback in Arabic, with a lurid drawing of a girl and a man on the front cover. His gestures, his leering grin, indicated clearly that this was a love story. The officer questioned him a few minutes longer, gave up and left. The plan was abandoned immediately.

Two weeks later the Palestine Philharmonic Orchestra gave a concert in the garden of the Evalina de Rothschild School in Jerusa-lem, under the patronage of Lady MacMichael. Two armchairs were set aside in the second row for Sir Harold and Lady Mac-Michael. Yaacob Bannai, one of those who had escaped from Latrun, sat in the first row directly in front of their chairs, a pistol concealed in his shirt. Other FFI youths were in the audience. The moment lights were dimmed, Bannai was to fire at MacMichael; the others were to set off smoke grenades and noisemakers; and all were to escape in the confusion.

Bannai, waiting, later described his emotions when he saw that sitting next to him was Colonel Arthur Giles, chief of the CID, the man charged with protecting the life and limb of MacMichael.

But the High Commissioner did not appear this night.

Five vain attempts had been made. MacMichael's reluctance to show himself in public—indeed, to end his self-imposed imprisonment in Government House—was understandable. Hardly a week had passed thus far in 1944 without bloodshed in the streets. All Palestine had become a terrorist battlefield—now the FFI, now the Irgun, now the British retaliating in every direction. . . .

On January 29, the Irgun, having ended its truce, bombed the government transportation car park in Jaffa; on February 12 and 13, it bombed immigration offices in Jerusalem, Haifa and Tel Aviv. On the fifteenth two police inspectors stopped a youth to question him: the boy, carrying FFI pamphlets, shot both dead and fled strewing his pamphlets over their bodies. On the morning of the twenty-fourth, Assistant Police Superintendent Morton, the man who killed Abraham Stern, escaped with wounds when a mine exploded under his car. That afternoon a second mine blew up as a police car passed, injuring four inspectors. On the twenty-sixth, government tax offices in the three major cities were blown up. On March 19, police cornered Elisha, a friend of young Hakim, on a staircase; trying to escape, he was shot dead. On the twenty-third, at the same hour, the Irgun bombed CID headquarters in Jerusalem, Haifa and Jaffa; three police were killed in Tel Aviv, three in Haifa. Assistant Superintendent of Police Scott of Jerusalem was killed in an exchange of fire when Irgun men dressed in police uniforms raided police headquarters. Suddenly photographs of FFI leaders, each with a price on his head, appeared in the Hebrew newspapers. The FFI had outraged both British and Jews by killing two Jewish merchants as informers, and announcing it would execute anyone else who informed on its members.

The struggle reached almost hysterical intensity. On April 1, in Haifa, a wounded FFI youth named Baruch hurled a grenade at a Jewish policeman firing at two of his fleeing colleagues: the man was blown to bits, the boy died of his wounds. On the sixth two FFI boys, wounded by police machine guns near Tiberias, turned their last bullets on themselves rather than be captured. In a village near Jerusalem police shot to death three FFI members the moment they discovered their identity. On the tenth, FFI youths, walking the streets looking for British to shoot in revenge for this act, fired through the window of a police station and wounded three men. On the eleventh, FFI boys tried to kill Deputy Superintendent of Police Fforde of Tel Aviv, the man whose little car Bet Zouri and his two friends once halted in a demonstration. The bullets missed.

Day by day word came of Jews in Europe burned to death, massacred, machine-gunned; new arrivals, eyewitness to these horrors, testified to what they had seen. It was impossible not to believe that what had been dismissed as atrocity stories were actually true. FFI youths, pistols in their belts, grenades in their shirts, walked about in cold fury. When one, working on a bomb, would say to a colleague, "Wait—it'll be ready in ten minutes," the other would cry, "Ten minutes! Do you know how many Jews are dying in these ten minutes!" On May 17, the fifth anniversary of the White Paper, three truckloads of armed Irgunists seized the Government Broadcasting Station at Ramallah; roads were mined; Irgun posters appeared overnight calling for a Jewish revolt. The British, using Indian troops, responded by raiding scores of settlements, virtually all of which were totally out of sympathy with terrorism (indeed, their members had been kidnaping terrorists and turning them over to the British police). Innocent farmers were herded into huge wire cages and searched, and beaten when they resisted; their wives hurled pots and pans at the soldiers and fought furiously rather than submit to arrest; hundreds were thrown into prison without charge or trial. On June 22, a British military court sentenced an FFI boy to be hanged for firing at a policeman: Sir Harold MacMichael announced that possession of a gun was now a crime punishable by death. The FFI issued an impassioned warning in a special number of *Hazit*:

This is how you British will walk the streets of Zion from now on: armed to the teeth, prepared for anything and fear in your eyes: fear from every dark corner, in every turn in the road, every sound at night, fear from every Jewish boy, fear day and night because the Jewish youth have become dynamite in this country. You shall walk on burning embers, our bodies will be the embers and our love of country the fire. No guards, no tanks, no fines, no curfews, no tortures and no hangings, no prisons and no detention camps, will help your High Commissioners, your officers, your policemen. We are fed up, we tell you. Your children will become orphans just as you orphaned the Children of Israel. Your mothers will lose their sons just as you made the mothers of Israel mourn for their sons. For every cry of a boy from the top of a burning boat, for every cry of a Hebrew mother when her child embarks on a broken ship in the middle of the sea, for every Jewish tear that is unanswered—we shall answer you. We came in fire and we were burned: we came in water and we were drowned: we the remnants walk in rivers of blood, the blood reaches our necks, our mouths, our eyes, and from the fire and water and blood, trembling arms are raised, voices cry out, and from the mouths and eyes and from the trembling arms and fingers, from the water and the fire and blood, from there we are coming up, we are coming. Woe unto you!

Then came a list of the dead of the FFI, of those tortured and maimed, of proclamations and government orders not printed in the newspapers, of arrests and deportations kept from the people by censorship:

As was ordered to us by our forefathers in our Holy Writings, we came to you with peace. It did not help. We came to you with money. We bought our water and our earth, the very air to breathe: it did not help. We came to you with prayer, in the name of justice and honesty and fairness; in the name of mercy we prayed to you in all the languages of the world. It did not help, not peace nor money nor prayer.

Therefore, this is the law of our war. So long as there is fear in the heart of any Jew in the world, so long as there are embers burning under their feet anywhere in the world, so long as there is a foreign policeman guarding the gates of our homeland, so long as there is a foreign master over our country, so long as we do not rule in our own land, so long shall we be in your way. You will look around you in fear, day and night. You will sleep in your uniforms, you will wear your arms, your life here will be hell, day and night, for we have had our fill of shame and exile, slavery and humiliation, we are fed up with waiting and waiting, begging and praying, for we have taken the oath —the freedom of Israel!

We have had enough!

Then, on August 8, the High Commissioner showed himself in public. He was, at last, to leave Palestine. He had been reassigned to Malaya. He would depart the country in a few weeks and be succeeded by Field Marshal Lord Gort, the hero of Malta. The Jaffa Municipality tendered MacMichael a farewell reception. He would have to drive from Government House to Jaffa. The FFI, its rage at its failure to kill MacMichael heightened by news that hundreds of thousands of European Jews had been helplessly trapped because of the White Paper, concentrated all its forces in a final attack on MacMichael.

On the way to Jaffa his military cortege would have to slow down at a sharp turn one kilometer beyond the city limits of Jerusalem. At dawn that day a group of FFI youths drove a car over the route to determine how long it took to negotiate the turn. They clocked the time at four minutes. Joshua made his plans accordingly.

Just before four o'clock that afternoon, on either side of the curve, a surveying team was again at work in their khaki uniforms. Down the road a bearded rabbinical student, in the usual flat black hat and side curls, sat on a boulder, alternately peering at the surveyors in a kind of half-witted curiosity, alternately swaying back and forth as he read his psalms. He was one of three lookouts. Eliahu Hakim, disguised as an Arab, was further down the road, armed with a Finnish tommy gun. He was to prevent MacMichael's car from backing away once it was halted by a hastily thrown-up road block. A third lookout was Hakim's schoolmate, David Shomron.

MacMichael's entourage came into view on schedule—first a police motorcycle, then a touring car filled with armed men, then MacMichael's limousine, followed by a tender of soldiers with tommy guns at the ready.

Shomron signaled frantically but they had miscalculated. The entourage traveled at such speed that it covered the clocked distance in only a minute and a half. The ambushers had hoped to pin down MacMichael's car at the barrier with a Molotov cocktail; instead, grenades burst directly in front of the motorcycle. The entourage halted in confusion; instantly FFI machine guns were in action. The soldiers leaped out and took refuge behind boulders, firing. The High Commissioner's car swerved off the road, then swerved crazily back again. There was a woman's scream of terror: Lady MacMichael. In the smoke and confusion, the FFI men fled into a nearby olive grove, bullets whistling over their heads. Joshua, running, saw Hakim at his side suddenly stop and turn as if to dash back to the scene. He grabbed him. "Where to?" he demanded. "The magazine from my gun," Hakim shouted over the gunfire. "I'm going back for it." Joshua held him in a grip of steel. "Come," he said. "We'll do without it." They began running and ducking again until they reached a neighboring suburb and dispersed. Within an hour CID agents were on the scene with police dogs. The trail led into the quarter, but nothing was discovered there. That night the radio announced MacMichael had been slightly wounded in the thigh and hand. Lady MacMichael was unhurt.

The next day *Hazit* leaflets appeared everywhere, slipped under the door of private homes, stuffed into mail boxes, tacked to walls, piled high in synagogues. The message, again in Eldad's fiery prose, read:

There was a double meaning to this attack. The submachine guns and hand grenades were aimed at the heart of High Commissioner MacMichael. He should pay with his life for his criminal acts. We look upon him as a murderer. He cold-bloodedly killed Jews, over 200 of the refugees from the *Patria* did he kill, more than 700 from the *Struma*. The blood of tens of thousands who never even reached the ships because they were killed in the gas chambers must rest on his soul because his soldiers shut the gates of the homeland. His leaving the country and his disappearance from the scene of the crime does not release him from his responsibility. What he did should be done to him.

169

We cannot throw him into the sea. Therefore we came to him with fire. We did not single him out because he is MacMichael: the punishment is not personal: the fire was aimed at the High Commissioner of a foreign rule. . . . The remnants of Hungarian Jews have a chance to leave their country. We can save hundreds of thousands from Hungary, Rumania and Bulgaria if only we can open the gates of our country. But the foreign ruler closes the gates in their faces. The occupier of our country sentences them to death. . . . Brethren, listen to this and listen well. We are fighting for your freedom. Let England listen, too. With blood you will pay for spilling the blood of our brothers. Let the whole world hear this. Jewish martyrs never shook the world: now perhaps the Jewish war will!

Four weeks later Eliahu Hakim, in British uniform, armed with false papers, arrived in Cairo to carry out the deed.

CHAPTER

15

THE SEVENTEEN-YEAR-OLD boy
who came to Cairo had been preparing for his role for a long
time. Five years younger than Bet Zouri, he was not too young in
1938 to pin a black ribbon on his shirt and mourn the hanging of
Shlomo Ben Josef. When seventeen-year-old Eliahu Bet Zouri
marched in public protest against the White Paper in Tel Aviv in
1939, twelve-year-old Eliahu Hakim marched in public protest in
Haifa. If the event itself did not make so vivid an impression on
him because of his youth, the tragedy he witnessed a year later
would burn a mark deep in him.

When the passengers aboard the S.S. *Patria* blew themselves up
in Haifa Harbor on the morning of November 25, 1940, he stood
on the terrace of his home on Panorama Road, high above the
bay, watching the terrible scene through binoculars. All over Haifa
people were gathered on terraces, on the flat roof tops of houses
built in serried rows on the hills climbing up from the sea.

That very morning, following the ruling of Sir Harold Mac-
Michael, the *Patria* was to take its passengers into exile. Shortly

after 9:15 A.M. Hakim heard a tremendous explosion*—and like all Haifa, rushed out to see. He saw the *Patria* list, then keel over; he saw the wreckage; he saw the headless bodies of men, women and children fished from the water with fishhooks by the very soldiers who had forced them aboard. At night, with giant flares burning, he saw them still hunting for bodies.

If he would never forget the sight, he would never forget the name MacMichael. Two hundred and sixty men, women and children died that day. He heard his teachers speak of the event in choked voices; he mourned the dead with others whose relatives had been aboard.

From his first years Hakim had not been one easily put upon. Always he was quick to take offense, quick to defend himself. As a child his outstanding trait was lack of fear. Simon Hakim liked to tell, with pride, how his youngest son, aged seven and not yet able to swim, would clamber up on the roof of a bathhouse overlooking the Mediterranean at Beirut, leap thirty feet into the sea, sink far below and to the cheers of spectators, splutter gleefully to the surface to be pulled out by his friends.

When the Hakims moved to Haifa the boy began classes at the Alliance Israelite School. Here he met another student, David Shomron, with whom he struck up a friendship not unlike that between Eliahu Bet Zouri and Adi. David and his family had just moved to Haifa from Istanbul. He was impressed by Hakim's generous allowance and endless variety of good clothes; and most of all by his vitality. Hakim had joined the Maccabees, the sports group of the General Zionist party; he was their best soccer player, their fleetest runner. He seemed made of steel springs, utterly tireless.

At thirteen he entered the Reale High School, a private institution operated by Dr. Max Biram, a German-born educator who conducted it on almost Prussian lines. Dr. Biram stressed obedience, military discipline, heroism—and above all, pride and self-

* Even today the exact nature of this explosion is unknown. Although some believe it was a final act of desperation—death or Palestine—others suggest that the aim was only to blow a hole in the keel, enough to prevent the ship's departure; and through error, too powerful a charge was used.

respect. In later years his students were to hold top commands in the Army of Israel. Eliahu Hakim grew up under his influence and in the midst of events—the Arab troubles, the endless difficulties with the British—which deeply affected him and shaped his development.

One day the two boys read of a particularly revolting Arab attack on a settlement not far from Haifa. The city's streets were placarded with posters counseling restraint: REMEMBER—HAVLAGAH! NO RETALIATION! BUILD—DON'T KILL.

Shomron had recently joined the Irgun. He asked Hakim, "Should we retaliate?"

"Yes," Hakim replied hotly. "We must fight back. I know the Arabs—I grew up with Arab boys. They're like the English, they think you're a coward if you don't fight back."

Shomron, testing him further, asked, "If you were given the chance to join the Irgun, would you?"

Hakim wheeled at the question. "Try me!"

Shomron, under orders to recommend promising friends, told his superiors. Hakim was recruited into the Haifa branch and inducted shortly after his fourteenth birthday. It was 1941. Four years earlier Eliahu Bet Zouri had been inducted in much the same fashion in Tel Aviv.

Young Hakim's three older brothers, Menachem, twenty, Joseph, twenty-two, and Ovadia, twenty-four, were all members of Haganah. His frequent disappearances to attend meetings of his own led them to suspect what he was up to. They tried vainly to persuade him to leave the Irgun.

"Its ways are wrong, it attacks our leaders, it is hysterical Zionism—" they argued. He would not listen. To every appeal, he retorted, "I am a soldier, not a politician." When his oldest brother, Ovadia, pressed him, he burst forth, "You cannot change me! The way I take is the right way. This is how a revolution begins—with a few followers, and then it spreads!"

His first underground duties were to put up illegal posters—among them the WANTED FOR MURDER placards bearing the photograph of Sir Harold MacMichael. Twice weekly he learned military discipline and use of arms. He became an expert shot. Shomron watched admiringly as Hakim would place a pop bottle on the ground, take ten paces, whirl, and while whirling shoot a bull's-eye on the bottle.

The split in the Irgun and its demoralization with Raziel's death in Iraq in June, 1941, found both boys at loose ends. After school they wandered about the streets of Haifa. The same apathy that fell on Bet Zouri, taking long walks with Adi in Jerusalem, fell on Hakim and his friend. They tried to fill their time with parties and other gaiety. They often visited a notorious waterfront dance hall, the Roxy Bar. Hakim was an excellent dancer. He was now tall, darkly handsome; he began cultivating a thin black mustache. Girls liked him. He had the exquisite Oriental manners of the Sephardic Jew, to whom reticence and modesty are part of family upbringing; at the same time, he was not anyone to be teased or mocked.

He had difficulty concentrating on schoolwork. "My head is too full—the British, the Arabs, the war," he would say to Shomron.

Once, when he was called upon in class, unprepared, his teacher remarked caustically, "Obviously, you don't want to learn. What will you grow up to be? A dancer?" Then, with a smile at his own joke, "Perhaps we should call you Roxy."

Young Hakim sat down, his face white.

He, too, began keeping a diary. He wrote better than he spoke. He put down fugitive thoughts, impressions, yearnings, which show him to have been thoughtful and introspective to an extent which would have astonished his teachers. He had just turned fifteen when he wrote:

I feel consoled when I read Achad Ha'am, Pinsker and other philosophers who speak of the ultimate redemption of our people in our homeland. I suppose a person feels helpless often in the course of his life. He will give up an ideal—and sit unhappy, depressed. Then suddenly something undefined comes along and saves him from that mood. That is how I feel now. I read so many articles setting up one political party against the other in our land and so many arguments about religion. . . . Is this the way our nation has always existed? Fighting, group against group?

He spent the summer of 1942 with his high-school class, working on a kibbutz in the Galilee. He and his fellow students hoed and harvested in the fields; when darkness came, because of the threat of German invasion, they took turns staying up all night, rifles across their knees, on guard, after the fashion of the heroic Hashomer of the past.

He wrote Shomron, "It's wonderful to sit with the gun, guarding the people and the land. But even this isn't what I want. I always dreamt I'd go out with the gun and fight, not sit and wait. . . . I miss our boys!"

Later entries in the diary reflect his state of mind. On June 15, 1942, still in the Galilee, he wrote, "Today I argued with one of the girls about the best road to independence." Five days later: "I must return healthy and strong, not only for my own sake but so that I can serve my homeland." A day later: "I must train myself so that I can control myself in small things, then later I shall be able to control myself in important things."

It was not long before this that Bet Zouri was writing in his diary adjurations to take himself in hand.

In July, Hakim filled a page of his notebook with a rhapsodic tribute, to the Galilee, which he, like Bet Zouri, loved.

I lie here on sacks of wheat and look around at the mountains of my country. I look at these hills where once my namesake Elija the Prophet, and the Kings of Israel, walked! The Galilee, where the tribe of Naphtali once lived! How glorious to remember our nation's past, to dream of the day when she will regain that glory! Yet, there are so many obstacles—the British, who want this land, the Arabs, who say that it is theirs, and we ourselves, divided into so many small groups. . . . My heart aches when I see how we waste ourselves fighting each other. If only we could unite, and fight as one for the restoration of Israel! I really believe this will come someday. But I must also admit that when I look realistically at the situation, I can feel only despair.

On August 5 he wrote, "Today, two years ago, Vladimir Jabotinsky died in New York. His ideas are mine. Today is a day of mourning for me."

More and more he was troubled by his own inaction. As the harvest holiday of Hanukkah approached, he grew indignant at

175

the idea that anyone would wish to celebrate in view of the *Struma's* sinking earlier in the year. He had released some of his anger by helping put up the MacMichael placards; now he wrote:

I was dumbfounded by that disaster. The 740 Jews who escaped the Nazis' sword, who escaped from lands where the iron fist rules, from lands marked by the triumph of pure savagery, thought they had escaped from the frying pan. Little could they know they would fall into the fire. How can I ignore them? They are our brothers! How is it even possible for people to think about parties and good times? If we do not mourn them, who will? The English, who ignored them? The Germans, who drove them out? How can a man sit contentedly in a café, how can he drink and be merry when he knows that only yesterday his brothers were on a rotting ship, living under impossible conditions, on the edge of death? . . . Such men who can do this lack a conscience!

He wrote with the special bitterness of a fifteen-year-old.

How *could* one remain idle?

When he returned from the Galilee he refused to re-enter school. "You are wasting your money," he told his parents. At their insistence, however, he did let himself be enrolled in an agricultural school. He stayed only a few weeks. Impatient, restive, not knowing quite what to do, he took a job in a military garage near Haifa. He was a first-rate mechanic, but one day when the British foreman ordered him to pick up rubbish, Hakim became outraged, got into a dispute and was dismissed.

What now? The night came when he and David Shomron were able to provide shelter to the escaping Shamir (then still known as Yizernitsky) and his friend Shaoul. Shamir had said little to Hakim then. He thanked him for the use of his brother's apartment, and for his help, and went on with Shaoul to Tel Aviv, and his rendezvous with Joshua Cohen in the orange grove. The news that Shamir was reorganizing the Stern group, which Shomron disclosed to him, electrified Hakim. This meant action. He wanted to join.

His family learned of his connection with the extremist underground in melodramatic fashion. Hakim was busily writing a note to Shamir in invisible ink when his mother unexpectedly opened the door to his room. She saw the starch, the container of water,

176

Hakim writing—he had no way out but to confess to her.

The Hakims were panic-stricken. The Jewish Agency was urging young men to enlist in the British forces and Mrs. Hakim used all her persuasiveness to make him volunteer. She begged him. Her youngest son's growing rebellion kept her in tears, the more so because he had always been obedient. She was the kind of mother who could not do enough for her sons: she prided herself on sewing all their shirts by hand. Once, months before, he came home with a cigarette between his lips and she had made him promise he would not smoke until he was nineteen. To please her he had given up smoking. But now he refused stubbornly to do what she asked.

"They don't need me," he said. "What shall I do? Shine up army trucks? Clean the rooms of a British officer?" Like Bet Zouri, he refused to join an army which would not accept Jews as fighters. In addition, the British wanted Jews and Arabs to volunteer on a one-to-one basis, but scarcely any Arabs, so the records showed, enlisted. The Palestine regiments therefore were virtually all-Jewish, but the British continued to describe them as Palestinian.

If, at least, they were called the Jewish regiments, if they could fight at the front like men, so the world would know . . . In the end he enlisted. "I couldn't stand my mother's weeping, the inactivity, everything," he told friends. "But I should not be in a foreign army. I should be fighting for my people's freedom. . . ."

Months later, on leave from Egypt, he visited David Shomron. "I'm going to desert," he said. He could take no more humiliation and frustration in the army. He tried to contact Shamir; the latter, who thought of him as only the rather spoiled son of a rich family, was doubtful. "Roxy," the dancer, in the FFI? Hakim had not as yet impressed him as a responsible youth to be entrusted with delicate matters. One moment the boy enlisted—the next he wanted to get out. This hardly suggested a stable personality. No conspiratorial organization could afford the emotionally disturbed or the thrill seekers: such youths would endanger the safety of them all.

When word came that Hakim desperately sought a chance, Shamir said, "Test him. Let him prove himself. Let him bring us weapons from Egypt."

177

This Hakim did—with spectacular results. Each time he came on leave, it was with an arsenal of arms and ammunition. All Egypt was a vast arms depot: guns, rifles, hand grenades, even submachine guns, were easily obtainable. Once he brought two full suitcases—a remarkable feat, since British Military Police patrolled the trains between Egypt and Palestine and every soldier was subject to search at any moment. To carry this off called for considerable courage and aplomb. The penalty for smuggling arms was at least court-martial; for Hakim it could well mean death.

On one trip he was directed to bring his bags to one of Shamir's hideouts. The FFI leader was impressed. He told a colleague, "I saw a man eager for action who had matured since I last knew him. I said to myself, This man is not sufficiently used."

Hakim, to his delight, was informed by Shomron that he would be welcomed into the Fighters for Freedom of Israel. He was to join them in Tel Aviv.

On a December evening in 1943, Hakim returned from Egypt for a fortnight's furlough. It was his last day in the British Army. At home he found his sister, Yardina, twelve, and their housekeeper. His parents were away on a vacation; his brothers were in Beirut overnight.

"I came for my civvies—I'm going to a dance tonight," he told Yardina. He packed his clothes in a bundle with a cigar box of ammunition and a pistol he had hidden in his room, and went to Shomron's house a few blocks away. Shomron greeted him cautiously. He, too, was preparing to leave. A young couple—a boy and girl about fifteen or sixteen—had been loitering nearby. They had been across the street from his house three evenings in a row now. During the day, too, he had been aware of a fellow student who rarely left him out of sight in school. He was sure that all three—the couple and his schoolmate—were Haganah scouts keeping him under surveillance. At the time Haganah was kidnaping FFI members in order to immobilize them. He and Hakim would go to Tel Aviv together.

At dawn the next morning the two shook hands ceremoniously and took a bus to Tel Aviv.

There Hakim was inducted into the FFI.

Three weeks later a jeepload of Military Police descended upon the Hakim house. The Hakims were beside themselves. Their Eliahu a deserter? His brothers, unable to locate him anywhere, finding no one who knew his whereabouts, placed an advertisement in *Haboker,* a Hebrew daily, reading, "Eliahu—come home. Father is ill. Menachem."

Young Hakim read it in the little room in Tel Aviv in which he was hiding. That night he slipped into Haifa, to be greeted tearfully by his mother and with cold anger by his father. The elder Hakim was a dark, self-contained man who had always been a remote figure to his sons. He suffered from asthma, and as far back as the boys remembered, he was to be found reclining in a lounge in the far end of the parlor, smoking his antiasthma cigarettes. Now there was a dramatic scene. That his son had deserted was shame enough; but that he had gone into the lunatic fringe of the underground . . . "You *are* insane!" his father cried. Eliahu would not be shaken. As Moshe Bet Zouri had done with the other Eliahu, so Simon Hakim did with his son: he tried every argument. "I don't ask you what you do," he said, "but if you will leave this madness, I will give you money, I will set up a shop for you in Beirut—" No, said his son. "The day the war ends I will send you to Europe," his father exclaimed wildly. "Think of it! The time of your life in Paris—"

The boy smiled sadly. "No, it is my duty to save my nation. I stay where I am." He promised that he would visit them as often as possible, but if he were gone, even for weeks, they must not worry.

Twenty-year-old Menachem, the second brother, tried to reason with him as his oldest brother, Ovadia, had tried some time ago. "Excuse me, but you are stupid," he said, taking him aside. "What are you doing, you and your little party? What can you do against the great British empire?"

Hakim looked at him. "You have read what the Irish did? I promise you that in a short time we will throw the English out of Palestine."

In spite of his anguish, Menachem had to laugh. Eliahu regarded him unsmilingly. "I would warn you, my brother, that if you have the idea of telling the Haganah about me—do not do so. I have already been in actions which, if they were known, would not be good for our family—"

Later Menachem was to say, "The moment he joined his movement, his character changed. He became serious; overnight he grew up. It was his whole life. He asked nothing of us; he told us nothing; we knew nothing."

Nevertheless, before he left, Menachem gave him fifteen pounds —sixty dollars. He would send the same amount to him every month, in care of a friend. Eliahu shrugged his shoulders. "As you please," he said.

When Hakim returned to Tel Aviv he gave the money to the FFI treasury. A week later Menachem sent him a new suit of clothes. Days passed—and one afternoon, in Haifa, Menachem saw the suit on a strange youth walking down the street. Everything Hakim received, he turned over to the movement.

Presently he was assigned to the FFI operations division under Joshua, who soon had nothing but praise for him. He reported to Shamir: "This boy is an excellent marksman, he has absolute control of his weapons, his hand never wavers. I find him a chivalrous and dependable young man." Shamir agreed, "Yes, he is developing." In addition, Hakim possessed another advantage in those days of sudden interrogations. He gave the impression of a peaceful, everyday youth, interested only in fun and girls.

His family had no idea of his days and nights at this period. Now not only an army deserter but a terrorist, Hakim was doubly hunted, by the CID as well as by the British Army. For weeks he rarely slept twice in the same place. This was the early spring of 1944, when the first attempts were made on MacMichael and terrorism was rampant in the streets. All through the night police tenders with blinding searchlights roamed the city hunting terrorists, and no corner, no shadow, was safe. It was impossible for Hakim to stay anywhere more than a few hours. Anyone trying to rent a room was suspect; anyone found on the streets after dark was likely to be pinioned against the wall by a dazzling shaft of light and searched at the point of tommy guns trained on him not only by the soldiers before him but by others posted on nearby roofs. One night Hakim slept in an empty air-raid shelter. On another, he rented a rowboat on the Yarkon River, rowed into a little cove and slept in it there. Many nights his bed was a roof top. At one point, preparing for the final attempt on MacMichael, he and a few others slept in bunkers, shored up with lumber, which they dug in the sand dunes outside Tel Aviv.

Finally he found temporary housing in his home city—Haifa—with two comrades, Baruch and Bannai. Baruch was nineteen, born in Poland, a somber, brooding boy whose family had been wiped out by the Nazis. Bannai, twenty, was in sharp contrast—a husky, outgoing youth, one of the twenty-one to escape from Latrun Camp, who had been appointed by Shamir to reorganize the FFI in Haifa. Bannai, too, had been the man chosen to kill MacMichael the night he failed to appear at the Palestine Philharmonic concert. Bannai usually posed as a Haganah officer—he invariably wore heavy boots and a leather jacket, clutched a rolled-up copy of *Davar,* the labor newspaper, carried himself with a military bearing and frequented cafés popular with Haganah members. His appearance was even more deceptive, for in a holster under his left arm he had a revolver, tucked into the back of his belt a small automatic and in each pocket of his jacket a pair of grenades made from cigarette boxes and gelignite.

He, Baruch and Hakim lived in one room and had to manage on FFI rations—the equivalent of twenty-five cents a day for food. They ate one meal a day. The rest of the time they munched radishes. At night they tried to satisfy their hunger by stuffing themselves with stale bread dipped in boiled water—the diet on which Joshua had lived for weeks in his orange grove. They prided themselves that they never yielded to the temptation to steal from a vegetable vendor, or to snatch fruit from a sidewalk stand—for such acts would be a descent to criminality. Though Hakim regularly received the sixty dollars his brother sent him, he never used it for himself or his roommates. The money went straight to the FFI treasury. In their hideout the boys maintained the most elaborate precautions against discovery or arrest: each slept with his weapon under his pillow; each never opened a door without drawing his revolver first; they never moved anywhere without a gun.

One day early in February, 1944, while Hakim and Baruch were in their room, Bannai burst in and slammed the door shut. Two police officers had halted him on the street. He knew he was lost, for he was armed and only FFI men were armed at this time; in addition, he carried a package of some two hundred of the latest copies of *Hazit*. "Let's have a look, laddie," one of the men had said. Slowly Bannai turned the package over to them; they opened it and as they started to glance through them, he whipped out his revolver and shot them both through the heart. They fell to the ground, the leaflets slowly fluttering down on them. That was how he left them, their dead bodies covered with illegal leaflets, as he rushed away, racing through back yards, leaping fences, until he reached the room.

The three knew police would be after him, undoubtedly with dogs. Their room was a virtual arms cache; there were fifty grenades, four submachine guns, revolvers, packages of cartridges. They dared not attempt to carry all that off; nor could they contemplate leaving it there to be seized by the police. They held a council of war and decided to remain where they were. They stayed awake all that night, sitting with their rifles in their laps, prepared to sell their lives as dearly as possible. They heard the barking of the dogs, now near, now distant; slowly morning came; they were still safe.

Baruch ventured out to buy a newspaper. Bannai had fatally shot Inspector Green, head of the Jewish Department of the Haifa CID. The other was the hated Sergeant Ewer who had shown the bullet-riddled body of Abraham Stern to Moshe Svorai.

The double killing lifted the curtain on the round of attack and reprisal that marked that bloody spring and summer of 1944. The *Hazit* appeared with even more fiery warnings and denunciations. Two weeks later one of Hakim's friends, Elisha, an eighteen-year-old Haifa Technium student, who had begun to be known as a short-story writer, waited for a bus in Tel Aviv, in his briefcase fifty copies of the *Hazit,* which he was taking to distribute in the other end of town. Out of the corner of his eye he observed a police patrol watching him; he began to walk, and when he saw they followed him, he threw his briefcase away and ran. He dashed into an apartment house, raced up the stairs to the roof and across the roof tops, followed by three police with tommy guns; in the chase he led them down another flight of stairs into a yard; he knew his fate if he were caught; he turned, emptied his gun at them and fled into another apartment house and up the stairs to the roof—only to find the door locked. He was trapped. As he tried frantically to force the door open, there was a burst of tommy-gun gunfire from below. He fell dead, face down on the stairs.

Then nineteen-year-old Baruch, Hakim's roommate, was killed on April 1. As he worked in an underground warehouse, his revolver fell to the floor and went off. The bullet struck him in the stomach. In great pain he managed to make his way to a nearby house. Two FFI boys came in a taxi to take him to safety. Baruch waved them away. "No, no, leave, the people in this house have already called the police!" His friends refused; as they struggled to lift him from the sofa on which he lay, the police broke in, among them a Jewish sergeant named Paloni. The two youths fled, Paloni rushing after them, firing. Baruch, on the sofa, cried out, "You're a Jew, stop shooting, how can you shoot at fellow Jews!" When Paloni continued to fire, Baruch, with a superhuman effort, pulled a grenade from his pocket and hurled it at him. Paloni was instantly killed. Baruch managed to roll off the sofa and tried to crawl away, but collapsed. He lay on the floor, a few feet from the mangled body of the man he had killed, wailing, "Why didn't you stop shooting? Why didn't you listen to me! . . ." He died the next day in Rothschild Hospital with police at his bedside trying in vain to get information from him.

To Hakim, the deaths of Elisha and Baruch were heavy blows. Baruch left a diary, and an entry for March 12—three weeks before he died—gives an inkling of what was going on in his mind at that time.

The danger of death hovers over me every day, every hour, every minute. Each day I remain alive is like a present from God, but I am ready at any moment to leave this wretched world which had no room for my nation, my people, my sisters and their children, who were innocent. But there is a difference between them and myself. They had no choice about their fate. God has given me a choice and I am master of my fate, like a prisoner who, in his last moments, may ask for what he wishes. I ask now, and I can also get what I ask: the death of Samson on a small scale. Let me die with the Philistines, not die as a martyr in the name of God! Let me not die as a sheep brought to slaughter. As long as my hands are not tied, they will hold a gun, and perhaps it will bring us our redemption. And if my people were tortured in vain, perhaps by my death I can be of some use to my nation. I am happy at last that I have removed this heavy guilt—that I was living a quiet and peaceful life when their share was continuous nightmare and danger of death. It is possible that at any moment this diary will stop and continue only in the cemetery with a name on a stone that may not even be mine. Only in the press will well-fed boys and girls my age, full of life, learn about some youth who was killed in a struggle with the police, and they will go about their pleasures. . . .

This is my fate. This is the fate I have chosen for myself and I march toward it with full awareness. There is no other way to arrive at our longed-for aim. But to you, of the Lehi—if you are still alive—the news will come to you, you will feel the moment, you will know who is that unknown soldier who fell anonymously for his people. And your tears will follow me to my grave. . . .

Did Hakim read this? He may have, for it was a last testament addressed to him and the others.

Whatever the case, Hakim, as we have already seen, took part in two attempts on MacMichael's life. After the High Commissioner was wounded on August 8, such elaborate protection was given him that no further attempts were made. On August 29 he made a farewell address to the country, and soon after left Palestine for his new post in Malaya. A fortnight later word came to Hakim. Shamir wanted to see him. Shamir talked to him briefly and earnestly. There was a deed to be done—not in Palestine but in Egypt. Would he put on his British uniform once more and go to Cairo? He would be given proper identification papers. In Cairo he would learn his assignment. Shamir gave him a slip of paper to read, memorize and burn. It bore the cryptic name, Ezekiel, and below it, a Cairo telephone number.

CHAPTER

16

IN CAIRO, Hakim had no idea of his mission. He knew only that it was an action far more important than smuggling arms. Shamir had spoken cryptically of "the deed." This was what Hakim desperately wanted: to be entrusted with a deed of stature, of overwhelming significance. One can only speculate why the FFI leadership did not tell him immediately. An obvious reason was that, at this early stage, vulnerable as he was, a deserter in uniform carrying false papers, torture might have elicited his purpose and enormous harm would have been done to the cause. What he did not know he could not tell. It was one matter to engage in terrorist actions, however bloody, in Haifa or Jerusalem, themselves a battlefield, but any inkling that the FFI were preparing to engage in international action would have had tremendous repercussions. The picture of Palestinian assassins loose in the capitals of the world could be a terrifying one.

It was just before noon when Hakim arrived. He knew he was to contact "Ezekiel"; and he had been told the telephone number was that of an FFI girl from Jerusalem. Her name was Nadja Hess. She had enlisted in the ATS, the Auxiliary Territorial Services of the British Army. This was comparable to the American WAC, the Women's Army Corps, and Jewish girls from Palestine served as clerks, interpreters and ambulance drivers.

Hakim called the number; without asking questions Nadja met him that afternoon and took him at once to the house of Raphael Sadovsky.

Sadovsky is worth examining, for he plays an unusual role in this story. He was a romantic, a would-be Byron, eager for any der-ring-do—yet of all men the least constituted to be a conspirator. He was a short, squat, unlovely man, about twenty-nine, with a round face given a certain distinction by a trim black mustache and goatee. He was a bachelor, he taught English, French and mathe-matics in a government school; charming, cultivated, full of enthusi-asms, belonging to an old Jewish family, he knew everyone and could open many doors. He was, in addition, secretary of the tiny Zionist Revisionist party in Cairo. This position sounded more im-portant than it was, for Zionism was a hobbled movement in Egypt, and its members could do little more than sympathize silently with their brothers in Palestine. Although the Egyptians thought of themselves as belonging to the West, as Europeans rather than Arabs (Egyptian law students invariably attended French univer-sities and Cairo's finest department stores were Le Printemps and Aux Trois Quartiers), as between Jews and Arabs in the Palestine struggle, their sympathies fell naturally with the Arabs. Egypt's leading Jews, highly placed in commerce and the professions, were vehemently anti-Zionist.* As a result, the Zionist organization in Egypt was virtually without influence. It existed on sufferance and dared not speak out. Even more so, then, a Revisionist party, one standing for a Jewish state on *both* sides of the Jordan, was con-sidered a kind of blasphemy.

But Sadovsky, secretly and to his delight, was involved in more special matters. They dealt with a Sergeant Joseph Galili. To every-

* When in the summer of 1942 a woman Haganah agent called on Cattaui Pasha, millionaire industrialist and President of the Jewish Community of Cairo, to ask him to help finance Jewish immigration into Palestine, he threatened to set his dogs on her.

one else Galili was a file clerk in RAF headquarters in Alexandria —a heavy-shouldered Jewish farmer from Palestine who had enlisted in 1941 and whose quick intelligence had won him his present post. Sadovsky, however, knew better—and it was all he could do not to tell his friends. He knew that Galili was a very important figure in the Palestine underground, engaged in mysterious, daring activities which had to do with winning independence in Palestine. It made no difference to Sadovsky whether he was helping the Haganah, the Irgun or the FFI: he knew only that he wanted to aid the cause of freedom. He was sure Galili belonged to the Irgun.

Actually, Galili was chief of the tiny FFI cells in Egypt. He had succeeded Sergeant Benjamin Gefner, who had organized the first branch in Egypt at Shamir's request. In June, 1943, Gefner had left Cairo to take part in the British invasion of Sicily; before going he had introduced Galili to Sadovsky, with a warning: for all his good intentions, Sadovsky was a chatterbox who could not be trusted to keep a secret. He was vainglorious, emotional to the point of neuroticism and, under pressure, likely to blurt out everything. Gefner, by way of example, told Galili of an incident. He had been walking on the street one day when he saw Sadovsky approaching him, accompanied by an FFI girl. As soon as Sadovsky saw him, he sprang in front of the girl, trying to shield her with his body and cried excitedly, "Go away, you're not supposed to see this girl I'm with—" It was ridiculous. She might have been any girl. Sadovsky had brought about exactly what he wanted to avoid: he had called attention to his companion and at the same time suggested that she was involved in secret activity. Sadovsky had no idea that Gefner was in the FFI and knew the girl well. "I realized then what this man is made of," Gefner told Galili. But because Sadovsky knew Cairo, because he was an encyclopedia of information, because he could carry out errands impossible for a foreigner, because he lived with his pious, highly respected parents and his home could be used as a meeting place, Gefner had enlisted his help. Now, after Gefner's departure, Galili made use of him too. He knew it was a calculated risk and so told Sadovsky as little as possible. To keep him happy he assigned him to small diversive tasks: to count the cars parked outside the British Embassy, to ascertain with what Egyptian actress a certain British colonel was sleeping and finally —as if it were of no more importance than his other assignments —to learn the location of Lord Moyne's residence and the license number of his car. Sadovsky, infatuated with the notion of working for the underground, had carried out these duties efficiently.

He greeted Hakim warmly, wringing his hand. "Shalom, shalom," he exclaimed, his eyes bright, all but placing a warning fingertip on his lips to counsel Hakim that he knew they were both in a high, fine conspiracy. Of course he knew where to find the man called Ezekiel. He had been informed by Ezekiel himself that a young soldier named Benny would come to him for this information.

"This is what you must do," he said. Hakim was to take the first train to Alexandria, three hours distant. In the lobby of the Jewish Services Club there, he would see a bulletin board where soldiers left notes for each other. He was to be there at nine o'clock, write the words "Ezekiel—Benny" on a slip of yellow paper, and tack it to the board. Then he was to sit nearby and wait.

Hakim did as he was told. In the club at Alexandria, at the hour named, he waited, sunk deep in a leather armchair, watching the bulletin board.

A few hours before, Sergeant Galili sat in his office at RAF headquarters, Alexandria. He could look out his window at the curving bay, more beautiful than Naples; almost as beautiful, he thought, as Haifa. In the distance, stately and powerful, rode HMS *Emperor,* an aircraft carrier. An American ship, she had been given to Britain in lend-lease and now with her white-jacketed officers clearly in view and her covey of tiny planes nesting at one end of the long deck, longer than a soccer field, she was moving slowly out to sea. He watched as she dropped anchor a mile off shore and the exercise began.

The planes, one by one, moved into position; then, suddenly, each catapulted sharply off the deck, like rigid butterflies propelled by an invisible power; then, describing an enormous U-turn into the distant horizon, they returned to swoop down and plow to an explosive stop against quivering guide wires stretched taut, one every few feet, across the deck. It was as though each plane played a gigantic hop-skip-and-jump until it halted, coming up sharp against the guy wires which stopped it and held it, fluttering like a bird, until it reached perfect, shuddering rest. Through another window, as the afternoon wore on, swiftly now, he saw the ivory domes and towers of Alexandria turning rose and mauve, vanishing in a pastel fairyland of color, half sunset-ridden cloud, half violet water reflecting the turquoise spires.

Sergeant Galili was thinking hard.

He had seen Shamir in Jerusalem. He had been summoned there a month ago; at the appointed hour, Shamir's fiancée, Shulamith, waited for him in front of the Orion Cinema in the heart of Jerusalem to lead him to Shamir's latest hideout. His pursuers were so hot on his trail that the man changed his quarters every few days. When Galili saw him in a little Arab stone house, Shamir was pale and sallow from lack of sun and air. His beard now was long and black, and he had taken to wearing gold-rimmed spectacles which made him look even more the retiring man of the cloth, lost among the vistas of his own meditations. From this stone house Shamir was directing a series of actions against High Commissioner MacMichael. Several had already been attempted and failed. Shulamith, a Bulgarian girl, brought him food and cared for him. Save for his courier, she was his contact with the outside world. Key FFI men never lived alone, for they could be jailed without anyone knowing, a police detail placed at their hideout and any visitor immediately seized. Each FFI leader either roomed with another member or lived, fictionally or actually, as man and wife with a girl sympathizer.

In this discussion, held in early August, 1944, Galili for the first time heard the name of Moyne. The FFI was looking for an act to shock the world, Shamir told him. They had agreed to move on Moyne, when the time came—Moyne, after MacMichael. Step by step. If the action against MacMichael were successful, there would be a hiatus before any move was made against Moyne. A tremendous cry would be raised; the Zionist leadership would find itself confronted with a major crisis; it would have to make its peace with the British, who would insist, as they always did, that the Jewish Agency secretly knew the FFI's plans and could have stopped them if it wished. This was manifestly nonsense. Dr. Weizmann and Ben-Gurion detested the terrorists, looked upon them as irresponsible desperadoes who jeopardized the Zionist cause: as for the terrorists, the last persons to whom they would confide their plans would be the Jewish Agency, which was doing all in its power, short of civil war, to destroy them. "We shall have to explain much, then we shall have to lie low," Shamir said. "Then we shall be able to start up again."

As they talked, Shulamith brought them coffee and cake.

They discussed first, how would the deed help the nation?

Second, who would carry it out?

As to its value to the nation, Shamir said: "The community thinks of us as outlaws bent on personal revenge. This is a perversion of our political objective, which is to oust the British. Our attack on Moyne will clarify exactly who the enemy is. Are we fighting the British Administration in Palestine as does the Irgun? Does the blame for our predicament lie here? Or does it lie in London, from where the orders are passed to Cairo, and from Cairo to Jerusalem?

"Most Zionist leaders," he went on, "believe Britain intends to carry out her promises to us. If you accept this premise, then the reason that promises are not being kept is not London's fault, but that of local officials who are stubborn colonials, or anti-Semites who deliberately misinterpret their instructions; or who refuse to act because they have succumbed to the spell of Arab romanticism. We are convinced this has nothing to do with it," said Shamir. "We believe Great Britain simply cannot carry out her promises to both Jews and Arabs. We believe the British have been feeding themselves and us illusion and wishful thinking.

"If, therefore, we go to Cairo and liquidate the British Minister, it will make clear to the entire world that the struggle in Palestine is not a misunderstanding between natives and a local administration—but a major conflict between a fighting nation which demands national freedom and an imperialistic power which denies it.

"At the same time, the deed against Moyne will bring the whole issue into the world forum, where it will merit the attention of world opinion and world diplomacy."

They discussed Lord Moyne. The man was not favorable to Zionism. As MacMichael's superior, he directed or approved every major decision of the High Commissioner. He supported the White Paper. He had once, in Parliament, eloquently argued the Arab case. He had been Colonial Secretary at the time of the *Patria* and *Struma*. He was against further Jewish immigration into Palestine: he could not understand why displaced persons would not want to return to the country of their birth. He had even questioned whether the Jews were actually Semites and had any claim to Palestine. No, he was not a friend. But this was not why he had been marked for death: he had been chosen as the chief representative of the foreign ruler—the symbol of foreign rule itself. The entire Middle East was ruled from his office in Cairo.

As to who should carry out the deed—ought they choose someone from their tiny group already in Egypt or send members from Palestine? And if from Palestine, how get them into Egypt?

Galili had listened with close attention. "I would prefer to pick some of our boys in Cairo, but it would be too dangerous. You cannot rely on soldiers. They can be transferred at any moment. And if we do use our boys and they are caught, we endanger every Jewish soldier in Egypt. I think we must use civilians, not soldiers, and they should come from Palestine."

He recommended two men—one to carry out the act, the other to cover him.

Shamir said, "One is better. It is easier to smuggle in one man, it is easier for one man to hide. The fewer who know, the better."

They compromised. Shamir would send one man first.

Who?

As though it were destined, each thought of the same youth—Hakim. Shamir himself had seen how efficiently the boy had smuggled arms from Egypt. And Joshua had spoken glowingly of him as "an ideal fighter and revolutionary terrorist, strong in will, proficient in weapons, quick in action, dedicated in purpose." Joshua, not easily impressed, was to say later of Hakim: "He was a youth who left behind a good home and an easy life to embrace the dangerous way of the revolutionary, because though it meant a cruel, difficult life for himself, it carried the hope of a new future for his people and his country."

Galili knew Hakim, too. Once, when Hakim smuggled ammunition from Egypt into Palestine, it had been Galili who gave the ammunition to him. The boy had taken it, filled his suitcases and—his face as guileless as though he were carrying oranges—had gone off to board the train to Palestine.

Ever since, Galili had kept this quiet, Arabic-looking youngster in mind. When Shamir mentioned his name, they looked no further. Hakim would be the first to be sent to Egypt. He would prepare the action. Then a second man would be sent. . . .

Galili, in his office, glanced at his watch. It was seven o'clock. He rose and made his way to a small restaurant. He dined leisurely. Then he took a pleasant walk through the streets of Alexandria until he came to a solid, olive-colored building. This was the Jewish Services Building.

He entered exactly at nine o'clock.

Hakim, waiting, sitting in the deep club chair, watched the soldiers strolling by the bulletin board. At nine o'clock he saw a tall, powerfully built British sergeant with an imposing handle-bar mustache come in and scrutinize the board. He recognized him vaguely as the man—he had never learned his name—who had once given him ammunition to take to Palestine. The sergeant casually removed the yellow note, tucked it into his pocket and moved to the bar. Hakim, after a moment, followed and took a stool next to him. He pulled out a pack of cigarettes, lit one and then, as if on impulse, offered one to his neighbor. The latter accepted it with an impersonal smile. Hakim said, "I come with greetings for Ezekiel."

Joseph Galili said, "I will buy you a drink. What would you like?"

At that meeting they spoke for nearly an hour. They left the bar and continued their conversation as they walked through side streets. Galili plied Hakim with questions. Finally he asked, Had he any idea why he had been sent to Cairo? Hakim said no, but added, surprisingly, "I have the feeling that it will be an action for which I must be ready to pay with my life."

They were passing a brilliantly lit shop as Hakim uttered these words, and Galili saw his young companion's face. The purpose of his questions had been to test the boy, to size him up. Perhaps, at the last moment, plans had been changed; perhaps Hakim had been arrested, released, was even now being followed; perhaps he had become an informer—and Shamir had not had a chance to send a warning. But the glimpse Galili now had of Hakim's expression, the determination and doggedness that emanated from this dark-eyed, intense youth, made Galili realize that there was no reason to doubt.

Slowly, then, he told him what "the deed" was.

Hakim stood stock still. His face flushed. "Yes!" he said. Then, almost with awe, "That they should have chosen me—"

Galili went on to assure Hakim that the FFI had an elaborate network of cells in Cairo; arrangements for the action would be carried out to the letter. He could have explained, had he wished to burden Hakim with the knowledge, how carefully he had nurtured the tiny organization in Egypt, building it up from five to its present twelve members. All were in army services—nine boys, three girls, divided into cells of three, no two cells in the same camp. Elaborate precautions, similar to those in Palestine, had been taken. Galili knew only the cell leaders and no one knew anyone in the other cells. In case of arrest a member could implicate only the two others in his cell—and if he were cell leader, Galili as well. But Galili to protect himself went by half a dozen aliases—Ezekiel, Ben-Zvi, Fellach, Amram, Selah and Yad. Each cell leader knew him by a different name. Thus, though he was known to Hakim as Ezekiel, the other FFI members took their orders from superiors named Ben-Zvi, Fellach, Amram—all the same man, Galili.

Galili glanced at his watch. He had made thorough preparations.

He had told a most respected man, Rabbi Yehoshua, director of Cairo's Ashkenazim Synagogue, (whom he had met through the invaluable Sadovsky) that he needed a room for two students who were coming from Jerusalem to work for a few months in the NAAFI, the British Army canteen. Rabbi Yehoshua had found a place in a private house in the Mousky, the ancient bazaar quarter. Now Galili said to Hakim, "It is time for you to return to Cairo." He told him his room had been reserved for him under his new name—Itzhak Cohen. Hakim, with a grin, tried it on his tongue. "It will do," he said dryly. Galili drew from his pocket a Government of Palestine Identity booklet bearing Hakim's photograph over the name Itzhak Cohen, born 1927, Jerusalem. From now on Hakim would be introduced by his new name to everyone—even to other FFI members.

Galili lay down strict rules. Hakim was never to speak Hebrew save when they were alone. He was to eat at small, out-of-the-way Arab restaurants. He must scrupulously avoid any café, dance hall, park, synagogue or other gathering place popular with Palestinian Jewish soldiers, lest he be recognized. The less explanation the better. He must keep out of sight during the day. Within the next forty-eight hours Galili would introduce him to another FFI member—a girl, an ATS ambulance driver. She would accompany him when he appeared in public. In the guise of a couple in love, they could stroll anywhere in the evening without rousing suspicion. They could take long walks in the vicinity of Moyne's home in Zamalek; they could wander near Moyne's offices in the city. He, Hakim, would have every chance to familiarize himself with the habits, the comings and goings, of His Excellency, the British Minister Resident in the Middle East.

It was nearly midnight when Galili shook hands with Hakim in Misr railway station and saw him off on the last train to Cairo.

The date was September 14, 1944.

In Tel Aviv, that September evening, Eliahu Bet Zouri was at a party given by Ada Ron for their schoolmate, David Danon, on his twenty-third birthday. Eliahu brought Hannah, and all his friends saw that she wore his ring, a ring that had been on his finger since he was sixteen. Ada, thinking how beautiful Hannah was, how bubblingly happy Eliahu appeared, recalled the day, years ago, when she first noticed the ring. It was ornate and Oriental, bearing a small purple stone and exquisitely made.

She had exclaimed, "What a striking ring! Let me look at it."

Eliahu extended his hand, then, as she examined the ring, pulled his hand back. He grinned at her. "No use your admiring it," he said. "To get this you must marry me." Then he told her his grandmother had given it to him after his mother died. It had been an heirloom in the Baruch family.

Seeing him now, and his girl wearing his ring, she drew him aside. "Don't tell me you're thinking of getting married—"

Eliahu laughed. "Look, it's time," he said. "I'm going to be an old man of twenty-three myself in a few months." And he used the same words he had used to Tamar when he first brought Hannah to meet her. "I think she's going to be the one."

That night, taking Hannah home, he said suddenly, "If I could arrange my life, we could get married tomorrow—" She knew that he had to help support his family, that he was anxious about his motherless, eight-year-old brother Uri, that he had many problems. She was not too sure what he really meant when he said, "arrange my life," but she could understand why they could not get married immediately. Perhaps, if he got a raise, if other matters she could not fathom—and would not pry into—were settled, they might be married before the year was over. They walked, arm in arm.

CHAPTER

17

MORE THAN 30,000 Palestinian Jews were enlisted in the British forces. Some 15,000 were stationed in Egypt; and of these twelve were members of the FFI. Of the twelve, three were girls; and one of the girls was Yaffa Tuvia. She was to be Hakim's companion.

Yaffa was twenty-one, tall, slender and graceful, with long dark hair, blue eyes and a narrow face of extraordinary sweetness. She might have posed for a Modigliani Virgin Mary. Her home was Haifa. She had enlisted the year before and served as an ambulance driver in the military camp at Tel el Kebir, forty miles from Cairo. In her apparently fragile wrists and hands she possessed surprising strength, and she was utterly dedicated.

As the other FFI members, she had devoted herself to small tasks and to the smuggling of arms and ammunition into Palestine each time she went home on leave—once every three months. She hid them in a money belt around her waist, in her handbag and in her valises. Each time she returned to Egypt, she brought back hundreds of copies of the latest issue of *Hazit* which she—as did each of the other eleven—surreptitiously distributed through the camps to be read by hundreds of Jewish soldiers who thought the FFI all but mad, but nonetheless found Eldad's fiery call to arms, his Old Testament denunciations, stirring stuff to read. The *Hazit,* in addition, was highly informative. It announced the latest FFI exploits, but it also interpreted world events and printed news rigorously censored out of the Palestine press—arms searches, trials, letters to the High Commissioner charging police torture of elderly Jews and the beating up of youngsters with shouts of "If it's Dachau you want, we'll give you Dachau!" The *Hazit* featured scholarly columns on philosophy, literature, Messianic movements in history, and politics.

Once a week Yaffa took the military bus to Cairo to see Galili. This was usually on Friday, when Jewish personnel went into town to attend Sabbath services as guests of local families.

On the evening of September 15 she met Galili at the Jewish Services Club in Cairo. He had been waiting impatiently. "We go at once to the Astoria," he said. This was a milk bar near the main Kas'r el Nil barracks on the Nile.

On the way Galili explained. "The Central Committee has decided to liquidate Lord Moyne." Yaffa could not suppress a gasp. Lord Moyne! The highest British official outside London, British Minister of State, member of the war cabinet, Churchill's friend! Galili sketched Moyne's importance as a symbol of British rule in Palestine. The explanation was hardly necessary. The words *Patria* and *Struma* were enough to kindle fire. Yaffa thought, If this man, however exalted his position, can have so many lives on his conscience, not only those on the *Patria* and *Struma* but the uncounted thousands in the camps of Europe who were so discouraged that they no longer attempted escape, surely justice should be done. . . . In any event, the Central Committee had decided. She asked no questions.

"The one who will carry out the action has arrived," Galili went on. "We go to meet him now."

When they entered the Astoria they took a table for four. From where they sat they could see, reflected in a wall mirror, the entire length of the restaurant, including the single tables in the rear crowded with soldiers.

Galili ordered milk and raisin cake. As if this were a signal, in the mirror they saw a slender youth who had been reading an Arabic newspaper rise and make his way toward them. Now he was at their table, shaking hands with Galili. With his dark skin, glowing black eyes and thin black mustache, he looked as Egyptian as anyone in the room. Galili presented him. "This is Itzhak Cohen, the friend I spoke about."

Yaffa almost started with surprise, but caught herself. She knew this boy; she was sure of it. His name was not Cohen. But try as she would, she could not recall his real identity. Yet—no question of it—he came from Haifa, too. Even more of a coincidence, they had belonged to the same sports group, the Maccabees, just a few years ago. She could even place his branch—the Hasmonians. She had been in the Galilee branch, made up of older boys and girls. The last time she had seen this unknown Itzhak he had been a youngster in knee pants dashing after a ball. Now, as they talked, she was astonished to see how mature he had become. He listened with dignity, he smiled often, quiet, self-possessed, and he spoke sparingly but to the point. If he remembered her, he gave no indication. She liked him at once.

They talked casually, the three of them, of everything and nothing in particular, but not once of the purpose which brought them together. She noted how comfortable he seemed with them, as if with old friends. She was impressed. Small as the FFI movement might be, how powerful it really was if despite manhunts and informers and hangings, despite every skill of wartime intelligence, it could dispatch a member for such a task, arm him, prepare him, get him into Egypt! And what sort of a fellow was he who, knowing the awful deed before him, could be sitting here with them, strangers in a strange, hostile country where discovery meant death, sipping his Turkish coffee, a smiling, confident, resolute man . . . and yet, if her memory were right, hardly more than seventeen!

Galili broke into her reverie. They would take a walk. Half an hour later they turned into a thoroughfare. Before them was an en-

198

tire area surrounded by barbed wire. "This is Sharia Nabatat, the street in which he works," Galili said. "You are both to learn all you can about his habits." They could see the British Embassy, with its white pillared entrance, and some yards away, an apartment building, before it a military police sergeant on guard duty. "This is the place in which he works," said Galili casually.

When Yaffa left the two men shortly before eleven o'clock, she and Hakim had agreed on how to meet in the future. They would choose a rendezvous—a café, never the same one twice—and an hour, always in the early evening. Hakim would be inside the café at the appointed time. Yaffa would enter, look about as though seeking someone who was not there, then turn and leave. A moment later Hakim would pay his bill, saunter out and follow her, slowly catching up with her. To an observer it would appear to be a casual pickup.

The major problem was to determine where the deed should be done. Several times they stood near the embassy, gazing over the billowing coils of barbed wire, weighing the possibilities. If Hakim could act there—perhaps when the Minister emerged for lunch— it would involve the least personal risk, for Hakim could easily lose himself in the noonday crowds. But the entire area was an armed enclave; it would be impossible to get close enough to Moyne. Even were Hakim to succeed, there were other considerations. His orders, as passed down from the Central Committee, were not to hurt anyone else, under any circumstances, for this would becloud the meaning of the deed. Therefore, no grenades; only a pistol could be used; the bullet must find its way unerringly. Could this be done at a distance and in the midst of the constant military traffic within the area?

Together Hakim and Yaffa followed Lord Moyne's route from his office to his home. They noted every traffic intersection, every turn where his car might have to slow down. Here, too, escape would be easy, but complete success doubtful. Hakim would have to leap on the running board in order to take sure aim at Moyne— a foolhardy act—or else assume that he could fire into a moving car and still find his target. Here again a problem posed itself. Moyne rarely traveled alone. Usually a woman sat in the back seat with him, and a British officer sat next to the driver. How could Hakim be sure of striking Moyne, and only Moyne, in a moving car?

What complicated matters for at least a week was the fact that they had no clear idea of what Moyne looked like. Hakim turned to Sadovsky for help and Sadovsky, asking no questions but eager to do what he could, managed to find a *London Illustrated News* with a small photograph of Moyne in it. It was blurred and not much use. A few days later by courier, Galili received a letter from Palestine with a clipping from a Palestine news weekly, which showed Moyne presiding at a ceremony. This photograph was a little better. But to confuse matters more, both Moyne and his aide-de-camp were of similar build: in the distance it was sometimes difficult to tell them apart.

By the second week they had seen Moyne and his aide frequently enough to have ironed out this problem. Yaffa and Hakim by now knew that at 8 A.M. each working day the two men left the residence, accompanied by Moyne's woman secretary; a long black limousine drove them to the embassy. They returned between 12:45 and 1 P.M. for lunch and siesta. At five o'clock they left for the office again, returning shortly after eight. Sometimes, in the morning, the two men left as early as six, carrying golf clubs or tennis rackets, bound for the Gezira Sporting Club before going on to the embassy.

As Hakim studied the problem, he grew more and more certain that the deed must be done at the residence—either when Moyne emerged from it or returned to it. The house was one of several on the Nile; behind it lay the river; before it, a narrow street led to a main thoroughfare, King Fuad Boulevard; 200 yards distant was the Bulak Bridge. If one could make the bridge and cross to the other side, he would be in the heart of the teeming native quarter, a labyrinth in which one could easily lose oneself.

Not far from the residence was the small Bulak police station. Now and then an Egyptian policeman lazily wandered in or out. Hakim seemed unconcerned. "They'll cause no trouble," he said. A stone's throw away was a small park with a zoo and aquarium.

Hakim and Yaffa joined the evening crowds, slowly walking about. "I want to know my way blindfolded here," Hakim said. Yaffa discovered that he went armed at all times. One night as they were sitting in the shadows on a little bench opposite Moyne's villa, he actually produced his pistol and took it apart for her, naming each part as he did so, then putting it together again. His hands moved with amazing swiftness and skill.

On one occasion, to check the action of his gun, he took her by trolley to the pyramids, about an hour out of town. As typical tourists, they climbed the pyramid of Cheops, and entered the tomb of the Egyptian king who reigned fifty centuries ago. Then, descending and going into the desert beyond, where they would be alone and unobserved, Hakim drew his revolver and emptied and loaded it, and even took a number of practice shots. On their way back to Cairo, they had a narrow escape. As Hakim sat in the trolley, the gun protruded from his belt. With horror Yaffa saw a passenger staring at it. They descended at the first stop and took the next trolley.

Yaffa found herself fascinated by Hakim. What sort of a boy was this who awaited so calmly the moment he would kill a man? Although she, too, was involved, her role was remote. He would aim the weapon; his finger would press the trigger; he would watch Lord Moyne—a living man, a man who was loved, who would be mourned and grieved for—he would watch this stranger die at his hand. What had brought about this transition from the happy-go-lucky boy she had once known?

Hakim at first was not responsive to her questions, although she put them carefully. One night, however, for no special reason, he began to speak about the FFI movement. His face lit up. "I've never met finer fellows," he said. As they sat on the wooden bench across from Moyne's residence, one more couple among scores in the park, he confessed that he was homesick for his comrades. She began to glimpse something of his loneliness, to understand how important was his identification with his fellow Sternists.

Perhaps, she thought, this stemmed from the fact that Hakim

was a Sephardic Jew—an Oriental Jew in a community whose leaders were Russian, Polish, German and South African. The sense of discrimination he felt—more fancied than real—was a subtle one, but nonetheless there. How necessary, then, the conviction that he belonged to a movement which entrusted him with a great deed. It fitted in, too, with the sense of dignity which is the mark of Oriental Jewry.

Almost impulsively she asked, "Why did you join the Lehi?"

He measured his words thoughtfully. First there was Ben Josef's hanging and his admiration for the way he went to his death. There were the Jews who had been and were being massacred in Europe. As he talked, Yaffa knew how he felt. To live in one's own country, yet see a foreign flag float over every public building, foreign policemen patrolling the streets; when you were brought before a judge, to have the proceedings go on in a foreign language—indeed, you, the natural son of the country, had to make use of a translator to make yourself understood; to use currency with foreign words on it, to mail your letters with stamps of a foreign government . . . Why? Why should one tolerate this? Were they backward natives needing a foreign raj to rule their lives for them? What was it Disraeli had said in the House of Lords when he was taunted as a Jew: "When the ancestors of the right honorable gentleman were brutal savages in an unknown island, mine were priests in the temple of Solomon. . . ."

Galili was impatient. He dispatched a letter to Shamir. Had they chosen the second man yet?

Galili's restiveness stemmed from his concern that Hakim and Yaffa were seeing too much of each other. They were thrown into each other's company—she came from camp each weekend and stayed two days—they were young people, linked by the same cause. If they fell in love, the entire project would be endangered for then they would see each other when it was not necessary. He must bring the second man from Palestine and start the action. He bombarded Shamir in Tel Aviv with messages.

When the deed was to be done had not yet been decided. Once the second man arrived they would perfect the final plan and the retreat. A stolen automobile, perhaps even Yaffa's ambulance . . . Sadovsky knew a South African physician sympathetic to the cause who might even be persuaded to see that an army first-aid car drove by Bulak Bridge at the proper moment. But how arrange this without divulging everything to Sadovsky and the physician?

Then, unexpectedly, Galili was arrested.

It happened in late September, a day after he had separate talks with Hakim and Yaffa. He had told Hakim that if he and his partner in the action were caught, they must conceal their true identity for at least three days—long enough to allow others implicated in the plot to take whatever measures were needed for their own safety. Galili had revealed to Hakim that packages of ammunition, waiting to be smuggled into Palestine, were hidden in ten private homes in Cairo, whose owners had no idea what the parcels contained. This contraband had to be cleared out to protect the guiltless.

In his talk with Yaffa, Galili had assigned her to pick up two new identity cards to be used by Hakim and his companion when they fled Cairo after the deed. The plan was for the two to go as soldiers, on the same day as the deed. She was to bring the cards to Galili as he waited in the Misr railway station in Alexandria.

The afternoon following these conversations an officer dropped in at RAF headquarters. Would Sergeant Galili be good enough to accompany him? Galili suspected the worst. He had sufficient presence of mind to ask permission to go to the nearest NAAFI canteen for a cup of tea. It was teatime; the officer nodded and went with him. Galili was able to murmur to a girl behind the counter, an attractive, red-haired member of the FFI named Dafna Leib, "I'm being arrested. They'll find nothing on me." She was to pass the word.

Galili was taken to Field Security headquarters in Alexandria and questioned exhaustively about political parties in Palestine. No mention was made, no question hinged, on any plot against Moyne.

He began to breathe easier.

All the next day he was kept incommunicado. On the third day his interrogator said suddenly, "Tell us about the Pan-Arab Conference."

The conference? He only knew what he had read about it. Mr. Anthony Eden had suggested months ago that Arab representatives meet in Alexandria to discuss creation of an Arab federation or league. Its purpose would be to protect their mutual interests—and, presumably, to pinpoint Arab political strategy after the war. At this very moment diplomats from Syria, Lebanon, Iraq, Transjordan, Yemen and an observer from Palestine Arabs were meeting at Antoniades Palace on the outskirts of Alexandria. It was no secret that Zionism and Palestine was a major item on the agenda.

"Our information," said his questioner imperturbably, "is that you and a colleague plan to blow up the palace."

Galili denied this vehemently. "It is not true!" And it was not true. But they continued to press him. In their questions there was no suggestion that they knew of the existence of an FFI branch in Egypt.

Yaffa, the identity cards in her bag, waited anxiously at the railway station. Galili did not appear. After an hour, she hurried to the Jewish Services Club. He was not there. Now deeply concerned, she sat down at the snack bar and ordered coffee. She overheard a Palestinian soldier who had just entered with several others say in Hebrew to one of his friends, "What do you think of the arrests?"

Almost in panic she turned to him. Also in Hebrew she said, "I couldn't help hearing you—please tell me what happened."

The other shrugged his shoulders. "I don't know the details, but some of our boys were arrested."

Yaffa left quickly. Galili had once said, "If ever we miss connections, find Dafna Leib in the air force." It took her two hours to track down Dafna, to introduce herself and learn from her that

Galili had been arrested but that nothing incriminating would be found on him.

She rushed to the station. She had missed the train to Cairo, and an appointment with Hakim, who was to have met her that night. The next morning she took the first train available and hurried to Sadovsky's house. He alone would know where Hakim could be found, although he did not know where he lived. When she told Sadovsky of Galili's arrest, she at once realized that it was a mistake, for he turned pale. He wanted nothing of trouble. Yes, he was to see Hakim at six o'clock that night. She could go in his stead.

Hakim, when she met him, took the news silently. They strolled into a public garden and there Hakim wrote a note to FFI headquarters in Palestine, relating what had happened and asking for instructions. Yaffa must find a way to get the note to Tel Aviv.

That night, back at her camp, she learned that Sonia Hauser, daughter of a distinguished Mapai leader, a girl completely unconnected with the terrorist underground, was going home on leave tomorrow. Yaffa made up a vivid tale. Would Sonia do her a great service and take a letter to Yaffa's fiancé? It was a most personal note, Yaffa said, embarrassed—then, in what appeared to be a burst of confidence, she told Sonia that she was preparing to get married; it would have to be a secret for she had not received permission from her commanding officer; she wanted to discuss important marriage plans in the note—under no circumstances was Sonia, therefore, to let it fall into anyone's hands, and most especially, not the military police. If there was a search on the train, Sonia was to destroy the letter.

Sonia, smiling at this exaggerated fear, said, "I promise to guard it with my life."

Yaffa gave her the letter and the address, a restaurant in Tel Aviv.

Sonia went on leave: when she returned a week later she could only say, staring curiously at Yaffa, "I gave your letter to your fiancé." Yaffa's FFI contact in Tel Aviv was a wizened, sour, middle-aged man who worked as a dishwasher in the restaurant. Sonia could not resist adding, "I must say you have strange tastes in boy friends." Yaffa blushed prettily and thanked her.

In Palestine, Hakim's letter precipitated matters. It led to a series of FFI meetings being held despite new waves of terror and reprisal that kept many quarters of Jewish Palestine cordoned off with barbed wire. The final meeting was held between Shamir and Avigad. Word had come that Galili had been released after seven days: he had not been allowed to return to Alexandria—even for his possessions; instead, he had been transferred that day to Ismailia, on the Suez Canal, fifty miles south of Cairo. He would find it difficult to go to Cairo now, for the police might follow him.

Clearly, the second man must be sent from Palestine—the man who would take over the action against Moyne, direct it and bring it to a successful conclusion. The machinery had been set up for the deed. Now the question remained, Who was to go?

They discussed candidates. In the end it was Avigad who said slowly, "The only man who fits these requirements—the only man upon whom you can rely—is Eliahu Bet Zouri."

Shamir knew how difficult it was for Avigad to utter these words, for he loved Eliahu as a brother. Nor was it a light decision for Shamir. He, too, placed a high value on Bet Zouri. He had watched him develop. When he had first met him in the National Cells, Eliahu was little more than a child. Now, Shamir thought, he was emerging as a man upon whom you could depend in any situation —he had the sensitivity of spirit, the strength of character, the intellectual capacity, the technical skill. Yet, on the other hand, these very qualities made him a man to be cherished and preserved. One had to consider, too, that he had no experience in such matters. . . .

But Shamir said, "Speak to him."

CHAPTER

18

Not long after this conversation, on a warm night early in October, 1944, Avigad and Bet Zouri sat on the terrace of a roof-top apartment in the town of Ramat Gan, near Tel Aviv. Here Avigad lived with his wife, Miriam, and their two-month-old daughter. Eliahu was virtually one of the family; he dropped in at all times: usually he arrived by bus and was taken home by Avigad on his motorcycle. He dined with them and played with the baby. Since Adi had married and still lived in hiding, Eliahu had become a kind of substitute brother.

Avigad had promised he would tell Eliahu about Moyne. Yet he hesitated. It was a heavy responsibility. He knew—he was certain —how Eliahu would react. From that moment on he, Avigad, would bear the knowledge of the part he had played. He had pondered about it and finally decided that he would not suggest that Eliahu volunteer for the mission. He would simply mention the deed, simply state the fact. Then it would be up to Eliahu.

As the two sat in their chairs, smoking, to the right they saw the dark waters of the Mediterranean; to the left, the parks of Ramat Gan; before them, two miles distant, the dim illumination and shapes of Tel Aviv, in the wartime blackout rising like a mirage out of the flat desert plain. "Eliahu," Avigad said suddenly, wanting to be done with it, "I must tell you—there is a plan afoot to get rid of Lord Moyne in Cairo." He saw Eliahu stiffen. "I have been talking with Shamir. The plan is already worked out in general; there is already one man there to carry out the action. He has done the groundwork. Now we must send a man to cover for him, to take responsibility—"

Eliahu leaped from his chair. *"Beshem Kol hashedim!* By the name of all the devils! That's for me, Avigad. I must be the one— I must go!" He began pacing back and forth. "What a thing to do!" he said again and again. "What a thing to do!"

Avigad's heart sank. He knew it would be this way. There was no way back now. Eliahu would insist: he had been set afire by the idea. He would do it. He might never come back. "My soul gave a prophecy," Avigad remembered later. Eliahu would not come back. Was Moyne—was anyone—worth Eliahu's life? But was it his, Avigad's, duty to judge this? They were at war; they were not children playing games. Their people had been killed and they killed in retaliation. This was the decree of reality. This was how it had to be. Bet Zouri was Avigad's dear friend, but whoever else might go to Cairo, he would be someone's dear friend. . . .

Avigad's reverie had little chance to go on. Eliahu was too excited. Avigad could not see him clearly in the darkness but he knew Eliahu: his face would be flushed, his eyes shining, he would be full of ways and means. Suddenly Eliahu stopped pacing. "I've been thinking, how shall I arrange it with my family, with my job? I have it. I'll tell my family I'm going on a surveying trip and I'll tell my employer I'm going on family business. As simple as that."

He placed his hand on the shoulder of the silent, brooding Avigad. "Avigad, it will be done. It's fated!"

Had one been strolling past the railway station in the town of Rehovoth a week or so later, he would have seen a British soldier saying a fond good-bye to his girl. She was a typical kibbutz teenager, sturdy-legged and solid in her blue shorts and embroidered white peasant blouse, her hair falling in long black braids down her back.

The soldier was a little below medium height, in khaki uniform. Under his visored cap his hair was blond, his eyes blue. He had a crisp yellow mustache, his complexion was fair, and at the moment, flushed. If he was nervous, he showed it only by the quick puffs he took on his cigarette as he chatted with his girl.

Eliahu had reason to be nervous. The uniform he wore, the papers he carried, the name he had taken—even the girl friend—all were counterfeit. The girl was Shulamith, Shamir's fiancée, and she had accompanied him so that his departure would appear to be that of just another soldier returning to Cairo from leave in Palestine.

Eliahu's appearance here, in this uniform at this moment, waiting for the Haifa-Cairo train in this little town thirteen miles south of Tel Aviv, had taken hours of intense preparation. Rehovoth station had been chosen because Lydda, the main depot, swarmed with soldiers, secret police and MP's. It would have been all but impossible to smuggle him into Egypt as a civilian; he had to go as a British soldier, in uniform, armed with proper papers to pass muster in the train, where MP's would examine them and take him through customs and border guards, both British and Egyptian. . . .

An hour before the train left from Rehovoth that afternoon a Private Yacob Hermon, on leave in Tel Aviv, ran frantically into the police station a few blocks from the beach at the foot of Hayarkon Street. He was clad only in his bathing trunks and hardly able to speak for indignation. Someone had run off with his clothes while he was in the water—uniform, shoes, pay book, everything. He had come down to the beach wearing his trunks under his uniform, as everyone did. He had slipped off his clothes, piled them neatly on the beach and gone in for a long, leisurely swim. When he came out he could find nothing. Private Hermon, explaining his plight, did not reveal that he belonged to the FFI; that he had been chosen to have his uniform stolen because he was the same size and build as Bet Zouri, or that in his uniform was a valid return pass to Cairo.

Even as he was giving details of the theft to police, a fifteen-year-old FFI scout with Hermon's bundle of clothes on his lap was in a car en route to Eliahu, waiting at a hideout. Eliahu donned the uniform, packed his civilian clothes in his suitcase and hurried across the street to a taxi in which Shulamith waited. They were driven to Rehovoth station.

The train came. They played out their farewell scene. *"L'hitraot* (See you again),"* said Eliahu, smiling, and climbed aboard. She waved after him. She could report later that he was in excellent spirits.

Before checkposts could be notified of the stolen uniform, before name and number and pay book could be sought all through Palestine, long before this, Eliahu would have reached the Egyptian border. His papers would have been checked. And the bogus Private Hermon would have been passed by unsuspecting officials. He would be in Egypt.

By the time Military Intelligence might be inspired to search for him in Egypt Eliahu would have discarded the uniform and become a civilian under another name.

Days before, Eliahu had made his farewells. He said good-bye to his father and his older sister Deborah at the post office, where both worked, telling them he was off on a surveying trip in the desert near Gaza. At home he found his two younger sisters, twenty-year-old Aviva and Lea, now fourteen. He began to pack his military kit and his suitcase. He told Aviva, "This time I may stay longer—perhaps two, maybe three weeks." Aviva, combing her hair in the bedroom, could see him in her mirror. She wondered had she washed enough clothes for him for three weeks? As he packed she observed that he had bought two new shirts. Why would he need new shirts in the desert? She lifted her eyes to meet those of her brother: he had given her a swift, sharp glance; suddenly she realized that she was staring at him in the mirror. He was the first to drop his gaze and begin to fumble, almost imperceptibly, with the shirts, as if to put them out of sight. She thought, Why should he want to hide them from me? And why doesn't he simply take work clothes—

But one never pressed Eliahu on personal matters.

"Eli, will you write?"

"Yes, of course I'll write."

He finished packing, kissed her and Lea, said "Shalom," and hurried down the stairs. Then, halfway down, Aviva heard his voice. "But really, why should I write? What will I have to say? There won't be any need of it—only if I stay longer than three weeks."

"All right," she called down. And she called after him again, "Shalom." Lea ran to the window, Aviva following her, and both girls stood there, watching him as he waited for the bus, turned to wave to them, then boarded it and was gone.

The night before he had made other farewells. He had spent the afternoon with Hannah. He had insisted on taking her to the cinema —as if afraid, perhaps, that he might talk too much. He was in high spirits. He told her, too, that he was going on a surveying trip, probably two weeks, at most three weeks, in the Gaza area, near the coast. He would be back on a Friday. He explained that the coastal freighters sailed only on that day. They talked a bit more, and when he said good-bye, at the door of her apartment house, she thought he looked at her strangely. "Why do you look at me like that?" she asked.

"Oh, it is nothing."

"Shalom," she said. He had brought her a copy of his favorite novel, Voynich's *The Gadfly*, the book he had been reading the day Esther Raziel brought him into the Irgun. He gave the book to her, kissed her, said, "Until I come back," kissed her again, and left.

Now he called on Avigad and Miriam. To Miriam he said, "Well, you know I go away. What shall I bring back for you?"

Miriam, who was aware that he was being sent on an underground mission to Egypt but had no idea of its nature, asked jestingly, "What can you bring back from Egypt? Stone? Sand? Heat?" And then, fondly, "I only want you to bring yourself back."

211

He laughed. "I will, don't worry." He was still in fine spirits. She gave him the address of her aunt, Mrs. Helen Blanca, and a little cake to take to her. "Tell her it comes from her daughter," she said. "You may be able to stay with her your first night until you find your friends."

Avigad took him home that night on his motorcycle. They spoke together a few minutes in the darkness before Eliahu went upstairs. In the distance they heard sirens: somewhere British tenders were descending on a neighborhood; the pitiless spotlights were at work, police, tommy guns in hand, were searching. . . . Avigad said, "I don't know the lay of the land; it would be silly for me to advise you, Eliahu. I can only suggest that you double-check your information and if possible have a third person to help—one to execute the action, the second to cover, the third to drive the runaway car."

In Palestine they often made use of stolen cars. Two masked FFI youths would hold up a motorist; while one drove the car away to be used in an action, the other stood guard over the owner so he could give no alarm. In an hour the action would be over, the car would be back, the two would vanish. . . .

"But if we cannot get a car?"

"Rent one. Steal one," said Avigad. "Not too long before the action because the police must have as little headstart as possible." Bet Zouri was unable to drive but he had been taught how to start a car without keys by short-circuiting the ignition. In any event, he must attach a false license plate, the car must wait in the next street, he must reach it by back yards, by leaping a fence—never by the open street. He must cover his escape with smoke grenades —and he must plan two or three alternate routes of escape.

Before he left, Eliahu went to Jerusalem to meet Shamir for the last time. It was a velvet September night. Shamir materialized out of the darkness in an alley behind the Straus Health Center. It was an ideal place for an assignation: narrow and tortuous, the shadows cast by the buildings enormous, the entire area catacombed with tiny alleyways, yards leading to yards.

Shamir had been greatly impressed by Eliahu's attitude. Eliahu had said, "I must do it—it is for me." Shamir attached great importance to the eagerness of men sent on dangerous missions. The deed was not a military operation in which, should one unit fail, a second could succeed. The individual's will, his confidence in his ability to succeed—these were of paramount importance. Especially so when the action took place in a hostile land where decisions had to be made on the spot, where approval or advice could not be sought or obtained.

He said to Eliahu, "There is little for me to tell you. You will receive all pertinent data from your comrade. But this I do tell you, Eliahu—you must come back. This is not a suicide action. You are to make a reasonable plan for retreat and escape—"

"I will do all that is necessary," said Eliahu.

Shamir went on to talk of the need for a car in the retreat. He and Avigad were both concerned. "No matter how difficult it is to get one, I would prefer you to wait a month, two months, until you get a car."

"And if we get no car?" Bet Zouri asked. "A bike?"

Shamir shook his head. "No bikes. A man on foot has better control of his movements. He can disappear among houses and alleys. A bicycle leaves few tracks but a man leaves even less."

Eliahu was silent.

A sense of uneasiness tugged at Shamir as they said good-bye in the alley. But he did not pay too much attention to it. When a man went on an important action, a certain resistance, a certain hardness, showed itself. It had to be so. Eliahu must not be shaken in himself or in his confidence that whatever decision he made would be the correct one. Above all, Eliahu was possessed of the most important conviction of all. Shamir had expressed it before: a man who goes to kill a man whom he does not know personally must be convinced that by his act he changes the course of history.

Shamir knew that Eliahu Bet Zouri believed this with all his heart.

The end of that week a letter came, by ordinary mail, for Avigad. It bore a Cairo datemark. It had been routinely passed by Egyptian censors in Cairo, British censors in Palestine. It read, "All is well. I feel fine. We only await the moment to greet Uncle Jacques."

It was signed "Zebulun"—Eliahu Bet Zouri's underground name.

CHAPTER

19

EVEN MEN who bear history on their shoulders find that time can move slowly.

Hakim, spending hours in one cinema after another, was lonely. This partly explains why, despite Galili's orders to remain inconspicuous, he looked up relatives in Cairo. But there was more to it than this. Hakim was also in something of a dilemma. He had now been in the Egyptian capital several weeks: what money he had was used up. He had been taking Yaffa out on weekends, for lunch and dinner, to cafés, to Arab dance halls, on outings to the pyramids and he had indignantly refused, despite her protests, to allow her to pay her way. It ran counter to everything in his upbringing, influenced by Oriental custom, that a man should allow a woman to share in this fashion. Now he needed money. To borrow from Yaffa was inconceivable; he dared not write to Palestine on such a trivial matter; and as the son of a wealthy family, it would demean him to ask Sergeant Galili or Sadovsky for it.

Whereupon he committed an act which his superiors would certainly have considered foolhardy. He telephoned Moses Hallek, whose wife was his mother's cousin, told him he was in Cairo on vacation and asked if he might have a loan of ten pounds—forty dollars—until he received money from home.

Hallek, a well-known accountant, was delighted to hear from him. "Of course, of course, you know you have only to ask," he told him. "Come to my office now and I'll give you the money immediately."

Within the hour Hakim was shaking hands with the older man.

"I'm only too glad to be of help," Hallek said warmly. "And now that you're here, you must meet the family." Before Hakim could protest, Hallek was on the phone to his nephew, Joseph Romano, a twenty-five-year-old construction engineer.

"Joseph," he said, "Eliahu is here and wants to meet the family."

"Eliahu?" responded Joseph. "Who is Eliahu?"

"Eliahu Hakim—the young brother of the three Hakim boys from Haifa," his uncle replied. Joseph had met the older brothers and recalled vaguely the baby of the family, a boy who must now be of high-school age.

"Fine," he said. "Send him over and I'll take him home to lunch."

Shortly after noon young Hakim walked into Joseph Romano's office. Romano saw a slim youth in khaki shirt and shorts, wearing a green beret. He could be perhaps sixteen or eighteen, it was difficult to tell, with a slender face, dark eyes, a black mustache and a slow and infrequent smile. He impressed Romano as shy, even restrained, but with perfect manners. He spoke carefully and answered questions only after giving each one due thought.

Romano greeted him cordially and drove him to his apartment —by coincidence in Zamalek, less than four blocks from Moyne's villa. Young Hakim gave no indication that he knew the neighborhood as Romano pointed out important buildings and landmarks on the way.

Over a lunch of rice pilaf, Joseph and his wife, Lois, who was soon to have a baby, and their three daughters, Rachel, fourteen, Myrtle, twelve, and Leah, ten, talked animatedly with their cousin from Palestine. The girls were full of questions. Why was he in

216

Cairo? He came for a vacation, he said, but as he did not like to be idle, he had taken a job in the NAAFI. This was his day off. How was he spending his time? He had gone quite a bit to the cinema. He had seen Greta Garbo in *Camille,* also a gangster film starring the American actor, Edward G. Robinson. He had been riding the trolleys, exploring the city. He had visited the zoo and wandered through the Egyptian museum, where he had been especially impressed by the solid gold sarcophagus of King Tutankhamen, one of its showpieces.

With some amusement he told how he had been staring at that glittering treasure—a solid gold mummy case enclosing a second solid gold mummy case enclosing a third, and in that, the wrapped body of the Egyptian king—when an American general and a tall lady had approached. She looked at the treasure very briefly, then casually turned away.

When they left, a guard sidled up to Hakim and said in Arabic, "Do you know who that was?" It was the American, Miss Doris Duke, the world's richest woman.

Hakim told his cousins with a smile, "Then I understood why the gold did not draw her eye. She looked at it as though it were nothing at all."

The conversation turned to Palestine, and Mrs. Romano spoke up. "This trouble that fills the newspapers—it confuses me. Can you explain the Irgun to me? And also the Stern group? Why do they do such terrible things?"

Hakim shrugged. "I am too young to know about that," he said. "I think maybe so far as the Stern group is concerned, the newspapers exaggerate a little."

Romano observed, "Maybe you are too young to understand such things, my cousin, but I know they are doing a good job."

Hakim looked at him, his face expressionless. "What do you mean, a good job?"

Romano said, "Look, they are scaring the Arabs and they are shaking the sleeping Jews all around the world."

Hakim said, toying with his fork—later Romano was to remem-

217

ber the exact intonation of his voice, the slightly challenging note, "Yes, but don't you think that what they do in the country is bad for the Jews?" Then he added, "I am against terrorism."

The talk went on to other things. After coffee he bade them a courteous farewell, but not before they had insisted that he must be their guest for Sabbath dinner two weeks later.

On that Friday evening Hakim was as restrained as before. He watched as Mrs. Romano lit the two Sabbath candles just before sundown, and then, standing before them, shielding her eyes—for their light symbolized light from God, too dazzling to look upon—intoned the traditional blessing, "Blessed art Thou, O Lord our God, King of the Universe, who hast commanded us to kindle the lights of the Sabbath." At the table he sat quietly as Romano broke the bread, uttering over it the prayer, "Blessed art Thou, O Lord our God, King of the Universe, who hast brought forth sustenance for us out of the earth," then putting a piece in his mouth and passing a small piece to everyone else at the table. When Romano said "Amen," he heard Hakim's deep voice join in, and at that moment it seemed to Romano that Hakim was really part of their family.

As the evening wore on, Hakim began to relax. He and the three Romano girls romped about the floor like children. Later, he took on all three at chess, sitting back and looking on tolerantly as, with much giggling, they consulted minutes at a time over every move. At one point in the evening Romano said, "Eliahu, you are not going to join the Haganah when you go back?"

"No," said Hakim, unsmilingly. "They are not for me."

"Then the Stern?"

"Terrorism?" Hakim shook his head. "Never."

When he said good night he told Romano almost formally, "I expect to be leaving soon and I wish all happiness to you, your wife and the baby to come."

Romano asked, "Will you be going to Italy with the brigade?" The Jewish Brigade, so long urged upon the British by the Jewish Agency, had finally been approved in London, and would soon go into action on the Italian front. "No, I don't think so," Hakim replied, and changed the subject.

Two days later Romano was driving in downtown Cairo when he saw young Hakim waiting at a trolley stop.

"Can I give you a lift?" he called out. The boy got into his car. He was on his way to Moses Hallek's office to repay the money he had borrowed. There was little conversation as they drove. Romano asked if he was staying in the barracks in the suburb of Heliopolis, headquarters of many Jewish soldiers from Palestine. If so, he would wait until Hakim saw Hallek, then take him there. It was quite a distance to go.

"No," said Hakim briefly. "I'm staying with friends." He did not say who they were. He thanked him for his offer. Romano let him out in front of Hallek's office and watched him vanish into the building.

He thought as he drove on, A curious boy. He tells little. He holds it all to himself. Only twice had the boy seemed to soften, to yield—at the blessing of the candles and the bread, and when he played with the girls. Why should a young boy who would have everything in life handed to him on a silver platter be so heavy, so serious?

Then he thought no more about him.

CHAPTER

20

I_N THE C_{AIRO} wineshop of one Gershon Green, Hakim waited for the unknown comrade who would join him from Palestine.

It was a few minutes before seven o'clock the night of October 20, 1944.

In Palestine, a great terrorist roundup had taken place twenty-four hours earlier. Before dawn, moving by some kind of sixth sense which anticipated trouble but was unable to pinpoint it, the British unexpectedly descended on Latrun Camp, roused 251 suspected Irgunists and Sternists, chained them at the ankles and flew them to the Sudan. Some of the prisoners had been at Latrun two or three years. None of them had ever been charged or tried on any count. No notification was given their families. No reason was given for the deportation.

Simultaneously, a new order became effective. The moment a terrorist outrage was reported, air raid sirens would sound throughout the city. All persons on the streets had to freeze in their tracks and remain where they were until the sirens sounded again. In this fashion, terrorists would literally be caught in the act.

Hakim, far from all this, smoked a cigarette and waited.

Bet Zouri's orders were clear. He was to make a rendezvous with someone called Benny at 7 P.M. at the Carmel Oriental Wineshop. Exactly at that hour he was to enter, walk to the counter and survey the bottles as if trying to decide what to buy. At that moment Hakim should also be standing there. Hakim was to offer Bet Zouri a cigarette, which he was to accept with the words, "Thank you. My name is Zebulun." If the other said, "It is a pleasure. My name is Benny," the contact would be made.

Bet Zouri had arrived in Cairo the previous evening. In the men's room of the Benha station he quickly changed into his civilian clothes. He was now Moshe Salzman, student, born 1922, Jerusalem. Proof was in the beautifully turned out Government of Palestine identity booklet he carried, given him by Shulamith as they rode to the station in Rehovoth. It had been prepared by the same FFI artist who had made Hakim's identity card—a lithographer with a genius for reproducing any kind of document, complete even to watermarks and cancelled stamps.

Bet Zouri made his way at once to the home of Mrs. Blanca, as Avigad's wife had suggested, gave her the nut cake and spent the night there. Next morning he took a room in the Tipperary Hotel, a tiny English lodging house. He kept to his room through the day and as darkness fell that Friday night he set out for the wineshop.

He found it—one shop among many in a rather poor neighborhood—a small place on Amin Sheikh Street with a modest blue neon sign reading, CARMEL ORIENTAL WINES. The grapes of Carmel are famous in Palestine; they come from the first vineyards planted by the settlers of the 1880's.

Gershon Green, the owner of the shop, was a stocky little man who had been expelled from Palestine by the Turks during World War I for his Zionist activities. To him, a few months ago, there had come a Sergeant Ben-Zvi, a huge fellow, who also hailed from Palestine and knew the grape country well. The two became friends. Green had no idea of Sergeant Ben-Zvi's extracurricular activities—he could not know that he also went by the name of Sergeant Galili—but he liked him and was glad to let him use his shop as a meeting place for friends from Palestine, and even allowed them to leave messages there.

The two Eliahus met face to face for the first time. There was no witness to their meeting. A few minutes before, Green had greeted Hakim, then gone to the rear of the shop to unpack a case of liquor. Bet Zouri walked in and a moment later the two were strolling down the street, talking. We can only speculate as to their first impressions of each other, how they began to take each other's measure, to develop a mutual trust knowing they were linked in an act which meant life or death for them both.

At eight o'clock they were sitting at the Café Astoria, waiting for Yaffa, on her Sabbath leave, to walk by. When she did they followed her. Once around the corner, Hakim turned to her and said simply, introducing Bet Zouri, "This is my comrade in the action."

The two shook hands with the sharp, jerky handshake of the Palestinian. "Shalom," Bet Zouri said. His voice was low and well modulated, she remembered, his smile a quick, engaging one. The three took a fiacre, so that Bet Zouri could see the British Embassy and the surrounding area, then to Zamalek, so he could view Moyne's villa and familiarize himself with the neighborhood. Then, after Yaffa left, Hakim took him to the room which had been rented for them in the old bazaar quarter. It was very small, on the second floor of an old house: it was unfurnished; the boys slept on blankets on the floor. The street was little more than an alleyway of leather stalls, cheap jewelry stands and tiny, cavern-like shops in the depths of which men hammered brass and copper-ware all through the day. Twenty yards away was an ancient synagogue.

Galili, now virtually exiled in Ismailia, dared come to Cairo only rarely. The two boys were very much on their own and spent hours in discussion, working out ways and means. Obviously, the British Embassy and the area around it, with its barbed wire, its innumerable military personnel, was out of the question: it would be almost impossible to carry out the deed there. As Hakim had concluded weeks before, it had to be done at the residence.

They could not attack at night: darkness would hamper them. In addition, a police guard was on duty at Moyne's villa through the night. Up to a month ago there had been a daytime guard as well, and a police patrol escorted Lord Moyne's car to and from his office. Moyne himself had dispensed with this extra protection because it had become a nuisance.

To attempt the deed in daylight, however, meant endangering themselves all the more. This gave them pause. They were to carry out their assignment without being caught. "This is not a suicide mission." Bet Zouri remembered Shamir's words. . . . In the end, they decided, whatever the risk, to act in daylight. Success was more important than safety.

For days they tried to work out a way of retreat. At one point, when Yaffa was with them, Bet Zouri turned to her. "If necessary, could you wait for us near the bridge in your ambulance?" She was prepared to do this, but Hakim opposed it. As the boys discussed the question, she discreetly walked some distance away. She wanted to know as little as possible. Finally Bet Zouri agreed that any involvement of Jewish personnel in Egypt would endanger every Jewish soldier there—the very reason both of them had been sent from Palestine.

By late October they had decided to attack Moyne when his car brought him home for lunch. Again they weighed the problem of their retreat. The Bulak Bridge offered the only practical way. There were no back yards, no alleyways, no corners to duck into. They would have to make a frontal daylight attack on Moyne, as the car deposited him at the villa door, then they must retreat. But what could they use? A car seemed out of the question. Even to inquire about renting one would cause suspicion; they dared not trust a native driver to wait for them. Stealing a car would also involve risks they dared not take. What was left? Escape by foot? This was impracticable, especially if there was no place to hide. If they attempted to run for the bridge, a fleet pursuer could bring them down without trouble. A motorcycle? It posed the same problems as a car: license plates, identification papers, registration, large amounts of money which they did not have. The one remaining possibility was a bicycle. Not far from their room was a repair shop with bikes for rent. A bike, too, had its drawbacks, but it could not be traced, it required no license, no documents—all one had to do was pay a small deposit and use a false name. . . .

Thus the two boys finally agreed on bicycles. Perhaps impatience, too, played a part, in view of the fact that Shamir had said to Bet Zouri that even if he had to wait a month for a car, it would be worth it. Hakim had already been waiting a long time. Bet Zouri had sent a note to Shamir a few days after his arrival, in which he had said, "We should be finished with Uncle Jacques within two weeks." Shamir, receiving it, felt concerned. Eliahu's letter was obviously written in a spirit of decision and confidence, but Shamir thought he seemed a little hasty. Was it, perhaps, too much a matter of ambition for him? But how was one to judge? Only the two boys knew the full situation.

On Friday, October 27, the week following Bet Zouri's arrival, Galili ventured a trip to Cairo. Through Sadovsky, who did not know where the boys lived but knew where they would be likely to be found, Galili met the two in a coffee house opposite the opera. They strolled together while the boys briefed him. They had agreed on three possible dates: 1 P.M. the following Monday, October 30; if not then, the same hour on Tuesday, October 31 and if not then, the same hour on the following Monday, November 6. The irregular spacing of dates seemed, in some fashion, to assure them a measure of safety, to throw suspicion off the trail.

Galili returned to Ismailia that same night.

Then—unexpectedly, inexplicably—Moyne vanished.

He disappeared. He was nowhere to be seen—not at his residence, not at his office, not at his club. They could not know that on this very Friday, the day they had met, Moyne had flown to Athens to talk to Anthony Eden about the critical situation in Greece. The two boys continued to watch the house; through the windows they saw servants, deliveries were being made. The place had not been closed up. Moyne must simply have gone away on a visit. They pored over the Egyptian newspapers, hoping to find some mention of him in the social and personal columns. They waited.

At this point Yaffa received a week's leave. With her usual quota of small arms and ammunition she took a letter from Bet Zouri to her FFI contact in Tel Aviv. Hakim, always the perfectionist, was not happy with his weapon. Would the FFI please send back with Yaffa a second pistol—a Nagan, the tried and trusted Polish revolver? It fitted his hand well, it never failed, he would be more at ease with it. Bet Zouri also asked for smoke grenades to cover their retreat. They might need them.

Before Yaffa left she brought them two gifts—a comb for Bet Zouri, whose hair never stayed down, and a chocolate bar for Hakim, who had a sweet tooth. Then she said good-bye. She would be back with gun and grenades on Sunday night, November 5. "Now, don't do anything until I return," she said.

Bet Zouri smiled. "Our hands are tied," he said. "He is not here."

On November 1 the boys rented two bicycles from the little shop near their room, and rode again and again through the area near Moyne's villa. They kept careful vigil. Suddenly, at eight o'clock on Friday morning, the third, they saw the familiar figure once more emerge from his residence. They moved swiftly. That night they met for the last time with Galili. Monday, November 6, was their date; they had missed October 30 and October 31. Yaffa would be back in time.

The two boys spoke only of the task before them at their meeting with Galili. Bet Zouri seemed sure of success and a return to Palestine within twenty-four hours. Hakim seemed equally confident of the deed itself, but when Bet Zouri talked of the retreat, Hakim was silent. Galili, bidding them good-bye, recalled Hakim's words: "I have the feeling that it will be an action for which I must be ready to pay with my life." He thrust the idea out of his mind, shook hands with them and returned to Ismailia to wait.

Sunday night, November 5, the boys dined at Sadovsky's house with his parents. They had dined there several times before. Sadovsky still knew nothing of their mission, had no idea of their true name nor of their membership in the FFI. The evening moved pleasantly: after the many courses, served by native boys, the older people retired and the three adjourned to Sadovsky's study, where he spoke animatedly and enthusiastically of his work as a teacher, and went on at great length about the satisfaction he received in helping the cause of freedom in Palestine. Would it be at all possible, he asked at one point, for the Palestine underground—he was vague, but they knew he meant the Irgun—to send him a letter sometime in the future when such things were possible, certifying that he had been of assistance? In later years he would be proud to show it to his friends. He chattered on.

As midnight neared, Bet Zouri rose. So did Hakim. When Sadovsky took them to the door, Bet Zouri said, "Won't you walk with us a little way?" At the end of the block, he stopped. "Mr. Sadovsky," he began, "I think I should tell you what we are about." Then for the first time he revealed their purpose. Why he did so will never be known. The most obvious reason is that he felt that telling Sadovsky that he was involved in a man's death would seal his lips as no other warning could. Sadovsky's reaction bore this out. He was thunderstruck. He began to tremble there in the darkness. "Great God in Heaven—" he gasped. Bet Zouri put his hand on his arm. "Mr. Sadovsky, we want to thank you for everything you have done. I should tell you that usually we don't thank in the underground, but you are not a member of the underground, so we thank you. We want you to know that you need have no concern. Whatever happens to us—if we are captured, tortured or anything, you can be quite sure that never will your name be mentioned."

A handclasp—and they were gone. Almost unbelievingly, Sadovsky watched them lose themselves in the darkness. Then he went back to his home and to his room, and prayed.

Yaffa had been detained. She was to have met the two boys to give them the gun and grenades on the morning of the sixth.

But she was not in Cairo. Sunday night, when she should have arrived, when Bet Zouri and Hakim were dining at Sadovsky's, she was still miles away in Palestine, distraught at her bad luck. At the last moment she had decided to return to Egypt in an ATS truck convoy rather than by train. It would be far safer; she dared not endanger the deed by risking search on the train.

Autumn is the rainy season in Palestine and Egypt. The night of her departure on the twenty-four-hour drive, it poured. Only one truck was protected by a tarpaulin. The convoy halted and several ATS girls hurried up and down the line of trucks, picking up luggage and knapsacks and transferring them to the covered truck. When one of the girls approached Yaffa, she clung to her bag. "I'll keep it with me," she said.

"Are you crazy?" the other demanded. "It's soaked now."

Yaffa, fearful of causing suspicion, allowed her precious cargo to be piled with the rest.

They drove for hours through the rain. Then it stopped; but just outside Beersheba, a sandstorm blew up. This halted them on the road until morning. Yaffa was nearly frantic. The boys were waiting and she was late. Finally, after more hours of slow progress and frequent halts, the convoy reached her camp at Tel el Kebir. It was already the night of November 6.

Yaffa hurried to the covered truck to retrieve her knapsack. It was gone. Almost hysterically she searched for it. Had MP's found it? Were they even now seeking her out? Then she recalled that each time the convoy stopped in Arab towns on the way, children had swarmed over the trucks stealing whatever they could. They had undoubtedly taken the bag: they had stolen the gun for which she had made the entire trip. There was nothing to do. Trying to control herself, she went to her bunkhouse, undressed, tried to sleep, could not, dressed again and wandered into the recreation hall.

On the table was a copy of the *Mid-East Mail*. The headline read:

LORD MOYNE SHOT TO DEATH

Under it were the photographs of the two, with the names she knew them by: Itzhak Cohen and Moshe Salzman.

Over and over, in her bunk, trying to stifle her tears, she asked herself, If only she had not been late. If only they had waited. Why did they not wait? Perhaps they would have escaped. Perhaps, perhaps, perhaps . . .

CHAPTER

21

At ten o'clock the following night, in Ramat Gan, Avigad emerged from the shadows behind a news kiosk on the corner of the road leading to Tel Aviv. A pack of newspapers had just been tossed off by a motorcycle delivery cart. It was raining heavily, but Avigad was bareheaded. He waited, almost diffidently, until the dealer unbound his papers. Then he bought one and slipped back into the shadows again.

Moments later, in his roof-top apartment, he held the newspaper in silence. He did not open it; all that fascinated him was the front page. He stared at it in despair.

The newspaper was the Cairo *Bourse Egyptian,* and in the center of page one were photographs of two boys—one dark, one blond.

Over them the headline read: ACCUSED OF MURDER.

Below the photographs were their names and the words:

Anyone having any information of the identity of the above men, their addresses, or of persons who have been in touch with them, is earnestly requested to communicate with CID, Governorate, Cairo, in person, by telephone, or by letter.

Avigad looked again at the photographs and the names. Itzhak Cohen? Moshe Salzman? He did not recognize the names, but surely one of the faces, distorted as it was with pain, must be, could only be, Eliahu.

He rose and walked into the next room where his wife was nursing their baby. "Miriam," he managed to say. "Look at this." He watched her as she read. She looked up at him with tears in her eyes. "It is so," she said.

That afternoon they had heard on the radio that Moyne had been shot the previous day, his assailants captured. But who were the assailants? Was Bet Zouri one of them? Who *had* been caught? Avigad knew that thousands of others had heard the news, for radios were turned on all through Palestine that Tuesday as people listened to latest reports on the Roosevelt-Dewey contest in the United States. He was sure that what he feared had come about, the prophecy his soul had given him—Eliahu's capture. In great agitation he had waited until late evening, then run down to get the first available Egyptian paper and make sure.

Now he and his wife sat, stunned.

Avigad said, "We must think." He paced back and forth. "We'll get them out, we'll find a way, I'll go to Cairo myself—" He paused. It suddenly had struck him. "But we are in danger ourselves. Eliahu went to your aunt's. If she tells the police we sent him—"

They must hide immediately. Miriam bundled the baby warmly and with no idea of what they would do, they ran out of the apartment and down the stairs. They stood for a moment in the downpour, then hurried to a taxistand on the corner, got into a cab and sat there, paralyzed. Where to go? "Just drive," Avigad said, and for half an hour they rode aimlessly through the wet streets of the little town. Then they decided to go to a relative in a Tel Aviv suburb. Their host said, "I can't turn you out into the rain with a baby, but you must be out of here by dawn."

They sat through the night, listening to the radio as bulletin followed bulletin. All Avigad could think was, I must tell his family. . . .

In a hideout in the Katamon section of Jerusalem, chosen because it was a non-Jewish neighborhood and so free from curfew, Shamir was visiting a Sternist named Dov. Among other things, they were planning the assassination of Sir John Shaw, Chief Secretary of the Government of Palestine, second to the High Commissioner and his executive officer. Sir John, as the administration's political expert, had worked closely with MacMichael on all matters dealing with illegal immigration, the deportation of refugees, the increasingly severe government restrictions. Now that MacMichael was gone, Sir John bore further responsibility for the deportation of 241 suspected terrorists to the Sudan on October 19—the day Bet Zouri left for Cairo.

As the two men talked, a droning voice on the radio was interrupted by a special news bulletin: Lord Moyne had been shot, his assailants had been captured. They suspended all plans at once. Shamir left immediately. Within the hour notes were on their way by courier to Friedman-Yellin, living in disguise just outside Tel Aviv, and to Dr. Eldad, still in jail. "The police and the Haganah will undoubtedly take strong measures," Shamir wrote. "We must take every precaution to counter them. I recommend, too, that we prepare a statement explaining the action in Cairo."

The word flashed through Palestine to all Sternists: Take cover.

In his cell Dr. Eldad prepared the first draft of the FFI statement.

In Haifa, Menachem Hakim was in his shop on Herzl Street when his brother Joseph hurried in, a newspaper in his hand. It was noon. Joseph had gone to Tel Aviv only that morning and was not due back until nightfall. His brother looked at him in some alarm. Joseph was deathly pale. He spread the newspaper out. "Look," he said despairingly.

They closed their shop and went together to their parents' house. They took their father aside and told him. The shock almost stupefied Simon Hakim. He could not speak. They dared not tell their mother until hours later.

Menachem and Joseph were not particularly religious men. But they went to the synagogue and prayed for a long time. Then they held council. What could they do?

In Tel Aviv, in the house of Ada Ron, the newspaper lay on the table. "No, it can't be," she was saying. And then in a voice of dismay, "But the tie—I recognize that tie. I don't know about the face but I know that tie." It was difficult to recognize Bet Zouri. He had been photographed before being given first aid for his bullet wound.

Ada's father, who had so often teased Bet Zouri, drawn him out, challenged his politics, heard his daughter say, "Yes, yes, it is."

"Impossible," he said. "Not Eli."

"But it is."

"I say, impossible. But don't tell Mother."

He went to his office. But Mrs. Ron learned about it. She wept all night. "How can it be? How can it be?"

Ada said helplessly, "I don't know." She said again and again, "He was at our party only a few weeks ago and he was so happy with Hannah—"

When Ron came home that night he found his wife crying. "Why didn't you tell me?" she asked.

In her house in another part of Tel Aviv, Tamar Vered was reading the newspaper. Suddenly she cried out—"Oh, but this is—" Then she held her tongue. She began to tremble and could not stop. He had been surveying. In Gaza. What was he doing in Egypt?

The next morning Adi came to her house. He was still in hiding but he was so concerned that he dared emerge in full daylight to see her.

"Do you know?" he asked.

"Yes, I saw their pictures."

Adi said, "We still have a little time until they identify them."

Would she go to Eliahu's house and destroy any papers she thought necessary?

Tamar did so. She found the family red-eyed and weeping. Eliahu's sister Aviva was able to say, "He has something in a trunk in the basement." Tamar brought up a small box and hurried home with it to examine it there. It contained personal letters, a few snapshots—one of nine-year-old Eliahu triumphantly clambering to the top of a high gasoline tank—and letters in rhyme he had received from two girls. She found odds and ends of essays he had begun. There were several sentences in his handwriting—was it something he had copied or was it his own? It read, "In the time given you to live, live so that you will not mislead yourself or anyone whose life touches yours. Look for the good in all things. When you find it, bring it into the light and let it be free. Encourage all good virtues with a brave heart." She found, too, the diary he had begun, the two or three paragraphs he had written—after the first or second attempt, he had never touched it again. She destroyed whatever she thought might link others to him.

That night Tamar, Adi and Aviva walked through the streets of Tel Aviv aimlessly. The girls could not stop crying. Adi seemed dazed. Repeatedly he said, "I don't understand. How could he join Lehi? He was so interested in the Canaanites—he was almost one of us!"

Aviva, too, had heard the original radio bulletin. For no reason she could pinpoint—perhaps the way in which he had tried to conceal the white shirts when he had packed—her mind had leaped to Eliahu. She immediately telephoned Hannah at her office. Had she or her employers heard from Eliahu?

Hannah suddenly remembered. Eliahu had told her he would be back from Gaza on a Friday. This was Tuesday. "Oh, yes," she said. "He'll be here in three days."

Aviva, in great relief, said, "Will you come and tell that to Deborah?" Her sister had shared her presentiment. Now they could both breathe freely. If Eliahu had been in touch with Hannah, he could not be a prisoner in Cairo. . . .

Deborah and her husband had moved to a new apartment. When the two girls came there, she was out. Hannah promised to return in the evening and give the precious message in person to Deborah. She left Aviva. But as she approached her own home,

Hannah saw Tamar and Adi waiting for her, their faces stricken. All at once the awful realization flooded over her. She, too, knew the news from Cairo, but she had not associated it with Eliahu. Standing in the street, staring at her friends waiting for her twenty yards away, she began to cry.

Tamar said, when they were together, "You must come back with us to tell Aviva."

"No, no, no, I can't. I'll go with you but I couldn't—"

Tamar and Adi went to Aviva and told her, while Hannah waited downstairs. Then Aviva came down and the three girls, beside themselves, walked the dark streets, weeping. Aviva asked, How can it be true? I don't understand. He isn't one to do a thing like that. Tamar tried to comfort her. All was not lost. There would be a trial, every civilized nation knew that political murder was not ordinary murder, surely they would show mercy—

In the house of Moshe Bet Zouri, the police searched. They smashed through walls with their gun butts, ransacked closets, ripped up floors. They took eight-year-old Uri on an outing to the zoo, plied him with apples and popcorn, and questioned him. They showed him a photograph of Eliahu. "Who is this?" "My brother Eli." "Do you know his friends?" "I saw his friends but I don't know their names." They showed him scores of pictures of Sternists. He recognized none of them. They took him home.

Moshe Bet Zouri had been on his way to work in the post office Tuesday when he passed a newsboy. The newspapers were upside down under the boy's arm but something about one of the faces on the front page struck him. He bought the newspaper, and then he knew.

He continued to work that morning, as always, because he could not afford to be absent. In his lunch hour he went from lawyer's office to lawyer's office. He could find no one who wished to help.

Deborah, too, was employed at the post office. The day they searched her father's house, she came to work to find the police waiting. They had not found her at her father's and did not know that she now lived elsewhere. Because the post office frowned on

234

married women as employees, she had never revealed her marriage or change of address.

The police took her to CID headquarters, and left her alone in a room for several hours. A phonograph played incessantly in an adjoining room, hour after hour. She looked about her in dread. She thought, They are watching me through some glass I cannot see, they will torture me to find out what I know, and the music is here to drown out my screams, and I know nothing of what Eliahu has been doing.

But after questioning, they released her, unharmed.

Twenty-four hours later the Hakim family came from Haifa to Tel Aviv and called upon Moshe Bet Zouri. Like the Bet Zouris, their home had been searched, floor by floor, wall by wall: each member of the family had been separately interrogated; if the brothers had learned months before that the boy had come under the evil influence of the FFI, why had they not reported this at once to the CID? They would have done the boy a great service—a great service. Ovadia, the oldest brother, spoke with restraint. "Denounce my brother? Sir, though I am against the methods of the Lehi with all my heart, how could I denounce my own brother to the police?" Now the Bet Zouris and Hakims met in their common sorrow. Mrs. Hakim, a plump, motherly woman with enormous mascaraed eyes, was inconsolable. "We must do something," she said, on the edge of hysteria. "Let us go together to the Jewish Agency. Let us tell them our sons are not just outlaws—we must make the people understand they are not criminals; they acted from their hearts—"

So they held a council of hope and despair. Together and singly they made the rounds of the Jewish Agency, the Zionist institutions, the Chief Rabbinate, the newspapers, again and again. . . .

In Cairo, the Romanos had not given their cousin from Palestine a second thought until the morning of November 7 when the *Journal d'Egypte* was delivered to their door. The newspaper was on Joseph Romano's breakfast tray when he sat down. He stared at it with something like shock. Could that be young Eliahu Hakim's photograph on the front page? Yet the name, Itzhak Cohen . . . ?

He showed it to his wife when she joined him. She was not sure. Then they both looked at it for a long time and knew it was Hakim.

They left their food and went to their bedroom, so the servants would not hear, and talked together in whispers. The newspaper asked that any who had knowledge of the two should come forward.

They decided, after a long conversation during which Mrs. Romano threw up twice, to do nothing, to say nothing.

And everyone who knew the two Eliahus waited, fearful for them, fearful for themselves.

CHAPTER

22

You must see Hakim and Bet Zouri as I saw them, standing in the prisoners' dock behind sharp iron palings, behind bristling bayonets, guarded by six giant, impassive Egyptian policemen. They were bareheaded. They wore no ties, and their shirts were open at the neck. Their youth struck at one like a sword. Hakim, thin, tall, dark-skinned, with burning black eyes, his hands clasped behind his back, brooding and preoccupied in his martyrdom; and Bet Zouri, blond and sturdy and ruddy-faced, with clear blue eyes and British-cut mustache, his head up, chin thrust out and fists clenched at his side, trembling with power and indignation.

The trial had begun in an atmosphere of danger. Hours before, Cairo had been swept by wild rumors. Suicide squads of terrorists had infiltrated the city, they would attempt to rescue the boys, they had mined the courthouse—halfway through the first morning's session, the entire structure would explode, killing everyone: judges, spectators, foreign embassy observers, correspondents from a dozen countries, the two boys themselves—in a final Götterdämmerung to bathe the world itself in the flames of the Palestine tragedy. Twice police had ordered us out of the building while army engineers with mine detectors went over every foot. Nothing was found. The people, held at a safe distance outside, literally fought their way back, eager to attend even at their own peril. Admission was by card only—eagerly sought out and hard to come by—and extraordinary security precautions were taken to check the identity of every person allowed into the building. Once inside, I had to produce my card three times before I could reach the courtroom. Guards were everywhere—indeed, more guards than spectators. Soldiers with fixed bayonets were posted at every door, stood at the head and foot of every stairway; in the corridors leading to the courtroom parallel ropes were strung to keep the spectators in single file so each could be carefully scrutinized; on the other side of the ropes, for the entire length of each corridor, soldiers stood against each wall, shoulder to shoulder. It was an armed camp.

For eight weeks we had waited for the trial. During this time half a dozen simultaneous investigations went on—the British in Egypt, the Egyptians in Egypt, the British in Palestine, the Jewish Agency in Palestine—with no little interest taken by American, French and Russian intelligence. Was Moyne's assassination purely a Jewish terrorist act? Was any foreign power involved? The political implications led to feverish speculation. How would this be used, and by whom? How would the Arabs, the Jews, the British, the United States, react? Would Egyptian nationalists help turn the trial into an international anti-British spectacle? Would the British stamp all Palestinian Jewry with the despicable label of terrorism? How would the Arabs seize upon this to justify their cause? . . . Whatever and whoever had inspired it, how would the deed affect the Zionist future?

Against this complex backdrop the trial opened on a bright and sunny Wednesday morning in January, 1945.

Cairo's Common Pleas Courthouse is a massive three-story structure in the heart of the native quarter, built of enormous three-foot blocks of yellow ocher stone, the color of the desert. Stone steps lead up from either side to a central entrance. Long before the two boys were scheduled to be brought there, the crowd had been gathering outside. They waited impatiently for a glimpse of the two murderers. At this point, the two were regarded almost with awe by the Egyptians. They were the chief subject of conversation in the coffee houses and bazaars, where stories circulated of their fearlessness, their scorn for their own lives, their scathing retorts to Colonel Giles, chief of the CID of Palestine, who himself had flown down to question them. They had written their confession in Hebrew, then insisted upon translating it themselves into Arabic, so every word would ring true. Repeatedly they had disdained legal aid. If the Egyptian government appointed lawyers for them, they could not help it; but they would still conduct their own defense. They would refuse to recognize the court's competence. Their deed was beyond ordinary morality: they could be judged only by perfect justice. . . . Hearing all this, the impressionable Egyptians raised their glasses in toasts to the two boys. Even among the hot-headed students of the thousand-year-old El Azhar University, nerve center of the entire pan-Arab movement, one heard only talk about the two from Palestine.

All Cairo waited.

When, on the morning of the trial, the two boys appeared, it was in the midst of a fantastic military motorcade. As I stood in the crowd outside, I saw their arrival signaled from afar. First mounted police galloped into sight in a swirl of yellow dust. Then came a small red open car with police pennants fluttering at either side. Seated next to the driver, revolver in hand, was Cairo's chief of police. In the seat behind him, three constables holding submachine guns; behind, an army truck jammed with troops, bayonets fixed, standing shoulder to shoulder, facing every direction; behind that, a second truck, in the center of which the two prisoners, manacled hand and foot, sat on the floor surrounded by the armed soldiers. This was followed by a third truck of battle-ready troops. Bringing up the rear, a retinue of armed motorcycle police revving their motors in an enormous racket.

239

The motorcade halted before the courthouse.

The soldiers poured off; the prisoners rose; as they became visible amid the forest of shining bayonets, a great sigh swept the crowd. All about me I heard the words, "So young! So young!"

I stared at the murderers. They were hardly more than schoolboys! I do not know what I had expected, but the reputation of the Sternists, their identification with terror in its most ruthless form, had led me to think I would see two snarling desperadoes. Their wrists still manacled, the two Eliahus were led up the steps into the building and hurried past the gaping crowds inside, held back by ropes, to the trial room.

The prisoners' dock was a small, rectangular wooden platform, six by ten feet, surrounded by a spiked iron fence shoulder-high. Their handcuffs were removed and they stood there, dwarfed by their guards—Bet Zouri in khaki trousers, a gray slipover sweater over his open white shirt, Hakim appearing strangely formal in a double-breasted gray flannel suit, but with his shirt open at the neck, too. The boys stood calmly, though their guards kept a grip on their elbows as if they might suddenly fly off.

Gazing at them, trying to read in their faces some clue to what had brought them to this dock, I recalled how the deed had first broken into my own consciousness. Late that Monday afternoon, November 6, 1944, I had been hurrying toward Zion Square, in the center of Jerusalem, with no inkling that history was being made in Cairo, 400 miles across the desert. Perhaps I should have known. As an American war correspondent shuttling between Egypt and Palestine, perhaps I should have had some second sense, in those days of terrorist outrages, to anticipate something of the sort.

But, as it turned out, none of us had expected it—not the foreign correspondents, not military intelligence, British, American, Jewish, Arab, not even members of the other small Palestine terrorist group, the Irgun Zvai Leumi. Who would have dreamed that the Sternists would dare carry their insane war against Britain beyond the borders of Palestine? It was enough that all Palestine was embattled: more than once I had been trapped in gunfire between police and terrorists as they fought up and down the streets of the Holy Land.

Not many weeks before I had been having tea at the King David Hotel when a shriek of sirens broke the afternoon silence of Jerusalem. All uniformed personnel leaped to attention, and, preceded and followed by armed guards, Sir Harold MacMichael, the High Commissioner, entered. It was his first public appearance since his narrow escape at the hands of Sternist assassins on the Jerusalem-Jaffa road. He had been slightly wounded: it showed in his almost imperceptible limp as, a crisp, erect figure, he shook hands rapidly all around with a single, stiff handshake, and surrounded by his guards, vanished into the great dining room. He was soon to leave Palestine and this was a reception, followed by a farewell dinner, tendered him by the Municipality of Jerusalem. Sir Harold MacMichael, I thought, the arbiter of the refugee ships . . . Only the day before I had gone to Haifa to interview refugees just arrived from Rumania, Hungary and such places. I saw them, standing behind the barbed-wire fence of the Atlit reception center, still wearing the yellow Star of David of the Nazi concentration camps. These few had certificates; for everyone allowed in, thousands were kept out. You never see people really *look* until you see them looking out from behind a fence. I talked to one man, about forty. At one point he pulled out a snapshot. "These are my lost children," he said heavily. He used the German word *verlören*— a powerful word. The Nazis had seized his children, stuffed them into sacks and buried them alive; his wife had been killed by machine-gun fire and thrown into the same trench. I stared at the photograph. It showed two blond little girls, perhaps four and six, one clutching a doll. I heard the man's voice, without emotion or hope. "Against them Hitler declared war." . . . On my way to the reception center, I had talked to a British soldier. Stationed here, he had not been home for four years and two months. He, too, showed me pictures of his family. . . .

Now, hastening toward Zion Square, I passed the Rex Cinema, where the marquee announced that *Jane Eyre,* with Joan Fontaine and Orson Welles would open that evening, turned into the narrow lane on which stood the *Palestine Post* building and climbed the two flights of stairs to the city room. On this night preceding the American elections I was to dine with Julian Meltzer, *New York Times* correspondent in Palestine. When I entered he had just completed a dispatch to New York reporting the seizure of forty-six suspected terrorists in a raid on Petah Tikva, a town some forty-five miles away. I glanced through his story. British police, aided by Indian troops, had surrounded the town before dawn, set up huge wire cages, routed every head of a household out of bed, herded them into the cages and for hours searched for arms, ammunition and illegal literature. Possession of any of these could mean long prison sentences, even death by hanging. Floors were ripped up, walls smashed through, beds torn apart. Women wept and threw themselves at the soldiers while their men, jammed into the cages like so many cattle on display, raged helplessly. The police were grim. Shortly before, Police Superintendent J. J. Wilkins of Jerusalem had been shot to death, constable after constable had been killed, police stations bombed. . . .

"Let's go," Julian was saying. At that moment the Reuters' news ticker against one wall burst into a jangle of bells—signal of an important news flash. Half a dozen of us hurried over to it. Perhaps it was a last-minute election development from the States. But the flash was from Cairo. Lord Moyne had been critically wounded by two gunmen. Police had seized them. Their identity was unknown. But, "They are NOT repeat NOT Egyptians," the ticker spelled out.

It shocked us, crowded about the machine, reading each word as it appeared. Could it have been Jews?

A few minutes later we knew. The *Post* correspondent in Cairo had managed to get through on a military phone. A news blackout had been clamped down but he could tell us—the words spluttered over the wire—doctors were working on Moyne but held out no hope for him. The assassins were from Palestine—no doubt about it: the two spoke Hebrew, they gave obviously false names and they were obviously Sternists. Prime Minister Ahmed Maher had summoned the cabinet in emergency session. . . .

Now, on trial for murder, the two stood a few feet from me.

The courtroom had relaxed. The tribunal of judges had yet to make an appearance, and until they entered, there was a steady buzz of conversation. People walked about freely, talking with their friends. It was brought home to me, as so often in the past, that time has little or no reality in the Middle East, that all urgency is pushed aside. With several other correspondents I approached the dock to talk to the two boys. Presently we were all crowded about them. I offered Bet Zouri several American cigarettes, always a treat. He accepted them with a quick, smiling, "Thank you," in English, marked by a slight guttural accent, and a wry, "These are better than what we are supplied with."

He was alert, alive: I felt that he missed nothing of what went on about him, that he instantly understood and put into perspective whatever came to his attention. Hakim, in contrast to Bet Zouri's solid, almost stocky figure, was slim; his face was almost delicate: his features were aquiline, his nose finely formed, the flanges deep, his eyebrows very black, the thin mustache black too. His face mirrored his emotions far more readily than Bet Zouri's. Now both boys were parrying our questions, in the best of humor. "What is the news from Palestine?" Bet Zouri was asking, and a chorus of voices replied. An astonishing scene: the two boys, laughing and joking—even Hakim, who had seemed rather dour, was smiling now—the giant guards for the moment looking on benignly, but still keeping a firm grip on their prisoners' elbows. So might two actors jest in the wings with admirers before the curtain rose. A British woman correspondent in a gay flowered dress bustled forward and pushed her notebook and pencil through the iron gratings to Bet Zouri. She smiled brightly at him. "Do autograph it for me," she said. "And give me a message for my readers back home."

Bet Zouri, his blue eyes almost dancing, wrote with a flourish. When he returned her notebook she held it up for us to see. He had written in English, "What we did was right!" and signed it firmly, "Eliahu Bet Zouri."

A French correspondent asked, "What is your favorite reading matter?"

Bet Zouri replied in French, with a grin, "I shall disappoint you and remain nonpolitical. I read poetry—it is food for the soul."

It would have been impossible for any of us to believe that less than an hour before, the two had engaged in an intense argument with Palestine's best-known lawyer and had rejected his plan to save them from the gallows because they refused to accept his line of defense.

Suddenly there was a stir in the courtroom.

We hurried back to our seats, only to rise as the tribunal of five judges filed in to take their places. The courtroom was about thirty by seventy feet, long, rectangular, white-walled, brightly lit as the sun streamed in through three high, enormous, barred windows near the vaulted roof. With the variegated uniforms and robes of the officials—green, khaki, white—with the bright yellow, crimson, green and gold ribbons of office, the maroon fezzes, the white turbans, the cowls and headdresses of visiting sheiks, it was a brilliant scene. The three civilian judges were in forest-green robes, each with a bright scarlet sash diagonally down from shoulder to waist; the two military judges on either side were in khaki dress uniform, their chests gleaming with rows of medals. The President of the Court, Mahmoud Mansour Bey, a lean, sad-faced man of immense dignity, sat on a tall, thronelike chair with his associates ranged on either side a head below him. To the right sat an imposing bloc of about fifteen officials—the Public Prosecutor, Mohamed Towayar Pasha, and his staff, all with the maroon tasseled fez on their heads. To the left sat another phalanx—the three celebrated defense attorneys appointed by the state, and their staffs. With the array of faces, the placement of the principals, the arrangement of judges, attorneys, attendants and guards, and the extraordinary patterns of vivid color, it was a scene that wanted only a Titian to paint it.

The President sounded his gavel. The trial began. I glanced at my watch: it was three minutes after ten o'clock.

"Your Honor—" In his black gown of office a heavy-set, broad-shouldered man slowly rose at the counsel table. His face was leonine, his large eyes so gray as to seem almost colorless. He began to speak quietly. This was Abdula Fattah el Said, former President of the Egyptian Court of Appeals, chief of the defense counsel. The court, he was saying, was a military court and, as such, was not qualified to rule on murder. "The admission of murder by the accused can only come within the purview of a civil court, where sentence can be reviewed by the court of appeals, and if necessary, after that by the court of final resort." By "court of final resort," he meant the King.

The Public Prosecutor, a thin, intense man with furrowed cheeks, opposed the motion in a long and involved argument.

"Overruled," said the President, after a short conference with the judges on either side of him. "The attempt on the life of the constable is sufficient to confirm the competence of this court. We shall proceed with the hearing."

Egyptian court practice follows the French. The Prosecutor restrains himself while the President conducts most of the interrogation, seeking by every stratagem to elicit the truth.

"I shall now read the charges," President Mansour Bey announced, in Arabic, and adjusted his glasses.

Bet Zouri's voice cut through the room.

"Your Honor, we prefer to speak Hebrew."

The audience buzzed. The President looked at him over his spectacles.

"Arabic is the official language of this court and of this country," he said sharply. "You are in Egypt now."

"Hebrew is also an official language," Bet Zouri replied firmly. "It is the language of my country."

The President stared at him for a moment, then turned to Hakim.

"Accused Hakim, will you reply to examination in Arabic?"

Hakim's voice was very deep, with the same slight guttural accent. "I know Arabic and English also, but I can only express my-self fully in Hebrew. Like my friend I wish to speak in Hebrew."

The President rapped out an order and a thin little man hurried forward and was sworn in. This was the court translator, Leon Mehrez, professor of Hebrew at the University of Cairo. Bet Zouri was told to test him. He said in Hebrew, "I shall talk very simply, Mr. Mehrez. What am I saying now?"

Mehrez blinked. Then he asked, almost tentatively, "Do you speak Sephardic or Ashkenazi Hebrew?"

A slow grin appeared on Bet Zouri's face. It was impossible for anyone who knows the language well to mistake one for the other. "You realize, Mr. Mehrez," Bet Zouri said quite conversationally, "it is better if you are honest with me. I propose to speak for at least an hour and a half—"

There was a rustle as Egyptian turned to Egyptian. The court-room was to be treated to the usual terrorist harangue—so the pa-pers had predicted—traditional in Palestine when terrorists were tried, as it had been in Ireland when the IRA refused to recognize the authority of the courts, lashed out at their accusers and defied everyone in sight.

The interpreter, a little pathetically: "Perhaps you speak Yid-dish?"

At this Bet Zouri turned to the court and lifted his hands in a gesture of helplessness.

"We shall obtain another interpreter," said the President. "Court is adjourned for forty-five minutes." He led his glittering retinue from the room. Only then did the guards allow the audi-ence to stream out. While attendants went in search of someone who spoke modern Hebrew, all was confusion: police stood armed and watchful; the crowds in the corridors were kept behind their ropes; little white-robed messenger boys hustled back and forth with tiny cups of strong Turkish coffee, carried, each with a small glass of water, on hammered copper trays; voices in French, Ara-bic, English merged into a confused murmur of sound.

An hour later, a satisfactory interpreter having been found in one Leon Atibi, a Hebrew schoolteacher, the President read the charges:

"The accused are indicted on four counts. One: Murder with premeditation of Lord Moyne, by Eliahu Hakim. Two: Murder with premeditation of Lance Corporal Fuller by Eliahu Bet Zouri. Three: Attempted murder of Constable Mohammed Amin Abdullah by Eliahu Bet Zouri. Four: Possession of firearms and explosives without permit by both Eliahu Hakim and Eliahu Bet Zouri."

The tassel of his tarboosh swung gently as he asked, "Accused Hakim, did you commit this crime with premeditation?"

Hakim gave him a somber yes.

"Did you take part with Accused Bet Zouri in the murder of Fuller with premeditation?"

"No, but I was present when my comrade shot Fuller. We regret this very much."

Had he attempted to shoot the constable? No, because the latter was an Egyptian, "and we have no quarrel with the Egyptians."

Were he and Bet Zouri in possession of weapons without license? Yes.

The President went through much the same questioning with Bet Zouri, but when he turned again to Hakim and asked him to relate the events on the day of the murder, Hakim shook his head. "Your Honor, I wish to make a statement that will change the situation. We ask that this trial be held before an international court."

"That is impossible," said the President. He rattled the papers on his desk. The sun slanted in through the high barred windows, drilling shafts of whirling dust motes through the great room with its panoply of color, each bar helping make a pattern of parallel white and black. "On Egyptian soil, only the verdict of an Egyptian court is valid."

Bet Zouri spoke up. "Your Honor, we must state why we make this request. We have great confidence in Egyptian justice, but we maintain that our case is a special case, and outside the boundaries of any country. We cannot be compared to ordinary criminals who act against society. Our aim is to destroy a political regime after which society will exist under a better and superior regime. We cannot be compared to criminals acting for their own personal interests. Rightfully, therefore, we state that our case should be heard before a court responsible to no one country but to the world —a court based only on pure justice and pure morality."

President (with surprising calm): "Certainly the accused is aware that such a court as he describes does not exist."

Bet Zouri (smiling sadly): "We know it. But it should exist for the welfare of every person in the world and that is why we make our public request."

The audience around me rustled again: he had made his statement in measured words and the listeners had been absolutely silent. Now they turned and whispered to each other—some three hundred persons in all, distinguished Cairenes, observers from foreign embassies, important visitors who had been able to obtain tickets, Egyptian law students who hung on every word and waited eagerly for the legal drama that would be played out by prosecution and defense.

The President said dryly, "Since we both agree that such a court as the accused requests is not available, let us now proceed with the case in hand. Accused Hakim?"

Hakim began to tell his story, in his deep voice.

"I recognize myself as responsible for the death of Lord Moyne. But I repeat that we regret the death of the driver, Lance Corporal Fuller.

"On the day of our attack, my comrade and I rode our bicycles to the lord's house on Rue Gabalya. It was about 1:30. We waited for his automobile to arrive. We hid our bicycles in the shrubbery of the fence. When the car stopped we ran up to it. But scarcely had it stopped when we saw the officer descend from one side while the chauffeur came out the other. I approached the car to open the door next to Lord Moyne, who was seated beside a lady, in the back. I shot him, paying careful attention so my bullets would not strike her. I shot three times.

"At this moment I heard other shots from behind the car. These came from my comrade's revolver. Then we got back on our bikes to ride to the other side of the bridge where we hoped to lose ourselves in the traffic. We saw then that we were being followed by the constable on his motorcycle. My comrade was behind me. I saw the constable approach him and try to stop him. I would have been able to kill the constable easily, but I contented myself with going toward him and shooting several times into the air. I saw my comrade fall off his bicycle. The constable was almost upon him. Again I could have eliminated the constable with a single bullet, but I did not. Then I was caught."

The audience listened raptly. Bet Zouri's face, as he sat on the chair at Hakim's side, was expressionless.

"In what manner did you receive your instructions?" the President asked.

At this the briefest suggestion of a smile flickered on Hakim's face; then it resumed the thoughtful, almost strained expression.

"Our methods are secret, sir," he replied with great seriousness. "I cannot disclose them to anyone who is not a member of our organization."

"Are there any members of your organization now in Egypt? Did you have any accomplices?"

Still unsmiling, he said, "With all respect, sir, I am not permitted to tell you that, either."

The President, almost as though he had been rebuked, said, "The accused need not reply. It is not the court's function to force him to speak." He turned to Bet Zouri. Would he describe the events of that afternoon?

Speaking calmly, Bet Zouri confirmed all that Hakim had said. "My comrade speaks truth when he says we did not mean to kill Fuller. I ordered him to stand still, then to lie down, so he would not be harmed. Instead, he ran at me and tried to grab my gun. I was forced to shoot him. I did not try to kill the constable; I purposely aimed low, at the tires of his motorcycle."

Now the witnesses were called. First came Miss Osmonde, Lord Moyne's secretary. She spoke crisply and precisely, answering questions as though she had been asked to read back a letter just dictated to her. "The car came to a halt in front of the house. Suddenly I saw a dark man appear at the door of the car—the door on Lord Moyne's side."

"Is that man in this courtroom now?"

She pointed at Hakim. "That one. He leaped on the running board. I heard him say in English, 'Don't move!' Then he fired three times at Lord Moyne—and I heard three more shots coming from behind me, from in back of the car. Then Corporal Fuller's voice—'I'm badly wounded, please help!' I got out of the car and ran behind it to see him on the ground. He was dying. I bent over him and as it seemed there was nothing I could do for him, I ran into the house to telephone for help."

"Did you notice any other person on the scene?"

She pointed to Bet Zouri. "He was talking with the dark one when we drove through the gate. I remembered seeing them talking together near the fence but I thought nothing of it at the time."

There was a stir through the crowd as the next witness—a slim, handsome British officer—took the stand. Captain Arthur Hughes-Onslow told a similar story. It always took him a moment or two to open the door of the villa, he explained—it was an ancient, wooden door, brought from Syria, heavy with ornate wrought-iron designs, and required no little strength to swing open. Then he had turned and seen the attack. Cursing himself because he was unarmed, he had raced into a neighboring house. He couldn't make the servant there understand, so he dashed out and set off in pursuit of the two. He was badly outdistanced when a passing car picked him up and they continued the chase. By then Constable Abdullah had collared the gunmen.

In quick order three other witnesses testified: the owner of the bicycle shop, the cook at Moyne's house, the chauffeur who had been parked at the scene. Then the arresting constable, magnificent in a new brilliant green uniform (King Farouk had promoted him to sublieutenant on the day of the arrest) took the stand.

"Were you personally attacked?" the President asked.

"Yes, your Honor."

"By whom?"

Lieutenant Abdullah pointed at Bet Zouri.

250

"How do you know he wanted to kill you?"

"I have proof. A car was behind me passing me in the opposite direction and it received the bullet meant for me exactly at my height."

"He could have hit you then?"

The officer nodded vigorously. "It was only by Allah's grace that I am not dead."

He was followed by Youssef Mahamed el Khadem, owner of the car that was behind the constable. Yes, he had been driving to Zamalek, he heard a shot, he looked about, a bullet had ripped a hole in the back of his car just above the rear window.

Now came Mrs. Helen Blanca. She told of the package Bet Zouri had left with her.

The President turned to Bet Zouri. The two boys were seated in the dock on two wooden chairs, a guard seated between them, a guard on the other side of each and three guards standing, shoulder to shoulder, behind them.

"Accused Bet Zouri, as we know, that parcel contained explosives. For what purpose did you keep explosives at the Blanca house?"

Bet Zouri said evenly, "I regret, your Honor. I cannot answer that question." He was seated, his arms folded.

President Mansour Bey reached for his gavel. "This sitting is adjourned until three o'clock," he said quietly.

It was 1:15 and the first hearing was over. The spectators flowed out; those of us who had to report the story hastened to our telephones and typewriters in the Immobelia Building, international press headquarters in Cairo. The boys, manacled hand and foot, were taken in their armed caravan back to their cells.

Asher Levitsky, the attorney who attempted vainly to reason with the two Eliahus just before the trial opened, resigned from the case immediately after the first session. A heavy-set man with close graying hair and sharp blue eyes, Levitsky was Palestine's outstanding criminal lawyer. Hakim's father had retained him to fly

251

to Cairo and guide the boys' defense. Simon Hakim had announced that though his son had committed a crime bringing shame and tragedy to all Palestine, he would have no peace the remainder of his life if, as his father, he did not do all in his power for his son.

I joined Levitsky for lunch and he told me what had happened in his meeting with the boys. He had warned them that if they made "political declarations," they would only prejudice their case. "There is only one way you can be saved," he told them. "You must confess that temporary insanity brought on by Jewish suffering in Europe brought you to your crime. Throw yourselves on the mercy of the court." They were young, they were misguided, they had been driven mad by the events of the time—the horror of Hitler, the White Paper closing the gates of Palestine. He would invoke an ancient Turkish law which excused murder when committed under great emotional or mental duress. Who would be more sympathetic than the Egyptians, who had their own scores to settle with the British?

Both boys refused. Temporary insanity? Never. Seventeen-year-old Hakim was indignant. "What do you want to show?" he demanded. "That I am a child? No." Bet Zouri said, "Mr. Advocate, we carried out our act for a purpose. If we plead insanity, we proclaim that our act was an emotional accident. It was nothing of the kind. We committed a political act for moral reasons. If we risked our lives, it was because it was an important deed."

Levitsky tried another tack. Despite them, he would still save them from the gallows. Hakim, who fired the bullets that killed Moyne, was a minor, therefore not responsible. Bet Zouri himself had not touched Moyne; he was only an accomplice in the assassination. The death of the driver could undoubtedly be reduced from murder to manslaughter. With their skilled attorneys, it was quite possible the verdict would be life imprisonment, and in a few years, when passions cooled, they could hope for commutation of sentence, even a pardon—

"No, we cannot agree to that, either," said Bet Zouri. He spoke with infuriating calm. "I will tell the court that if Hakim had missed, I would have shot Lord Moyne."

"Then you will both hang," Levitsky said bluntly. "The Egyptians are sympathetic; in their hearts they applaud you, but they cannot allow the premeditated murder of a high Englishman on Egyptian soil to pass without punishment."

"Even so," said Bet Zouri. He added with slow emphasis that Levitsky was never to forget. "Some people live short lives in which nothing significant occurs. That is a tragedy. But to live a short life that includes a deed for one's homeland—that is a triumph." For "homeland" Eliahu used the Hebrew word *moledet,* difficult to translate in all its emotional context, but which has a far more poignant meaning, corresponding to the French *la Patrie,* the German *Vaterland*—the land, the soil, the history, the mother earth from which one springs and to which one gives all loyalty. "Isn't it better, Mr. Advocate, to lead a brief but significant life than a long but meaningless one? Therefore, I say that I am not sorry. I am very happy to sacrifice my life if it must be that way. I am convinced that our nation will benefit by our deed."

Levitsky played his last card. He still had a way out that would not compromise their honor. If they would state that the FFI Central Committee ordered them to kill Moyne, or be killed themselves . . .

The two boys, he told me, almost laughed outright. "You mistake our organization if you think that is the way we operate," Bet Zouri said.

After our lunch Levitsky took the train back to Jerusalem. He carried with him two notes from the boys to their families.

Dear Parents [Hakim had written], I feel the great despair I have caused you but I cannot help you. Like a soldier, I have been sent to the front and fallen prisoner. There is a great war now and many people are falling, but without a cause. Console yourself with the fact that I am not the only one who is falling, and also that as a result of our act a Hebrew flag will fly over Jerusalem. My father, to you I say, you have five children: let yourself now think that you have four. I send you, my dear mother and father, my dear brothers and sister, all my love—

Bet Zouri's note read:

Dear Father, I regret that I did not part with you when I left. I thought I would have returned to you long before this. Don't feel badly, my father—there is a chance that I will not receive the severe penalty and that we shall be able to see each other once again. Our guards treat us in a way that leaves nothing to be desired. They are most honorable and respectful to us. I embrace you and all the family—

In Cairo, the presiding judge received anonymous letters threatening him with death if his tribunal did not hand down a just verdict.

The trial took over all the newspapers.

CHAPTER

23

I<small>T WAS</small> B<small>ET</small> Z<small>OURI</small>'s day in court —the day of his speech.

The news had spread. It was impossible to obtain tickets for the trial.

Bet Zouri stood in the dock, his arms folded across his chest, facing the President. He was dressed as before—a gray sweater over his open-necked shirt—and his casual, almost collegiate appearance was in sharp contrast to the deadly seriousness of the moment. He began to speak quietly—his face pale but composed—and to our astonishment he spoke in English. The interpreters are "unable to translate my Hebrew as faithfully as I would wish," he explained, "and my Arabic, I regret, is not good enough. So I shall address you in English and I hope everyone will bear with my mistakes."

I was seated next to Fred Lee, the American Broadcasting Company correspondent. We looked at each other. Bet Zouri was making sure that we—the American and British correspondents—would understand, would miss no word. Through us he would speak to the world.

Bet Zouri told how he and Hakim met, how they followed Lord

Moyne, the photograph they carried, their debate as to where to carry out the deed. They agreed that Hakim would fire at Moyne because his revolver had a simpler mechanism than Bet Zouri's and rarely jammed. "It is the kind of a pistol known as a six-shooter and is very popular with American cowboys," Bet Zouri explained gravely. There was stifled laughter and the President sounded his gavel sternly. "But if my comrade failed in the attempt, we agreed that I would shoot the lord." Again he said, "We are not interested in killing anyone." Their idea was to force everyone but Moyne out of the car and make them lie face down on the ground. By isolating Moyne there would be no chance of hurting anyone else in the action. "However, we forgot to think that anyone would attempt to stop us. That is our fault. Nobody in the world is sorrier for the death of the driver than ourselves."

He was completely at ease now. There was no sound in the courtroom. He spoke slowly, carefully, as if to miss no point nor exaggerate any. His arms were no longer folded across his chest; now he leaned forward, one foot on his chair, his right elbow resting on his right knee, his left hand on his left hip, like a seminar instructor explaining a subject to a small group of students. He made few gestures. Hakim sat behind him, listening intently, now and then glancing over the audience as if trying to read their faces.

Bet Zouri told how the limousine rolled up to the gate, how he and Hakim ran toward the car—

"But when we were near it we saw that the captain had already gotten out and also the driver. My comrade was busy; as the driver came toward the car, I pointed my gun at him. He was a meter away. I told him, 'Stop. Lie down!' He did not reply but came nearer me. I ordered him again, 'Lie down!' Instead, he raised his hand to catch my revolver and I pulled the trigger. I remember exactly that when my brain gave the order to my finger to pull the trigger, it was not to kill him but to prevent him from snatching my revolver."

Speaking reflectively, almost as though thinking aloud, Bet Zouri went on:

"I have asked myself many times since, if I did not mean to kill

Fuller, why did I fire three times at him? I have not been able to find a satisfactory answer. I cannot say that I lost my mind. I was quite cold-blooded, and remember very well that when I pulled the trigger, I counted one, two, three." He paused for a moment. "It seems that the answer is that it was habit. When members of our organization train in Palestine, we are accustomed to fire three times to see how well we concentrate our bullets on the target. I repeat that I did not mean to kill Fuller, who was engaged in a war that had nothing to do with our war, and I regret it more than I can say."

He described how he and Hakim raced to their bicycles, how they were trapped on the bridge, how he was seized after an exchange of shots. Now he grew indignant. "I disagree with the court on the charge that I tried to kill the constable. The reason I fired at his tires was because I did not want to hurt him." And now he became doubly indignant. "It is not true that I tried to kill him but failed because I am not a good shot. When he caught up with us, it would have been easy to kill him at a distance of six meters. If you do not believe what I am telling you, it can very easily be proved." He leaned forward, resting his elbow in the space between two palings, gazing directly at the President. "If the court will place a revolver into my hand . . ." He raised his voice above the sudden hum of astonished amusement—"if the court will give me a gun, I promise to put six bullets . . ." He paused, and his eyes met those of the President directly in front of him. He stretched forth his arm as though his hand held a revolver, and pointed it at the President ". . . I will promise to put six bullets into the face—" Pause again. "—of that clock . . . above your head."

It was done dramatically and effectively. The audience chuckled. President Mansour Bey grinned almost sheepishly. The Public Prosecutor lost his gaunt, sad look for a moment and smiled; catching the President's attention, he tapped his own chest as if to say, They would be happy to place the bullets here, too. The President composed his face, turned to Bet Zouri and said gravely, "That will not be necessary." He rapped his gavel. "Will you continue, please."

Bet Zouri brought forth from his pocket a few sheets of penciled notes. He placed his foot on the chair and began, almost formally: "I shall now explain to you the reasons that caused me to act as I did."

The room was very still.

"For this purpose I must go back a few years to a scene I saw when I was a boy in Tel Aviv. I remember standing on the balcony of my father's apartment and watching many people gather in the street. It was an interesting sight for a boy of twelve or thirteen —this large crowd of grownups shouting, carrying flags and so on. Grownups standing near me said, 'This is a demonstration.' As I watched, I saw police, among them British police, come in from the surrounding streets with sticks and stop the demonstration. It was a little strange. I knew then that an English policeman is a man coming from England to be a policeman in my country. And when I saw one of the policemen bring his stick down on the head of a demonstrator, I asked myself, Why should a man leave his home and family in a far-off country and come three thousand miles to my country to be a policeman? Why can this Englishman hit my people and they cannot strike back?"

Again there was a rustling as Egyptian turned to Egyptian with knowing smiles. Not only Prime Minister Ahmed Maher himself had been involved in the Black Hand terrorist organization but even some of the members of the court had been nationalist terrorists in their student days. Hassan Djeddaoui, who had been the first of the defense counsel to visit Bet Zouri in his cell, had written an autobiographical sketch for the correspondents in which he listed among his achievements a year's prison term for "anti-British activities."

"I did not understand then," went on Bet Zouri, speaking slowly and precisely, "that the English are in my country because of the mandate of the League of Nations. They were given the rule over Palestine because they promised to help build a Jewish National Home. But instead of carrying out this duty entrusted to her, England seeks only to broaden her rule in Palestine. She imposes her—"

The President's voice interrupted him acidly. "The accused is making a political speech. If he persists, I must ask all correspondents to cease taking notes. The political aspects of this case are not within the competence of this court."

Commotion in the courtroom. Over the noise, Bet Zouri's voice:

"I am sorry, but I disagree with you. It is not a political speech."

He was standing, arms folded, facing the President.

The latter said, "I am sorry, too, but that is my ruling."

Bet Zouri: "I am making my defense, your Honor, and I must go ahead with it."

The President sounded his gavel. "No report of the proceedings beyond this point is to be published." He ordered the bailiffs to confiscate all writing materials of the correspondents. They would be returned at the close of the day's session. *This is incredible,* I thought; yet we witnessed the astonishing spectacle, we participated in it. I watched as the elaborately uniformed guards, each with a revolver conspicuously at his belt, moved among the correspondents representing the press of the world—C. L. Sulzberger of *The New York Times,* Christopher Lumby of the London *Times,* Relman Morin of the Associated Press, Walter Collins and Sam Souki of the United Press, Grant Parr of NBC, George Moorad of CBS, the correspondents of Agence France Presse, of Reuter's, of Palestine's *Davar* and *Haaretz, Palestine Post,* of all the press and radio networks of the free world. We yielded our notebooks, our sheafs of paper, our pencils and fountain pens, and sat impotent. Bet Zouri calmly resumed his speech, while the guards stalked watchfully up and down the aisles, to see that we did not surreptitiously put down a word he uttered. Bet Zouri and Hakim faced the gallows for killing a man; if they were unable to explain what motivated them, the deed lost its significance—and now we were barred from giving this testament to the world.

"I have studied the British Administration in Palestine," Bet Zouri was saying, and though he faced the President, it seemed that he was directing his words to us: we were the audience, no one else. "I learned that it is full of injustice, graft and anarchy. Every inhabitant is forced to obey the law but there is no law which the Administration or the police is forced to obey. Injustice, partiality and cruelty prevail everywhere." He gave examples: the administration had compelled all Palestinian citizens to sell to it gold coins at a fixed price; later, the same administration sold the same gold coins back to the citizens at a price four times as high. At the same time it announced that it was fighting war profiteers. "But when a poor Tel Aviv storekeeper sells merchandise a penny above the set price, he is arrested, fined and jailed for months. Does this law apply to the Administration? No."

Bet Zouri paused. He leaned forward: "I tell you, in Palestine the Englishman is master. He is a god. His word is the law. All the inhabitants, though they are the natural sons of the land, are natives who must obey the master. This is the consciousness the English seek to plant into the hearts of the peoples of all countries where they rule."

Looking off into the distance, speaking almost regretfully, now and then fingering his mustache as he paused to find the right word, he went on:

"I have never had the chance to visit England—that land whose sons fight all over the world for freedom, that land that is the mother of the Magna Carta, of habeas corpus—so I don't know what the Englishman is like in his own country. But I think that he must be like Doctor Jekyll and Mr. Hyde. In his own country he is a gentleman of the highest order, but when he goes abroad into the colonies, he becomes something else. He drinks the wine of power and becomes so drunk that he thinks he is the god of the native—"

"This is irrelevant!" the President snapped. "I warn you—"

Bet Zouri stiffened. "But strangers are doing things in my country as they wish! We can do nothing. They will not listen. What are we to do, to whom will we turn?"

In the silence that followed, he continued in an almost conversational tone. "The situation in Palestine reminds me of a book written by a great writer, Jack London. In *The Sea Wolf* he tells of a shipwrecked man who is rescued by another ship. He thinks his suffering is ended, but it is only beginning. For the ship that rescues him is a little state with its own laws, and the laws are the muscles of the captain. Everyone on the ship has to obey the orders of this captain. He is autocratic, a cruel man, without mercy. No one can dispute his word; the muscles of the captain are the law, and in Palestine, the muscles of the police are the law.

"I tell you that the conduct of the English government in Palestine is worse than that of the cruel captain on the ship. Millions sank in a sea of blood and tears, yet the English captain did not allow them on the ship that could have saved them. He stood on the deck and saw without pity how the people were sinking. If some of the drowning managed to hold on to the sides of the ship, he, the captain, pushed them back into the sea to sink and drown. And we who saw all this with our own eyes had nothing left but to surrender—or fight. We decided to fight—to destroy the foreign ruler, to drive out the cruel dictator—"

President (sharply): "Stop this! You are making propaganda! Get down to facts. What has this to do with the killing of Lord Moyne?"

Bet Zouri, suddenly losing his calm as he stood in the prisoners' dock behind the spike-tipped iron staves fencing him off from us, took one step toward his judges, leveled that accusing finger and in a voice so impassioned, and carrying the accents of such righteousness that it almost brought us out of our seats, cried, "Our deed stemmed from our motives, and our motives stemmed from our ideals, and if we prove our ideals are right and just, then our deed was right and just!"

Behind me I heard Egyptians say, one to the other, "A strong man! A strong man!" And then a woman's voice, "What a pity that a boy like that was led to do such a terrible thing!"

The President, taken aback, stared at him for a moment, then looked down at his blotter and said, in Arabic, his voice almost gentle, "Continue."

Bet Zouri stepped back. He was composed again. Subtly, in ways difficult to describe, he had the courtroom with him now: President, state prosecutor, clerks and interpreters, the audience, the correspondents. One cannot condone murder. He had committed murder. Yet the courtroom was his.

He continued to speak, turning to us, directing his words to us, the correspondents, as if to say, "If my words will be heard beyond the gallows, it is because one of you will carry them with you from here."

Patiently now, like a schoolmaster: "Some may say we have no right to attack the English because it is thanks to them that we live in Palestine. There is no truth to this argument. We, the Hebrews, the natural sons of the land of Israel, fought for Palestine before the Balfour Declaration. We are the natural and legal owners of the country. We do not recognize England's right to give us Palestine or to take it away from us."

He paused. "Let me make clear to the court: My ideas are not Zionist ideas. We don't fight to uphold the Balfour Declaration. We don't fight for the sake of the National Home. We fight for our freedom. In our country a foreign power rules. In our country England is a stranger who does what she wants.

"The crimes she commits are without number. I can give you names, dates, addresses: nothing can refute my accusations. To the English everything is 'the law.' When an English policeman clubs a Hebrew young man in the street in Jerusalem in nineteen thirty-nine and leaves him dead, 'that is the law.' When another English policeman shoots a deaf old man and leaves him dead on the ground —'that is the law.' When Captain Morton breaks into a house in Tel Aviv and murders Abraham Stern, shooting him in the back, 'that is the law.'

"In Palestine the Jews are trying so desperately to do wonderful things, but they are blocked and stopped. Young Palestine is full of initiative; its citizens seek its progress. But the English Administration is not ready to hear any suggestions. They will not listen. Whatever they want in our country, 'that is the law.' I wish I could tell you—my English is not good enough to express how badly the Administration rules. It rules with fear and torture. The English torture chambers are always full in Palestine. The CID tortures those who fall into their hands, to get information. They do it sci-

262

entifically; they know anatomy and the most sensitive parts of the body. They go far beyond what is called in the United States the third degree. I will call witnesses who will tell you the truth of what I say. And when the English arrest and torture, 'that is the law.' "

The President asked, "Was there no other way to protest but by the gun?"

Bet Zouri (hotly): "To whom could we protest? In a country which has a parliament, a cabinet, which has freedom of press and speech, you can protest against injustice, corruption and cruelty. But these freedoms do not exist in Palestine. If we have turned to the gun, it is because we were forced to turn to the gun! When we found every other effort would not help, we understood then that the only way to fight a rule based on violence is to use violence. That is why we decided to fight the English by using their own means, to attack the representative of their government, which is responsible for all our misfortunes."

President: "I warn the accused not to continue on this line—"

There was an exchange between them and then Bet Zouri's voice sounded above the other's, loud and emphatic, in words that rang through the court:

"Sir, I am not telling you why we fight, I am telling you why we fight so severely. If you think that what we want is to change a bad government to a good government, you mistake us. What we want is to tear it out by the roots and throw it away!"

It was electrifying. One almost expected some of the audience to break out in cheers.

Over the commotion, the President had to pound his gavel repeatedly. When he spoke, his voice was harsh:

"Accused Bet Zouri, if you have anything else to say pertaining to this trial, say it. Otherwise, stop. We have listened to you now for nearly two hours."

Bet Zouri looked at him. Then, with a gesture almost of disdain, he said dryly, "If the court is tired of hearing my voice, I will retire."

He sat down and folded his arms.

The President had to pound for order again.

"Accused Hakim, do you wish to speak?"

Hakim rose. He spoke in his deep voice, strained, hesitant, and the words, in English, came uncertainly. But there was a brooding power in the simplicity of his speech. "The Bible says, 'Thou shalt not kill.' Why for then did we kill?" There was no other way for them to make the foreign government respect their rights. "If we are asked to answer to the killing of Lord Moyne, we in our turn accuse him and his government of the murder of thousands of our brothers and sisters, of robbing our homeland and our property." He expanded on Bet Zouri's theme. What law was there before which Moyne and his government could be held responsible? To whom could Hakim and his people turn for justice? "That law— the law of justice—is yet to be written in the law books but it is written in our hearts." He said, his head up now, his shoulders back, his hands still clasped behind him, "In the name of that higher justice we ask the court to declare us innocent and let us go free."

He seemed about to add something to this but Bet Zouri leaned toward him and tugged at his jacket. Hakim sat down, silent.

There was the sound of the gavel. Court was adjourned. Defense counsel would take over on the following day.

I walked out of the courtroom with Relman Morin of the Associated Press. Morin, a dispassionate correspondent, was saying, "When he said, 'If the court is tired of hearing my voice, I will retire,' I wanted to go up and shake his hand. Quite a fellow—" We began to talk about the banning of the speech. Others joined us. We all agreed that the President had gone far beyond his authority in ordering us not to take notes. That was a question of censorship and outside his province. I was surprised at my own indignation. "We've got to get that speech down—then see what happens," I said.

In a few minutes we were all in the press room, sending out tortuously phrased dispatches which mentioned Bet Zouri's speech

264

without quoting it or summarizing its contents. The readers of Sulzberger's story in *The New York Times* read the following report:

> One is permitted to state that Bet Zouri delivered himself of what is permitted to be described only as a "political tirade." This "political tirade" lasted two hours and was coolly and calmly spoken by Bet Zouri in a fluent if frequently slightly incorrect English, so that all the foreign correspondents seeking to report the case could fully understand. . . . Bet Zouri's tale was long and dramatic, but the dramatis personae, in the sense of individuals or countries, cannot be mentioned. . . . It is permitted to state that Bet Zouri contends that "the ideas I am going to mention are very different from Zionist ideas."

After sending our own cryptic dispatches, we gathered in an anteroom. We were all incensed. Had any of us managed to take notes? Fred Lee of ABC had scribbled a few key words on his shirt cuff, in the best undercover-agent tradition; I had gotten some words down on a two-inch pad; Collins and Souki had also surreptitiously taken a few notes. I sat down at a typewriter, the others stood about me in a circle and we began to pool our memories to reconstruct the speech of Eliahu Bet Zouri.

Our point was this: If the court wished to keep Bet Zouri's charges confidential, the courtroom should have been cleared save for the opposing attorneys. But at least 300 persons had been in the room. Garbled accounts of his words were already circulating through Cairo. Since all we wrote would go through a panel of British, Egyptian and American censors, political as well as military, we should be allowed to report the speech as a legitimate part of our stories, and then allow the censors to do what they must. Censorship itself was bad enough, but muzzling the news at the very source was an outrage.

I set to work. Everyone wanted a copy of the speech. With an original sheet and six carbons in my typewriter, I began taking dictation alternately from one or the other about me. Generally we agreed on what had been said. Sometimes we disagreed as to Bet Zouri's exact words, but sentence by sentence, paragraph by paragraph, we resurrected out of the limbo of that courtroom in Cairo the words Bet Zouri had used to explain the deed.

I was busy typing when the door opened and Colonel John V. McCormack, British Press Relations Officer, entered. He looked at us sharply, but went on to his office in an adjoining room. We held a quick council. Some were for telling him; others were against it. Sulzberger said, "I'm going to tell him. Perhaps we can get him to help us get it out." At that moment Colonel McCormack emerged from his room and Sulzberger approached him. We were putting together Bet Zouri's banned speech, he told him; we proposed to incorporate it in our next dispatches. Since military security was not involved, would Colonel McCormack intercede in our behalf with Prime Minister Ahmed Maher?

He refused. If the court had ruled against taking notes, Colonel McCormack did not see that our request came within his province.

Morin spoke up. "We'll ask the Prime Minister ourselves."

I folded the top copy of Bet Zouri's speech and put it in my pocket.

That night a committee of three—Morin of the AP, Souki of the UP, and Sulzberger of *The New York Times* called upon Prime Minister Ahmed Maher. The Prime Minister sent out word that he was ill and could not receive them. The committee made an appointment to see him the following day. Again he was unavailable.

The denouement of this incident came a week later, when Major Patrick Welch, Public Relations Officer of the U.S. Army, Middle East, Colonel McCormack's opposite number, called me in.

"I understand that you and several others have been doing something you should not do," he said. "In fact, I think I should inform you that you are under contempt of court for having taken notes on the speech of Bet Zouri."

I could only stare at him.

"You're not the only one," he said, with a smile. "I have just received a letter from Colonel McCormack pointing out what you and the others did. But you're really the one they're after."

"Why me?" I managed to ask.

"Let me read you a line from McCormack's letter," said Welch. "In addition, Mr. Gerold Frank is preparing to fly to New York

266

this weekend and will most likely carry a copy of the speech on his person."

I had planned to return to the States that weekend. I *had* the speech on my person.

I remained in Cairo several weeks longer than I had expected.

In the infirmary at Tel el Kebir camp, where she lay ill of a virus infection, Yaffa Tuvia heard the other ATS girls from Palestine speak bitterly in Hebrew about the two Eliahus. They followed the trial day by day. "Such murderers we do not need!" one was saying. She threw down the newspaper. "They are a shame to all of us. The sooner they are hanged, the better!"

Another shook her head. "Do you read how this Bet Zouri talks about himself? No, he is not an ordinary killer—he has a brain, he must wait for his brain to tell his finger to pull the trigger—"

They could scarcely contain themselves.

Yaffa had destroyed the few names and addresses of her contacts. Sooner or later, she was sure, she would be arrested. No one could be more thorough than British intelligence. I must be strong, she told herself. She kept silent, and she waited.

CHAPTER

24

THE TRIAL had become the talk
of Cairo.

Bet Zouri's speech was quoted everywhere, though not a word of
it appeared in the world's press. Yet, in the coffeehouses, in the
bazaars, wherever people gathered, Cairenes, while delighted at
the spectacle of the British lion being bearded by the two from
Palestine, began to ask other questions: had the day come when
they would see the most brilliant lawyers in Egypt plead the cause
of Zionism? For so it appeared as the last days of the trial approached and the defense took over.

The attorneys themselves were names to conjure with. Never before had all three appeared in the same courtroom. It was known
they had rejected any fee for their services—these were rendered
in behalf of the state, and in the name of that justice to which all
men are entitled—but their very eloquence troubled many an
Egyptian.

First to address the court was the chief defense counsel, Fattah
el Said. The former President of the Cairo Court of Appeals, a man

famous for his knowledge of the law, had sat, his heavy frame almost motionless, throughout the trial. Except for the opening day when he rose to challenge the competence of the court, he had said nothing.

Now, toying with his pince-nez, he began. "I confess, Mr. President, that I had to struggle with myself before I decided to accept this case. I share the regret of our government at the murder of Lord Moyne. He was a great Englishman and died in the accomplishment of his duty. It is my difficult task to convince the court that Hakim and Bet Zouri acted out of moral ideas: it is because of this conviction that I finally decided to take their case. My clients' sole motives were their ideals: theirs was a political crime. They had nothing against Lord Moyne personally. They had never met him, never spoken to him, never heard him speak. The shots they fired, the shots that killed him, were not aimed at Lord Moyne the man, but rather at the executor of his country's policy."

He analyzed the psychological condition of the Jews in Palestine, and those in the world. He cited the plight of European Jewry: in Germany, Rumania, Poland, Yugoslavia—pogroms, massacres, cruelty. "The Great Powers, as we know, did nothing to rescue these victims, though they had vast territories in which they could have given them refuge, had they wished." He spoke of the *Patria* and the *Struma*. "I call to your mind these miserable refugees aboard the *Struma* who had the sky overhead, the sea underfoot and before them Palestine.

"Had they been Germans or Japanese, they would have been put ashore and interned. I want you to consider that. Had they been enemies of the Allied Powers, they would have received a more humane treatment. It was easy for the Jews to conclude that England was responsible, since it was she who made the rules by which Palestine was open or closed. I remind the court that even the British Parliament has often protested against the British Administration's actions in Palestine. If the British themselves revolted, how not the Jews? Even we Egyptians must question a blind policy of pushing back refugees when the elementary dictates of humanity demand that they should be welcomed."

There were mutterings in the courtroom: who had written this speech? Fattah el Said, or Dr. Chaim Weizmann? He went on:

"I have admiration for the British character. It is that that gives me courage to say that the measures taken in Palestine were often defective. Events such as these undoubtedly had a destructive effect on the spirit of these young boys in Palestine, and if you add to that certain acts within Palestine—such acts as the accused have charged—it is possible to understand the reactions of the boys."

He recalled the cases of Schwarzbard and Frankfurter—the first, a young watchmaker who assassinated Simon Petliura, the anti-Semitic Ukrainian leader, in Paris in 1926, and was acquitted by a French court, and David Frankfurter, a student at the University of Berne who in 1936 assassinated William Gustloff, the Nazi gauleiter of Switzerland, and received a prison sentence. "These Jewish youths were similarly driven to murder because they felt there was no other path," he declared, "and neither of them was given the death penalty."

"But is murder the only way to protest in Palestine?" the President demanded, echoing the question he had asked of Bet Zouri.

Fattah el Said turned his great gray eyes on him. "The Jews tried everything, but nobody heard them. Some came to the conclusion that it was necessary to sacrifice themselves, in a savage act, so as to appeal to the world to save their people."

He concluded by stressing the fact that his clients must be believed in their declaration that they did not wish to kill anyone else, for they could easily have killed the two other persons in Lord Moyne's car.

Before he sat down, to give way to the second of the defense counsel, Tewfik Doss Pasha, former cabinet minister, Fattah el Said submitted documents to show that Hakim was not yet eighteen: indeed, had been seventeen years and ten months when he committed the crime. There was a dispute here—the Public Prosecutor insisted Hakim was twenty, as had been stated in the official charge. The President announced a physician would be called to examine Hakim and determine his age.

When court resumed on January 13, the President authorized the defense to call three witnesses from Palestine, whom Bet Zouri had requested, to relate the facts which had a "direct effect on the accused driving them to kill." The witnesses who would bear out Bet Zouri's charges—that cruelty and illegal acts of the Palestine police and CID were an integral part of life in Palestine—were Moshe Svorai, his wife, and one Eliahu Korb.

Then it was discovered that all three were prisoners in Palestine. It was Mrs. Svorai who had opened the door to Captain Morton and his men when they arrested and killed Abraham Stern in 1942; it was her husband, allegedly brutally treated by police, to whom Stern's dead body was shown at the hospital in Jaffa.

Korb, a twenty-one-year-old youth, had been in charge of an FFI arms warehouse when he was seized by the CID. His description of his torture during the week of March 21, 1944, to learn the names of his associates and the location of the warehouse, was stenciled on leaflets which were pasted on walls and telephone poles throughout Palestine, and sent to all newspapers by the FFI. The details caused a sensation. Sir John Shaw, Chief Secretary, called a press conference at which he denied Korb's charges and asserted that the CID did not use torture to elicit confessions. The FFI posted new leaflets demanding that an impartial inquiry committee be sent into the camps and prisons to gather testimony. Nothing was done.

What Korb had charged was that the CID kept him in a room outside Jerusalem Central Prison and when he would not speak, stripped him naked and for the next four days tortured him, flogging him with a leather-covered steel rod on his back, sides and genitals, reviving him each time he fainted; they had then placed a board over the lower part of his body and struck it repeatedly to injure his kidneys; then, thrown upon his back, four men stood on his arms and legs while a fifth man tried to lift him by his genitals, until he fainted; then they repeatedly plunged his head into a pail of water, reviving him each time. . . .

In the Cairo courthouse, President Mansour Bey announced

that the British Administration in Palestine had refused permission for the Svorais and Korb to come to Egypt to testify.

The defense dropped its request.

Tewfik Doss Pasha, a man with a thin, keen face, held the floor for two and a half hours when he spoke. "These boys believe themselves pure patriots seeking the independence of Palestine," he declared. "They are not concerned with Zionist ideals and the Zionist program. Their crime is like the crime of a deceived lover. Great Britain's act in closing the doors of Palestine deceived them; it prevented the admission of thousands of suffering Jews, and so they killed because they were deceived. We ask mercy for them."

Bet Zouri's voice cut sharply through the room. "Not mercy, but justice!"

The President rapped for order. "The accused," Doss Pasha said almost paternally, "refuse to ask for mercy but I have already told them they are like a doctor's patient. They cannot choose their own medicine."

Brilliantly he analyzed the crime of assassination. From the purely legalistic point of view, there was no difference between ordinary and political murder. But international law made a clear separation: it permitted the extradition of ordinary criminals but not of political assassins.

"Why?" he demanded. "Does international law encourage political crime? No! But it does recognize that they are very often prompted by passion, the criminal being influenced by sentiments which cause him to behave as if he were insane. That is the difference between a man who murders for self-interest and one who murders because of conviction.

"The accused have stated that they were instructed by a secret organization; that eliminates the hypothesis of the wilful murder of the chauffeur and of any intent to murder the constable. Their organization and the accused aimed only at killing Lord Moyne, because he was the representative of the British Government. They wanted a sensational deed to attract world-wide attention. The accused have stated specifically that their aim was the independence of Palestine, with or without the Balfour Declaration—it is therefore not an expression of Arab-Jewish rivalry, but an expression against Government abuses.

"As an Arab, I state that I reject the Zionist claims. But here we are judges and advocates before being Arabs. These boys were fighters for Israel's liberation. They are victims not culprits. They were children when they came under the influence of their secret organization which inculcated them with its desperate ideology. That influence is still with them—even now they are so maddened by passion that they will not divulge the name of the man who sent them on this terrible errand. I say to you, pity is above justice. I ask pity and mercy for these boys. I believe them when they say they have nothing to do with Zionism—they sought only freedom."

He ended on a high note. "During our own revolution twenty years ago, young Egyptians took the lives of Britishers. Our young men killed British officials on the streets of Cairo. I was appointed by the British authorities to defend several of the accused before British military courts. And in one political case, I remind the court, a British judge acquitted an Egyptian. In the name of my clients, I ask the court's clemency for these boys whose crime was brought about by a frenzy of passion that drove them to the borders of insanity."

Now the third of the defense attorneys, Hassan Djeddaoui, took up the pleading. During his long speech he broke down and wept. He reviewed the tragic odyssey of the Jews through thirty centuries. "Can we after this not pay heed to the state of soul of these young people? Day and night they heard of the suffering of their brothers and sisters; day and night that lamentation rose to their ears." With deep emotion he quoted Shylock's speech from *The Merchant of Venice:* " 'Hath not a Jew eyes? hath not a Jew hands, organs, dimensions, senses, affections, passions? fed with the same food, hurt with the same weapons, subject to the same diseases, healed by the same means, warmed and cooled by the same winter and summer, as a Christian is? If you prick us, do we not bleed? if you tickle us, do we not laugh? if you poison us, do we not die? and if you wrong us, shall we not revenge?' "

In the silence he said:

"Is it astonishing that the accused went mad? Is it astonishing that their spirit went astray? I recall to you that we are in the presence of two young boys born seven years after the Balfour Declaration. They grew up with that declaration in their eyes and in their ears; they drank it in their mothers' milk; they breathed it in the atmosphere of their Holy Land; and they saw with their eyes the realization of the four-thousand-year-old dream of a Jewish homeland. The passion of these young people is patriotism, patriotism exaggerated, perhaps badly guided patriotism, but patriotism nonetheless. These youths risked death according to their beliefs, for the sake of their country. They were wrong. But out of that very wrong rises the proof of their innocence of soul."

The entire world, he concluded, watched Cairo at this moment: it awaited the word that would be spoken by the judges in this courtroom, that would be flashed to the four corners of the earth.

"Three great capitals are involved in this deed: if the word that goes forth from Cairo will be a noble one, then Cairo will become the greatest of the three. In this time of carnage and death, of revolution and great disorder over all the earth, we will have taught the world a lesson of calmness and moderation, of pity and compassion—a lesson for all peoples and for all governments."

Eloquently, he asked for the lives of the two Eliahus.

The defense rested.

The Public Prosecutor, sitting these many hours, drew up to his full height. The day before he had altered the charge so that Bet Zouri was no longer charged with complicity in Moyne's death but, like Hakim, with his premeditated murder—a revision permitted under Egyptian law and based on Bet Zouri's statement that if Hakim had failed, he would have shot Moyne.

The Public Prosecutor turned his baleful eyes upon the boys. In contrast to the length of the defense arguments, he spoke tersely, sharply. The case was open and shut. The accused admitted the deed. They came to Cairo with a plan to kill Lord Moyne. They killed him—an old man, whom they gave no chance to defend himself—and they tried to escape. Fortunately, they were caught and must now pay for their crimes.

"I demand their heads, not because of the high position of the victim, but because death is the due penalty for their deed. If the accused had no pity for the murdered man, they are not entitled to pity. They premeditated the murder of Lord Moyne. They premeditated the murder of anyone who would interfere—for they were under orders to carry out their crime. In this case, it was Corporal Fuller. They killed him. They also wanted to kill the constable because he, too, would interfere.

"The accused have committed a crime against the Zionist cause. They have committed a crime against Egypt by spoiling her reputation, threatening her security, soiling her clean sheet. If they believe they have helped their race by their deed, all organizations, all associations, all authorities who speak on behalf of the Jews disown them and their action and ask for severe punishment.

"I call the court's attention to the Jewish Agency's denunciation of their act. The Jews in Palestine fear that it will have a bad influence upon their youth. I say to you that it can also have a bad influence upon our youth. I say to you that it is absolutely necessary to have the example of their punishment as a drastic lesson to others."

He turned to the defense counsel.

"My distinguished colleagues ask mercy for the two accused because they are 'children.'" He paused. "Two children! . . . My honored colleagues, you have seen the two children at play. The toys they played with are on the table before your eyes. One is called an automatic, the other a revolver.

"Two children!

"My honored colleagues, you have read the description of the other playthings, the other toys, these two children delight in? They left them at the house of Mrs. Blanca. Sticks of dynamite! A very curious pabulum!

"My honored colleagues. Do not delude yourselves. We stand before two of the most dangerous criminals in existence, without pity, without scruple. The murder of Lord Moyne and the murder of Corporal Fuller are simply the playful game of two children?"

He paced back and forth, still facing the battery of defense attorneys.

"My learned and eminent colleague, Tewfik Doss Pasha, tells us we must spare the accused because they acted so zealously in a cause dear to their hearts. Are we to allow murder in the name of propaganda? Are we to allow the spilling of innocent blood because it serves the aim of propaganda?"

He paused. "I say, let us get on with it! Egypt is not a country where one can kill with impunity. We have public order, we have public security, and of what use are these safeguards to the people if any individual can arrogate to himself the right to kill because of his convictions?"

He turned to face the accused in the dock.

"You, Bet Zouri, and you, Hakim, have come to Egypt and committed a dastardly deed. You must pay for it.

"I ask for the full penalty of the law."

The prosecution rested.

In the silence, the President looked over his glasses at the prisoners.

"Accused Hakim, do you wish to make a statement?"

Eliahu Hakim rose. He stood with his feet planted a little apart, his hands clasped behind him, his head down, staring at the floor, as if trying to collect his thoughts. Then he looked up at the court.

"I should like to explain why I joined the British Army and my reasons for leaving it. I concluded that the English war was not connected with our war—"

President (interrupting): "That is irrelevant."

Hakim: "But the reason I left the army was how I came to kill Lord Moyne."

President: "You should have mentioned that point when you spoke of your motives."

Hakim (throwing back his head): "Then I have said my word." He sat down.

President: "Accused Bet Zouri, do you wish to make a statement?"

Bet Zouri got to his feet. He spoke slowly. "Your Honor, I would like to comment on statements made by both the prosecutor and the defense. The prosecutor said that our action threatened the security of Egypt. So far as I can understand, he meant that Egyptians would have been held responsible for our action. But our organization always issues a proclamation after each action explaining why it was done and that it was done in accordance with instructions. Had we succeeded in retreating safely, such a proclamation would have been issued here at once.

"Secondly, I want to make clear that not all the views expressed by our defense counsel about Palestine are our views, and to repeat that our aims are not the same as Zionist aims.

"Now, in my name and in my comrade's name, I wish to thank our lawyers for their excellent defense. As far as Egyptian law is concerned, we are convinced that they are the best we could have had."

He sat down.

The President banged his gavel. "The court will take the case under advisement. This sitting is adjourned."

The trial had opened on January 10. It closed on January 16.

Two days passed—and on January 18, we received notice that the verdict would be given at noon.

We arrived in the courtroom to find the two boys already in the dock. They seemed quite cheerful: they nodded at us and smiled in recognition.

Moments later the five-man tribunal filed in. The President spoke briefly. "The facts in the case have been submitted to the Mufti," he said in Arabic. After this terse statement, court was adjourned and the tribunal filed out as solemnly as it had come in.

There was turmoil in the courtroom. It had happened so swiftly that hardly anyone seemed to know what the verdict had been.

The two boys had been found guilty. Only when the death penalty is involved are the facts referred to the Grand Mufti of Egypt, the nation's highest religious leader, for under Moslem law only the Mufti is empowered to order the death of a man.

Hakim did not seem to realize the import of the words. Bet Zouri, seated beside him, must have, for when the President spoke, for an instant he slumped in his chair, his mouth slightly open, his teeth apart. Two red spots began to burn in the center of his cheeks. The blush he had never been able to control spread over his face. He sat blankly for the space of a few heartbeats; then Hakim leaned over and spoke to him; he recovered himself, exchanged a few words with Hakim and then both smiled at each other and turned to face their judges, who were already filing out.

An attorney rose to his feet and began to walk toward the dock. A colleague stopped him. I heard him say in French, "If you propose to tell them what it means, do not do it now. I think they understand. But if they do not, let them not know it as long as possible."

Later I learned that when Hakim leaned over to Bet Zouri, he asked in Hebrew, "What does it mean?" and Bet Zouri replied, "It means death for both."

Four days passed.

In the streets of Cairo, the incredible took place. Egyptian students marched in demonstrations, chanting, "Free the Moyne slayers."

Then word came. The Mufti had confirmed the sentence with the traditional words from the Koran: "Who kills shall be killed."

Now the weeks of appeal, the prayers, the petitions. To King George VI, to King Farouk, to Pope Pius XII, to President Roosevelt, to Winston Churchill, to the League of Nations in Geneva . . .

The condemned were removed from Bab-al-Khalk prison—"The Gate of Creation"—to the more ancient and secure Cairo Jail, a massive stone structure with two-inch bars over every window and walls more than two feet thick. It still carried the name it bore under the Turks: *Kara Midan*—The Black Place.

In a little house on the outskirts of Tel Aviv, Avigad sat with Shamir. What could they do? "We cannot rest, we cannot rest," Avigad said. "We must try to rescue them."

The FFI, driven underground as never before, still had managed a few fugitive meetings. They had followed the trial by every means at their command. Now Shamir asked, "Do we have any chance of success?"

"I will go myself," said Avigad. He rose and paced back and forth. "Somehow, in some way—"

When Ben Josef awaited death in Acre Prison in 1938, a wild plan was proposed by an underground member the day before his execution. A youth similar in build to Ben Josef would disguise himself as an orthodox, bearded rabbi and gain admittance to Ben Josef's cell on the pretext of hearing his confession. The two would exchange clothes and Ben Josef would walk out twenty minutes later wearing the other's disguise.

Whatever punishment might be meted out to the man who dared this rescue, it would not be death; and Ben Josef would have been saved.

At the last moment the plan was abandoned.

Something of this was in Avigad's mind. Perhaps bribery, or major assault with tommy guns, grenades, bombs . . .

Shamir said, "Let me look into the matter."

A few days later he was closeted with Sergeant Gefner, the original FFI leader in Egypt, who had returned from service on the Italian Front. Shamir posed the problem. Why could they not send a few men to Cairo to attempt a rescue?

Gefner was against it. "You don't know Cairo. It swarms with spies and informers. Anything you do will be seen, any question you ask will be known to the police within the hour. That the boys had to use bicycles shows you what kind of a place it is. All you will achieve will be to kill the men you send."

Shamir said slowly, "You are wrong. Even if the attempt fails, it will carry tremendous significance. It will increase the echo of what has already happened."

Gefner said, "I am thinking in terms of human life and you are thinking in terms of the struggle. I recommend strongly that you do not try it."

Shamir rubbed his cheek reflectively. "My people in Cairo tell me there are no police around the jail."

"Not true," said Gefner. "There may be porters, street vendors, beggars—and they are actually police and detectives. Even a lemonade seller can hide a gun under his lemons."

Gefner had passed through Cairo in December, three weeks before the trial, and come upon Sadovsky on the street. The man looked like a shadow of himself—the shadow of a shadow. He walked bent over, utterly broken by what had happened. He told Gefner everything. He had nothing but admiration and love for the boys. "I was frightened when they left on the action," he said. "I showed it. They noticed how I felt and Bet Zouri said to me"—and here Sadovsky quoted the words—". . . Usually we don't thank in the underground but you are not a member of the underground, so we thank you. . . . Whatever happens to us—if we are captured, tortured or anything, you can be quite sure that we shall never mention your name."

Sadovsky had reason to be concerned. More than once he had entertained the two Eliahus in his home. They had eaten at his table many times. The Sadovskys had three Arab servants: they might well have recognized the photographs in the papers.

In any event, after all the discussion, no men were sent to rescue the two boys.

The aftermath of this particular phase of the story may be told here.

In January, 1945, Gefner was discharged from the British Army. Four months later, in May, as he was walking in Tel Aviv, he was surrounded by police, arrested as a suspected terrorist and sent to an internment camp in the Sudan.

A month later he was put on a plane and flown to Cairo: he was placed in solitary confinement. No reason was given him for his arrest. On his twenty-fifth day in prison, he heard Sadovsky's voice, quite clearly, through the wall. Sadovsky in the next cell? He put his ear to the wall: it seemed to him that they were questioning Sadovsky; the voices were British, the words were English, but he could not make them out clearly. They were shouting—and Sadovsky? . . . Gefner was not sure. Was the man weeping? Groaning? Was he being tortured?

The shouting, the questioning, the torturing, if that was what it was, went on for a few days. Then, silence.

A guard entered Gefner's room and took away his belt, his keys, anything he could use to hang himself with or to injure himself.

Why, Gefner wondered, had they not done this the day he was placed in the cell?

Only later did Gefner learn what had happened.

After the death of the two Eliahus, Sadovsky had gone into a deep depression. He could not get over their fate. One day, unable to restrain himself, he bought flowers and visited their grave. He placed the flowers on the grave and stood there, deeply moved. He began to weep. An Arab caretaker quietly notified police, and he was seized.

Why was he there? Had he been involved in the assassination? Was he a member of the Fighters for the Freedom of Israel? What, who, did he know?

He denied everything. But he trembled with fear as they questioned him. He could have said simply, "I weep because I am a good Jew and these are two Jewish youths who in mistaken zeal have done a terrible deed. They now lie dead, and I mourn them." But the more he denied, the more agitated he became, and the more suspicious the police.

He was thrown into a cell.

Next morning Sadovsky tried to commit suicide by slashing his wrists with a razor blade. He was caught in time but now the police were certain that he was involved in the plot. They brought his servants, his parents, to confront him; they beat him; they refused to believe his protests. He began to make up stories to save his skin. Then they knew they had a man who would talk. Before he was finished, he had told all. He named names—Gefner and Galili, Yaffa, Ada—everyone.

The difficulty facing the police was that all these persons went by different aliases. They had Gefner in their hands but never identified him as the man named by Sadovsky. They had had Galili in jail before: now they set up a dragnet for him in Palestine.

Galili had moved swiftly. The two Eliahus had been seized at 1:30 P.M. on a Monday, Galili read about it in the 7 A.M. edition of Tuesday's newspaper. By 10 A.M. Tuesday he was in Palestine, having hitched a ride aboard an RAF plane to a military airport near Tel Aviv. At noon he was in Tel Aviv. He threw away his British uniform, dyed his hair, obtained forged identity cards with a new name, donned civilian clothes and went underground in the FFI. He saw Bannai, and left a message with him that he wanted to see Shamir. Forty-eight hours later he met Shamir in the latter's hideout. Together they worked on a statement regarding the arrest of the two boys.

In the months that followed, he kept quietly in the FFI underground. After the trial he, too, discussed with Shamir the possibility of rescuing them. Again, it was decided that nothing could be done.

Then word came to Galili that Sadovsky had been arrested.

He had no sooner learned this than he was himself suddenly seized in Tel Aviv. One by one, after Sadovsky's confession, the British rounded up everyone involved in the plot. Galili was flown back to Cairo and taken to Maadi, the center of Middle East intelligence. For three months he was kept in a little room, naked, without clothes. "Perhaps to intimidate me or embarrass me," he said. "Perhaps because a naked man, feeling his shame and helplessness, will speak." Day after day he was questioned.

He denied everything.

His questioners said, "We will give you a passport to go to the United States and start a new life—to South Africa, to anywhere you wish—if you give us the information we want on the FFI."

He said he knew nothing.

Then they told him that Sadovsky had confessed and named him.

Galili, no weak man, treated the news contemptuously. "All he told you is lies. I want to see him. Let him face me and tell it to my face."

The police agreed, on condition that the two prisoners spoke only English.

But day after day passed—and no Sadovsky was brought to his cell. In the end, the British court-martialed Galili for desertion and exiled him to Eritrea and then to Kenya.

But before he was sent into exile he asked for religious consolation, and the Jewish chaplain visited him. As the latter was about to leave, Galili asked him about Sadovsky. The chaplain looked at him in surprise.

"Didn't you know?" he asked. "Sadovsky hanged himself in his cell."

He told Galili the date. It was the day after he had demanded that Sadovsky be brought to face him.

Galili never knew why Sadovsky took his life.

Was it because he dared not face him?

Or had he killed himself to save Galili's life?

Had he feared that if they were brought together and he testified, the truth would come out and Galili would be tried and hanged as an accomplice in the murder of Lord Moyne?

CHAPTER

25

Iɴ ᴛʜᴇsᴇ ɴɪɢʜᴛᴍᴀʀᴇ days before, during and after the trial, the Bet Zouri family lived as in another world. They questioned Asher Levitsky repeatedly to learn all they could about Eliahu. "He is in good hands," Levitsky assured Bet Zouri's father. "He has the finest attorneys in Egypt. They will do all humanly possible."

Moshe Bet Zouri had called upon, methodically, every important Zionist official who would see him. He was known as a devoted member of the Mapai party. All knew that he frowned on his son's activities. But who would speak up for terrorists who had gone so far? What was there to be said in defense of Eliahu Bet Zouri and Eliahu Hakim? Had not the Jewish Agency, had not every institution of Jewish government in Palestine and outside Palestine warned and warned again? Had they not pleaded with the Irgunists and the Sternists? Had they not done everything short of civil war? Madmen had sown, and now madmen reaped their dread harvest.

Moshe Bet Zouri found himself demoted in his post-office job.

He was transferred to a substation on the outskirts of Tel Aviv. He took his demotion uncomplainingly.

He spent his nights at the synagogue, praying.

Eliahu's twenty-year-old sister, Aviva, could not rest. She must go to Egypt to see her brother, to do what she could. She had no money to pay for the trip, nor was she sure the authorities, when she arrived, would allow her to see him. Nonetheless, a sum was advanced her by Eliahu's friends so that she could go to the Egyptian capital.

She went alone. Her first stop was at the office of her brother's attorneys. She had to wait several days before they could do anything for her. Under Egyptian law, families of condemned men were permitted to see them only the night before execution. But here a note of hope sounded. Prime Minister Ahmed Maher himself signed a pass allowing her to visit her brother in prison. In the office of Attorney Abdula Fattah el Said, she met Hakim's brother, Ovadia. He, too, had petitioned for the right to visit his brother.

The Prime Minister had signed both passes on the same day.

Briefly, Aviva saw the Chief Rabbi of Egypt, the aged and blind Rabbi Haim Nahum Pasha. The old man held her hand in his for a few moments. "Have faith, my daughter," he whispered to her. "I have it from the Prime Minister himself: whatever possible will be done; your brother will not hang. Ahmed Maher has given me so to understand. It will all pass over. Pray to God, and have faith."

The next morning Aviva and Ovadia presented themselves at the prison. They were greeted by the warden himself, Chudar Pasha, a heavy-set man with courtly manners. He shook hands with each ceremoniously and asked them to wait in his office. "It will be but a few minutes," he said. He clapped his hands, and when a servant came running, he ordered Turkish coffee. It was served them in tiny cups, strong and sweet. To Aviva he said, "Your brother is a most intelligent, a most admirable young man. He pleases all who know him. We honor him."

Then he added, "My lady, I have a favor." He pulled a letter from his pocket. He had had it for two days, but it was written in a strange language he did not understand. Would she translate it for him?

Aviva looked at it and recognized the language as Greek. She said, a little helplessly, "Excellency, I know that it is Greek but I cannot read it. I do not understand the language, either. I cannot help you."

Chudar Pasha's eyebrows lifted. He seemed genuinely surprised. "What," he demanded, "a sister of Bet Zouri, and you don't know Greek?"

They could not help smiling at that. Then the door opened and armed guards appeared. "You will have ten minutes, my lady," Chudar Pasha said. She was ushered down a long corridor and into a small white-walled room divided down the middle by heavy wire netting. Eliahu, his wrists manacled, appeared on the other side, entering from another corridor, looking much as when she saw him last, dressed in his own clothes, not, as she feared to see him, in the faded blue prison garb.

"Aviva!" His face shone. He bombarded her with questions. The armed guard stood nearby through the entire interview. Though he understood Hebrew, he was not adept at it and repeatedly cautioned brother and sister to speak slowly so that he could understand every word they said.

How was everyone at home? Eliahu wanted to know. Deborah and Lea and Uri? How was their father? "Is he very angry with me?"

"No, no," said Aviva. "He is proud of how you have conducted yourself. He is trying to get influential people to intervene so that you will receive a reprieve—"

"You will see," Eliahu said stoutly. "It will be all right." He smiled at her. "I am sure they won't give us the full penalty."

Aviva told him about the cables of protest, the messages for clemency on their behalf, signed by Toscanini, Sigrid Undset, distinguished men and women throughout the world—

"I know," Eliahu said, smiling. "I read the newspapers."

Then—had she seen—he avoided the use of her name, but

Aviva knew he meant Hannah. He also asked, in guarded tones, about Avigad.

"Yes, I saw them both. She sends you her love. She will try to come on a visit to you as soon as she can. And your friend—I saw him and also his wife and child. They all send regards."

She wanted to say more to comfort him, but she felt helpless. At home they had never shown their emotions. She could not show them now—the more so in the presence of the impassive Egyptian listening to every word. She yearned to kiss Eliahu, to touch him, but this was impossible too—the netting separated them. All she could say awkwardly was, "You look well. You seem to have gained weight."

Yes, he said, he felt fine. They fed him well. The bullet in his chest had been expertly removed. He was remarkably well treated by everyone—warden, guards, attendants. They tendered him favors: he had no complaints.

Then brother and sister were silent again.

Had she seen—he used Adi's alias—Jacob? She nodded. She had seen him and his wife. They were expecting a baby. "It is well they married," Eliahu said with a grin.

Then the same unbearable silence.

He said, "I would like to study while I am here." Would she bring him the same edition of the *Reader's Digest* in English, Spanish and Portuguese? By comparing them he could learn Spanish and Portuguese. And would she send more clothes for him? He had only the one suit. And a blanket?

Aviva had brought him cookies baked by his grandmother and a cake she had made herself. Warden Chudar Pasha had suggested that these be left in his office. He would have them delivered.

The time was up. "I will see that you have everything tomorrow," said Aviva. They made an attempt to touch hands through the netting. With his manacled wrists it was a sorry thing. He smiled at her and was led away.

Next morning when she returned, she was not permitted to see him again. She left what she had brought in the warden's office.

Ovadia Hakim's pilgrimage had been especially sad. His mother had been too distraught, his father too weak to come. Since the arrest, the family had fasted two days a week and attended the synagogue every morning. Before Ovadia visited his young brother in prison, his attorney drove him to the Bulak Bridge, and he heard again the story of how the two were captured: how Bet Zouri was wounded and fell, and how young Hakim had wheeled round on his bike to go to his rescue, and so both were caught. The lawyer paused.

"You know, of course, that your brother made a great sacrifice—"

Ovadia knew. Repeatedly he had reviewed the scene in his mind's eye. His young brother might well have saved his own skin. He had already made the bridge; he had only to continue pedaling swiftly, then leap off his bike and lose himself in the crowds. In appearance, manner, speech, he could have passed for an Egyptian. Indeed, it was quite possible the crowd itself would have protected him. All they had seen was what appeared to be an Englishman in hot pursuit of an Egyptian. Cairo crowds had been known to foil such pursuits, to save a pickpocket, a purse snatcher, a thief, from capture by the hated foreigner. Yes, thought Ovadia, he might have saved himself. . . .

His attorney drove him to Cairo Central Jail. They parked the car and walked around the great stone pile. Fantastic ideas of helping the boys escape ran through Ovadia's mind. But *Kara Midan,* the Black Place, was a virtual fortress. No one could break out without help from within. Could the prison officials be bribed? Bribery was an accepted means of persuasion in the Levant. Yet this was out of the question too. The officials might want to help, but they were too fearful of the British. He put the possibility out of his mind.

Once in the interview room, he prepared himself to encourage his brother if he should appear depressed. But young Hakim came in fresh, smiling and confident, unconcerned that his wrists were manacled and the guard was present to hear every word. It was Ovadia who found himself cheered up.

"How is the family?" his brother wanted to know. Would Ovadia beg their forgiveness for bringing such sorrow upon them? He had done his duty as a soldier: his one regret was for their suffering.

"They do not do badly and long to see you, especially Mother, who wished very much to join me," Ovadia replied. "But you know how Father's health is—and she could not leave his side."

And the reaction of the Jewish community? How did the newspapers speak of their deed? What was the attitude of their friends? The people in the street?

Ovadia told him there was sympathy, admiration and understanding. There was also fear, great bitterness and loud denunciation of them as misguided—yet no one, Ovadia said, denied that they were idealists.

Hakim said firmly, "I think our act has brought our people closer to freedom." Ovadia marveled at his calm. "I am well treated," his brother went on. "The authorities here are most courteous to me."

"Yes," said Ovadia. "Wherever I go in Cairo I find a most sympathetic atmosphere among the population. Everyone who hears our family name speaks to me with great respect."

Hakim smiled. "All will end well, you will see."

The guard stepped forward.

Each brother put his fingertips to his lips in token of a farewell kiss, and young Hakim was led away.

One never knows how history is written.

Not until the morning of February 24, 1945, nearly a month after the boys had been sentenced, was Moshe Bet Zouri well enough to make the trip to Egypt to see his son. He was received first by Chief Rabbi Nahum Pasha. As he had assured Aviva, now the old man assured the father. "Do not worry," he said. "I am in contact with Ahmed Maher. The Prime Minister has personally assured me that your son will not be executed. We can count on his word." He was also doing all in his power to intervene with His Majesty, King Farouk.

Eliahu's father felt a surge of hope. It was said that the Chief Rabbi, rich in years and service to Egypt, had great influence at the Royal Court.

"Shall I be permitted to see my son?" he asked.

Rabbi Nahum Pasha turned him over to the attorneys. Fattah el Said, chief of the defense counsel, saw him in his office. "My dear Bet Zouri," he said. "Please return tomorrow. I will go with you. I see no difficulty in arranging what you wish."

That afternoon, February 24, as Prime Minister Ahmed Maher crossed an arcade on his way to the Senate to present a declaration of war against Germany and Japan, a photographer stopped him for a moment to pose for a picture. As he did so, at a sidewalk café thirty feet away a man rose and fired four times at the Prime Minister. He fell, fatally wounded. An Egyptian political dissident, for reasons which had nothing to do with Palestine, had assassinated him.

Moshe Bet Zouri, reading about it in his modest hotel room, trembled.

Next morning he went again to the lawyer's office. Fattah el Said, shaking his head sadly, said, "My friend, we are now in a different situation, a very different situation. But let us try." He took Eliahu's father in his car and they spent the day visiting one government office after another. Before the last—the building which housed the office of the newly appointed Prime Minister, Nokrashy Pasha, Moshe Bet Zouri sat in the car for nearly an hour.

The lawyer came out.

"Sorry," he said. "They don't allow."

Silently, he took the wheel and drove Eliahu's father back to his hotel.

That night Moshe Bet Zouri took the train back to Palestine.

In the House of Commons, two days later, Prime Minister Churchill rose to report on his meeting at Yalta with President Roosevelt and Marshal Stalin. It was a major address, lasting most of the day, and in it he took cognizance of the unhappy situation in Egypt.

"I must at once express our grief and horror at the assassination of the Egyptian Prime Minister, Ahmed Maher Pasha," he said. "His death is a serious loss to his King and to his country." His colleague, Anthony Eden, had only recently had a long conference with Ahmed Maher. "The sympathy of Great Britain for the widow and family of the late Prime Minister of Egypt has of course been expressed, not only in telegrams from the Foreign Office but also by various personal visits of our ambassador, Lord Killearn. . . . I am sure the House will associate itself with these expressions."

Then he added:

"There is little doubt that security measures in Egypt require considerable tightening; above all, that the execution of justice upon men proved guilty of political murder should be swift and exemplary."

Then he went on to more urgent matters of the war.

At 1 P.M. on the afternoon of Sunday, March 18, a week before Passover, commemorating that night when the Angel of Death, smiting the first-born of the Egyptians, passed over the houses of the Israelites, two police officers came to the apartment of Moshe Bet Zouri in Tel Aviv.

They found Eliahu's father in bed. He had suffered a heart attack some days before; he was recuperating but still weak. He did not gather the import, at first, of what they were telling him. They wanted him to come at once to see his son in Cairo.

"See my son now? They will not let me see my son. I could not see him last time—"

They urged him. At last he understood, but he could not muster the strength to go. It was impossible for him to make the long journey to Cairo.

Deborah and Aviva would go instead. With astonishing speed—

by noon of the next day, Monday—they had obtained their visas. But Deborah had no passport: she would have to wait twenty-four hours for it. The officers urged Aviva, who had a passport, to go alone. She refused to leave without her sister. On Tuesday Deborah received the necessary document; a police car waited outside their apartment to take them to Lydda railway station. Train tickets had already been arranged.

The two girls moved like automatons. Such urgency could mean only one thing.

They left Moshe Bet Zouri in despair. He sent another telegram to Chief Rabbi Nahum Pasha in Cairo; he sent an imploring petition to King Farouk.

Once upon the train, the girls were escorted into a private compartment with drawn curtains. As they entered, their hearts fell. There, pale and resigned, sat Joseph and Ovadia Hakim. They greeted each other somberly, and sat in silence for a long time. At the Egyptian border, Egyptian guards entered their compartment and remained with them.

When they reached Cairo Wednesday morning, the four asked to be taken at once to their lawyers' offices, and then to the Chief Rabbi. Instead, they found the guards conducting them to the headquarters of the Egyptian Secret Police.

Aviva, gaining strength from she knew not where, protested vehemently. She must see the Chief Rabbi; His Eminence was their only hope. Finally, after numerous conferences among themselves, the Egyptians took the two girls to a hotel room. "My ladies, please wait."

Presently the door opened and there stood the Chief Rabbi.

The old man, blind, broken, could only reach for their hands and whisper hoarsely as they led him to a chair, "It is martyrdom, my children, martyrdom. It cannot be changed. There is nothing I can do now." Were Prime Minister Ahmed Maher alive . . . But Ahmed Maher was dead, dead—by some awful irony—of an assassin's bullet as well, and it was too much, too much. Had not Churchill himself in his speech, a strong speech, called for the hangman?

Egypt had no other choice. Indeed, it was a matter of wonderment that the government had allowed nearly three weeks to pass before deciding to act. . . .

The girls, now joined by Joseph and Ovadia Hakim, tried to compose themselves. They were driven to the prison. Once inside the little white room with its wire-netting barrier, Deborah and Aviva waited. They saw Eliahu coming down the corridor, accompanied by a guard. He walked almost jauntily, smoking a cigarette, exchanging pleasantries with the other. He had not yet seen them; he took a last puff, let the cigarette drop to the floor—his hands were manacled—ground it under his heel, then turned and saw them. His face broke into a wide smile. Obviously, he had been told nothing, he knew nothing. "Deborah! Aviva! They told me I had visitors but I thought it was my lawyers!"

With a great effort of will the two girls tried to make conversation. Eliahu said banteringly, "Well, you're certainly having a good time, Aviva, no doubt of it. Every now and then you take off time from work and come to the banks of the Nile for a little vacation. Who else can do that?"

He asked about the family, and then, "How is my girl friend?"

"She sends you her regards," said Aviva. "She's sorry that she hasn't been able to make it here yet—"

"Ah, well," said Eliahu. He smiled and blushed. No matter what, he could never hide his blushing.

"And Jacob? Did he have a little boy or girl?"

A girl, said Aviva. And Adi had named the baby "Anat."

Eliahu grinned. "A Canaanite name," he said. "And a lovely one, too." Then, awkwardly lighting another cigarette—the guard had to help him because of his handcuffed wrists—he glanced at them. "I see that you have a good High Commissioner now—" His eyes twinkled. Aviva knew what he meant. The political arguments that had been made so often: the trouble was not with British policy, but with the man on the spot; MacMichael had been a bad High Commissioner, Lord Gort was a good High Commissioner. Yet the barbed wire remained, the detention camps were filled, terrorism, arms searches, arrests without charge and trial went on. . . .

"How do you know all this?" Deborah asked. It was the first time she was able to speak. Less articulate than Aviva, more the victim of her emotions than Aviva, Deborah had been in a state of such shock and horror in recent weeks that she had almost been unable to function.

Eliahu grinned at Deborah's question. "Well, suddenly I realize that I can read French well. I've been reading the Egyptian French press." There had been many stories about the popularity of Lord Gort in Palestine. MacMichael had kept himself aloof from the people; Lord Gort was everywhere, visiting settlements and farms and villages, shaking hands with kibbutz secretaries, Arab muktars and sheiks—a smiling, friendly man.

As the session drew to a close, the sisters could hardly contain themselves. Their eyes stung, their cheeks began to flush. Like Eliahu, they were fair-skinned and their feelings easily betrayed them. "Have you had bad news?" he asked. "What is it—your faces —you look a little upset—"

"No, no, not at all." Aviva recovered herself. "Everything is fine. You can imagine; it's so hard waiting and waiting for good news to come—"

He laughed. "It will come," he said. He saw the guard rising to signal the end of the interview. He suddenly remembered: would they send him and Hakim matzos for Passover? This request was the hardest for the girls to take with equanimity, but Eliahu continued, "Please give my love to Father and tell him I hope that he will get well quickly. Tell him I'm perfect in every respect. I have no complaints. I'm treated well. They're very friendly to me." He spoke in a rush. "Indeed, I read and write, I do daily setting-up exercises—and do you know, I've discovered I know Portuguese, too. I read it very well, thanks to you, Aviva."

She remembered. The copies of the *Reader's Digest* she had brought him. "I simply compare, and I can read everything now," he said with a grin. "Why shouldn't I?" He laughed. "I have plenty of free time."

The girls said good-bye. They tried to touch fingertips through the screening. "Shalom," they said. And under her breath Aviva murmured, "Shalom, my dearest Eliahu, *Shalom Ad blidai*. Shalom without end."

He turned and walked away. The door closed behind him.

Surely, thought Aviva, he cannot know what will happen tomorrow.

And then she broke down, and Deborah with her, and the Egyptians had to help the two girls out of the prison.

In the night they took them back to their hotel. The girls went into their room. They heard the key turn in the lock. Outside, in the corridor, Egyptian police stood guard through the night.

In the hotel room Aviva stood as in a spell, by the high window, looking down on the peaceful square, bathed in moonlight, far below. A fountain was there: all night the water played.

Her sister slept fitfully, but Aviva could not close her eyes. She thought, If I do something desperate—please don't be cruel to my brother, he doesn't deserve it. Please. She thought, I will jump out the window. If they want a life to pay for Lord Moyne's life, let it be mine. She took a step forward as if in answer to her thought; she heard Deborah turn and twist and sigh, and she looked at her sleeping sister and thought, No, I cannot do it to her. I cannot do it to my father. But how shall I go on living? All the days to come?

He will be dead. They will bury him here. They will not give us the bodies. They are cruel. I will say, "You will do what you have to do, but give us their bodies." They will refuse. The British do not want their graves to be a shrine. The British don't want them to be martyrs.

Aviva thought, It will be so terrible. On the anniversary of his death there will be no grave to go to, to bring flowers to, to weep over. . . . She thought, On the anniversary of his death I will go to my mother's grave and pray to her. If she were alive now I would go to her and cry with her. She thought, Eliahu . . . He was deprived of everything. He did not have time to live, to love his girl, to know life. What am I doing, living? Eliahu is not here and I go on as if nothing has happened. He is already dead. I know it. And this part of me is dead, it is inside me, yet it does not let me go on living.

So she stood at the window until dawn came, and sunlight, and the hour that sooner or later she must meet.

CHAPTER

26

I<small>N</small> THE EARLY HOURS of the twenty-second of March, as Aviva stood weeping before her hotel window, a telephone call came to Rabbi Nissim Ochana, Deputy Chief Rabbi of Egypt. On the other end was the hushed voice of J. J. Hakim, Secretary of the Jewish Community of Cairo. Because his name was the same as Eliahu Hakim, he had had a difficult time these past months. It was soon proved, however, that he was not related to the accused, and the Egyptian authorities had allowed him to carry on with his duties.

Now he had word for Rabbi Ochana. An hour before daybreak a red police car with two officers would come to his residence to take him to Bab-al-Khalk Prison. He must be ready.

"It is not necessary to explain to you—" Mr. Hakim said. He went on to say that he had been telephoned shortly before midnight by the Under Secretary of State, who summoned him at once to the Ministry of the Interior. There the Under Secretary had informed him, in greatest secrecy, that the two boys would be hanged at eight o'clock the following morning. He had warned him: "We count on you to see that there is no demonstration among your people"; he was to say nothing to anyone; he must arrange for an undertaker to collect the bodies and he was permitted to notify Chief Rabbi Nahum Pasha to call upon the condemned to give them religious consolation in their last hour and accompany them to the gallows. Mr. Hakim had first telephoned Nahum Pasha, but the Chief Rabbi, aged and blind, did not trust himself to be adequate to this terrible moment. Mr. Hakim had therefore telephoned Rabbi Ochana.

The rabbi dressed. The red car arrived. It awakened his wife, who was alarmed, but the two officers were most courteous. "Do not be disturbed," they told her. "We shall return your husband safely to you within a few hours."

When Rabbi Ochana arrived at the prison, he was immediately escorted into the office of Warden Chudar Pasha. The latter rose and greeted him ceremoniously. "Sit down, Rabbi." He looked at his pocket watch. "It is my duty to inform you officially that within the hour we shall begin to carry out the sentence of death on the prisoners Hakim and Bet Zouri."

Rabbi Ochana, though he knew, paled at the words. Until the last moment he had hoped the verdict might be set aside. He could not help blurting out, "What a pity that these two splendid men are going to die through no fault of their own."

The warden said, almost apologetically, "It is a decree from the high authorities." Both men were silent. Then the warden asked, "What will you tell the condemned?" He added gently, "You will forgive me, but I know little of your religion, though I am told that in many matters it is not unlike our own."

"What shall I tell them?" Rabbi Ochana echoed his words. He labored under a great emotion. "In our religion a person about to die must confess himself before God in the final moment. He must recite the viddui: "Almighty God, forgive me for all my sins and transgressions from the day of my birth until this hour. May my death be an atonement for all sins that I have committed, knowingly or unknowingly, against Thee. May my soul rest in Paradise with the saints who sacrificed themselves to consecrate Thy Name and for Thy people Israel. May my body rest in peace in the grave and rise up to its fate in the Resurrection that comes at the end of all the days of the world."

Warden Chudar Pasha listened, silent, his head bowed.

"Then, afterward, they will say, each, 'Hear, O Israel, unto thy hand will I entrust my soul. Thou hast redeemed me, O God of Truth.' "

The warden sighed. "It is such a confession that my people, too, would make before Allah."

Precisely at 6:30 A.M., as the warden and rabbi sat talking, the door opened. A giant of a man with dark eyes in a pale face, and huge mustachios reaching almost to either cheekbone, entered. It was *Moalam* (Master Artist) Mohamed Shoura, the hangman. Middle-aged, the father of three sons and a married daughter, for twenty years he had carried out all hangings in Egypt. Now he bowed and took a seat.

A moment later a tall, gray-haired man wearing a general's uniform and a red tarboosh strode in. Everyone rose. It was His Excellency, Mohamad Haidar Pasha, Director General of the Prisons of Egypt, later to be Commander in Chief of the Egyptian Army.

He took his seat. Everyone sat again. They waited.

Now a shuffle of footsteps was heard outside. The door opened to show Bet Zouri and Hakim surrounded by towering guards. They were wearing their faded-blue prison attire. The two boys glanced about; when they saw the assembled officials, they knew. They stood side by side, somewhat remote, a slight smile on their lips.

An hour before, police had awakened Bet Zouri in his cell in the Cairo Central Jail, given him breakfast and, telling him he was going to see Rabbi Ochana, had escorted him to a closed police car. Inside he found Hakim. It was the first time the two had seen each other since the trial, and they embraced each other.

Their car came to a halt before the prison. They were led up the steps and through long corridors until they reached the warden's office, to enter and see the group awaiting them. In the group were several newspapermen. The night before they had been summoned by telephone to the governor's house. There each was presented with a small white envelope. Inside was a brief note: the verdict rendered upon the murderers of Lord Moyne would be carried out at 8 A.M. the following day. They were invited to be present so that they could report to the people of Egypt and the world that justice had been done.

Warden Chudar Pasha rose after a moment, and in a loud voice read the verdict to the two boys. They listened, standing: Hakim with his head down, now and then shifting his position; Bet Zouri, legs spread a little apart, staring at Chudar Pasha, his face pale, the same two red spots burning in his cheeks that showed when he first heard the words in the court: "The facts in the case have been submitted to the Mufti."

Now the boys were separated and Rabbi Ochana was permitted to spend a few minutes with each. First he saw Hakim. "My son," he said in a trembling voice, "you have to return your soul to your Creator. In a short time you will see the Master of the World."

"Yes, Rabbi."

"It is a decree from heaven, my son, and you must accept it with love."

"I accept it, yes, I accept, Rabbi." Hakim's voice faltered for a moment. "But I want to see my parents. I very much want to see my mother and my father—"

Warden Chudar Pasha, who had entered a moment before, said gently, "You have already seen your brothers. Why add to the grief of your parents?"

Hakim then asked if he might write a farewell note to them.

He was brought paper and he wrote with painstaking care, "My parents, I ask you not to grieve over me. I send my warm regards to all the Jewish people of Palestine and I ask for the redemption of our people in Israel."

Had he any other requests? Warden Chudar Pasha asked.

Hakim said, "I would like to shave my beard. It is very rough. I have not shaved for ten days."

"There is no time," said the warden. "I am sorry."

Then Rabbi Ochana asked Hakim to repeat the confession. Hakim rose and repeated it word for word after the rabbi in the little room.

Warden Chudar Pasha stepped forward. He had been waiting respectfully until the two had finished the prayer. "We must go now."

"I would like to see my comrade, if I am permitted," Hakim said.

Warden Chudar Pasha made no answer. He signaled, and *Moalam* Shoura, the hangman, approached with the traditional execution suit made of red burlap. He took off Hakim's slippers, so that he was barefoot, and helped him disrobe and put on the red suit. As he put it on, Hakim said, "This is the finest suit I have ever worn. I wear it with pride."

The warden signaled again and a guard approached with a pair of manacles.

Hakim drew back. "You do not need these," he said. "I promise you I will not resist." Then—"But, after all—" and with a ghost of a smile he extended his hands and his wrists were manacled.

Warden Chudar Pasha said resignedly, "It is the law."

Hakim walked with them into the prison yard to a small square brick structure in which stood the gallows. It was brilliantly lit. They brought him into the execution chamber, before the waiting witnesses.

He stepped forward and stood upon the trap. *Moalam* Shoura prepared to place the black hood over his head. Again Hakim protested: "There is no need for it—"

And again he allowed them to do what they wished.

Now the hangman was about to fix the noose about his neck when the hooded figure put his head back and they heard him begin to sing. He was singing Hatikvah, the Hebrew song of hope, later to be the national anthem of the State of Israel. The hangman stepped back a pace, his head bowed, and waited.

The song ended. They heard Hakim's muffled voice. "I am ready now."

The hangman stepped forward and placed the noose about his neck.

301

Again they heard Hakim's voice. "I ask you to bury me in Haifa."

They were his last words. The trap was sprung. The body fell.

There was a silence. A doctor placed his stethoscope to Hakim's chest. Then he announced, "This man is dead." It had taken four minutes and ten seconds.

The body was left on the rope for a few minutes more, then taken down, wrapped in the ceremonial prayer shawl of the Hebrew religion and placed in a waiting coffin.

While the hangman had his way with Hakim, Rabbi Ochana, who could not bring himself to watch the execution, was closeted with Bet Zouri. The rabbi is almost distraught: Bet Zouri will not recite the viddui. "I am sorry, Rabbi," he says, "but I do not believe."

Rabbi Ochana pleads with him. "I implore you, I pray you, make your confession."

Bet Zouri is firm. "I cannot. I will not, as I do not believe."

Then Chudar Pasha speaks to him while *Moalam* Shoura helps him into the red hanging suit and removes his slippers. "Have you any requests?"

"No—but I would like to write some letters. To my father, to my sisters, to my girl—"

"I am afraid you do not have any more time—" the warden says.

Eliahu adds suddenly, "I would like to embrace my father—"

The warden shakes his head. He remembers that Eliahu has no mother.

In the execution room Eliahu, too, protests. "Why must you chain me?" He, too, does not want the hood to cover his face. But he allows the hangman to do what he must. Standing on the trap, he speaks. "I thank you, Rabbi, for coming to me. I thank you, Warden, for treating me with dignity." Then he lifts his voice in the Hatikvah.

Everyone waits, their heads bowed in respect.

The trap is sprung. The body falls heavily.

After three minutes and fifty seconds, Eliahu Bet Zouri is pronounced dead.

Outside, slowly, at 8 A.M., a black flag is raised to the top of the pole high above the prison. At 8:25 a second flag is raised. The black flags hang there, fluttering slowly in a gentle wind.

An hour before, in her hotel room, Aviva wakes suddenly. The sun streams in the window. She has fallen asleep in her chair. Deborah still sleeps.

Was it a knock on the door that wakened her? Had she dreamed it?

She goes to the door and tries it. As she does so, it opens. The guards have just unlocked it: the sound of the key turning in the lock must have awakened her. Aviva rouses Deborah, and the two, as in a spell, attempt to leave the hotel. The guards refuse to allow them. Instead, they are kept in their room. Aviva pleads: they must see the lawyers, the Chief Rabbi—perhaps they can still do something. It is a few minutes after 7 A.M. . . . There may yet be time—

The guards shake their heads. They are sympathetic but their orders are to keep them there.

The girls are forced to wait. The lawyer arrives. Aviva runs to him. "We must go to the rabbi," she wails.

Her lawyer says, "No, they will not allow it." The guards say, "The rabbi will come here, ladies. He has been informed that you are here."

The minutes pass. Aviva and Deborah fix their eyes on the clock. Watching the minute hand move, they burst into tears. "The rabbi, where is the rabbi?" Aviva manages to ask.

"He will come, my ladies, he will come."

Not until nine o'clock does Rabbi Ochana appear. His eyes are red and he is a broken man. The girls look at him numbly.

He sits beside them and holds their hands in his. "It is all over, my daughters. They are martyrs."

Aviva asks, like an automaton: "And the funeral?"

The rabbi's voice breaks. "They are already buried, my daughters."

Aviva again, not knowing her own voice: "And how did Eliahu act? Was he strong?"

"They were heroes. They were both heroes, my daughters. . . ."

That afternoon, as it happened, Professor Harroun Haddad, professor of Islamic Institutions at the University of Cairo, made his customary call at the house of Mohamad Haidar Pasha, the Director General of Prisons. Twice each week Professor Haddad tutored Haidar Pasha's two young nephews in French and English.

When he entered, after the Sudanese houseboy had taken his hat, he was greeted by Haidar Pasha himself. The usually imperturbable Egyptian official shook his hand with surprising warmth. "Ah, Professor Haddad," he said. "What I have seen this morning—"

Professor Haddad, a little alarmed, looked at him questioningly.

Clasping his hands together in an astonishing show of emotion, Haidar Pasha said: "I saw two young lions die today."

Professor Haddad suddenly knew. The government *had* carried out the executions. He sat down heavily. "The two from Palestine?"

His host nodded. "Yes," he said. "This morning. At eight o'clock."

There was silence for a moment. "I did not know them, though they were of my faith," Professor Haddad said thoughtfully. "I never set eyes on them. I heard about them, I read about them—" He looked up quickly at Haidar Pasha. "Who did not? Yet, my heart goes out to them." He was silent for a moment. "Excellency, how did they die?"

Haidar Pasha said, "I have seen nothing like it before. They were very near to God all the time. They were in a high world, my Professor. They went to their death clean, clean as white candlewax. . . ."

That evening, in another section of Cairo, a physician, Dr. Isaiah Selim, was making a call at the home of Mohamed Shoura, the hangman. Mrs. Shoura was ill and Dr. Selim busied himself looking after her needs. As he was about to leave, Mohamed Shoura met him outside his wife's room and took him aside. Under the dark imperial red of his tarboosh, his face was pale. "My dear doctor, I must speak with you," he said. "You know, I carried out a duty this morning."

Dr. Selim nodded sadly. He had seen the report in the afternoon newspapers.

Moalam Shoura paced back and forth—a huge man, fingering his black mustachios nervously, trying to find words. "I must tell someone, someone who will understand," he began. "As you are a Jew and a doctor, I can speak to you. This is the first execution in twenty years in which I had the impression that I am a criminal for what I do. I was emotional for the first time."

He stopped. "Do you know, sir, what they said to me? They saw that I trembled. They said, 'Do not fear. We know you only do your duty. We will be of every help to you.'"

He resumed his pacing. "I accompanied them from their cells to the execution room. I helped remove their uniforms of prison and to dress them in the hanging suits. Such courage they showed, such bearing. Even then, as I attended to them, my hand trembled. I feared I would be unable to carry out my task when the time came, and I am very proud of my skill—" He paused. "I heard their singing before I approached their cell. Their rabbi was there, seeking to comfort them, and when they comforted him, he, too, wept."

He paused opposite Dr. Selim, his black eyes enormous. "You are a physician; what I tell you is indelicate, but it must be said. In every hanging, always, in the last moment, the bowels and the bladder open. There is a complete loss of control. In ninety-nine percent of the cases. But not these two. I say to you, my doctor, they were smiling and singing at the last moment when I placed the hood over their faces. Smiling and singing—"

He could not restrain himself. He suddenly threw his arms

around the man opposite him and kissed him on either cheek. "I embrace you. This is a kiss for the two boys. For them!"

In Palestine, in the major cities, the *Hazit* appeared. It read:

The curtain is not down. The hanging of Eliahu Hakim and Eliahu Bet Zouri is not the end: it is but one of the pages in our history. The book is open and its pages are written in letters of blood. We do not always see clearly the meaning of the blood that is shed. But these two names will illuminate our lives for there was a meaning to their life and a meaning to their death. They lived and died according to the laws of honor which bind all freedom fighters from one generation to another. They sacrificed themselves in our war for a better future. They died so that the will to freedom should be rekindled in the heart of the nation. The fire that burned in their souls they sent out to kindle other sleeping hearts, to wake them for the fight for freedom. This fire will not be extinguished.

The curtain is not down. At no time and at no place in the world did a tyrant succeed in putting an end to the fight for freedom by executing its fighters. The more he seeks to subdue us, the more hangmen he employs, the more the number of rebels, the greater the rebellion.

The two who died in Cairo were not alone. There are many more. We know that every youth in the homeland is like Hakim and Bet Zouri: ready to give their lives. We shall draw fresh strength from their bravery and self-sacrifice. Our generation has been educated to suffer and to sacrifice. In the end we shall stop the occupation of our homeland by strangers.

Their names will shine in the darkness.

They believed that the objective for which they gave their young lives will come true. And because they gave their lives for their country, they have the right to say to you, to order you: Fight until victory!

In Tel Aviv, Moshe Bet Zouri, leaving the post office at the end of the day, bought the latest issue of the evening newspaper. He opened it and on the front page a headline sprang to his eyes:

He went home, tore the lapel of his coat and sat on the floor, weeping.

In Haifa, Simon Hakim and his three sons rent their garments and their voices joined those of his wife and daughter in lamentation.

On the outskirts of Cairo, in an area time has long since passed by, is the ancient Bassatin Cemetery. Here those of the Hebrew faith have been buried for more than twelve centuries. Among those said to lie here are Moses Maimonides, greatest of the medieval Jewish philosophers, who died in 1204, and Rabbi Jacob ibn Hayyim, mystic and miracle worker, whose weeping followers brought him here one thousand years ago. The yellow sand has crept over everything.

Here, in a remote corner amid the debris and neglect of ages, one finds a single square stone, taken from the hills of Mokattam, the low mountain range near Cairo from which the Pharaohs quarried the stone to build the pyramids. It is not large—perhaps two feet high, perhaps three feet wide. There is no name on it, but only the words, chiseled in Hebrew:

PRAY FOR THEIR SOULS

Beneath it, Eliahu Hakim and Eliahu Bet Zouri sleep together, as they were buried, in one coffin, curled in each other's arms as children. They lie curled together, like sleeping children, under the eternal stone.

No one guards their grave now.

The sands of the desert blow. Nothing grows there—no weeds,

no foliage. Only the sifting, creeping yellow dust over everything, and in the cloudless sky, a molten sun.

In the ancient earth, in the nameless grave, they lie together, under the imperishable stone.

Few remember them now.

Avizur

My son, too, will be like him.
The sun of the mountains of Judea will tan him,
And the wind of the seas will coarsen his skin,
His eyes will glitter with the fire of freedom
As your eyes, Oh father!

My son, too, will be like him—
When he goes to battle my blood will boil in his veins,
And within him my mother's soul will flutter.

When I saw my ancestors forgather in my dream,
I knew then why I was so restless;
When I saw my ancestors forgather in my dream,
I knew: My son, too, will be like him!
            —Eliahu Bet Zouri

ACKNOWLEDGMENTS

Those readers who would like to learn more about the incidents and the background of this story are referred to the following sources, which I found useful in addition to personal interviews.

BANNAI, YAACOB. *Halim Almonim* (The Unknown Soldier). Tel Aviv: Circle of Friends Publishers, 1949

BEGIN, MENACHEM. *The Revolt.* New York: Henry Schuman, 1951

BORISOV, J. *Palestine Underground.* New York: Judea Publishing Co., 1947

COHEN, GUELA. *Sipura Shel Lochemeth* (The Story of a Woman Underground Fighter). Tel Aviv: Karni Publishers, 1962

ELDAD, DR. ISRAEL. *Israel, the Road to Full Redemption.* New York: Futuro Press, 1961

ELDAD, DR. ISRAEL. *Maasar Rishon* (The First Tithe). Tel Aviv: Circle of Friends Publishers, 1952

Great Britain and Palestine: 1915-1945. London: Royal Institute of International Affairs, 1945

KIMCHE, JON AND DAVID. *The Secret Roads.* New York: Farrar, Straus and Cudahy, 1955

MACMICHAEL, HAROLD. *The Anglo-Egyptian Sudan.* London: Faber & Faber, 1934

MERIDOR, YA'ACOV. *Long Is the Road to Freedom.* Johannesburg: Newzo Press, 1955

309

NEDAVA, J. B. *Olei Hagardom* (Those Who Mounted the Gallows). Tel Aviv: Shiloach Publishers, 1952

Palestine: A Study of Jewish, Arab and British Policies. New York: Esco Foundation for Palestine, 1947

SCHECHTMAN, JOSEPH B. *Fighter and Prophet: The Jabotinsky Story.* New York: Yoseloff, 1956, 1961

SHMULEWITZ, MATTITYAHU. *Beyamim Adumim.* (Bloody Days). Tel Aviv: Elisha Printing Press, 1949

Sefer Lehi (The Book of Lehi). A compendium of *Hazit* and other FFI underground publications

TREVOR, DAPHNE. *Under the White Paper.* Jerusalem: The Jerusalem Press, Ltd., 1948

Files of the *Egyptian Gazette & Mail,* Cairo

Files of the *Jerusalem Post,* Jerusalem

Files of *Le Journal d'Egypte,* Cairo

Jabotinsky Museum, Tel Aviv

Jewish Division, New York Public Library

Zionist Archives, New York City

INDEX

Souki, Sam, 259, 265, 266
"Special Night Squads," 87
Stack Pasha, Sir Lee, 26
Stalin, Josef, 122, 290
Stern, Abraham, 48, 72, 78-80,
    82, 91, 92, 101-09, 116,
    122, 123-24, 131, 262, 271
Stern, Roni, 106
Stern group (FFI) (Lohmey
    Heruth Israel), 8, 18, 27,
    31, 35, 36, 60, 93, 102-09,
    116, 121, 125-26, 129-36,
    139-42, 151-57, 161-69,
    176, 177, 179, 180, 181,
    187, 189-90, 193, 196, 198,
    201, 206, 212, 217, 231,
    240, 253, 271, 279
Struma, S.S., 109-11, 112, 113,
    114-15, 116, 156, 176, 197,
    269
Suez, 87, 88
Sulzberger, C. L., 259, 266
Svorai, Moshe and Mrs., 107-09,
    271
Syria, 46

Tchernichovsky, Saul, 52-53
Tel Aviv, Palestine, 19, 36, 38,
    40, 58, 70, 72, 77, 79, 84,
    100, 112, 114, 132, 134,
    151, 165, 232
Tiberias, Palestine, 39-40, 45
Tigerhill, S.S., 84-85, 116
Tito, Marshal, 16
Toscanini, Arturo, 286
Towayar Pasha, Mohamed, 244,
    274-76
Transjordan, 46, 47
Trumpledor, Captain Joseph, 48
Tuck, Pinckney, 18
Tuvia, Yaffa, 196-202, 203, 215,
    222, 223, 225, 226-28, 267

Undset, Sigrid, 286
Uziel, Chief Rabbi, 156

Vered, Tamar, 96-97, 117, 145,
    232, 234

Warsaw Ghetto, liquidation of,
    148
Warsaw Institute of Technology,
    105
Wedgwood, Sir Josiah, 115
Weizmann, Dr. Chaim, 27, 46,
    47, 89, 155 n., 190, 270
Weizmann, Michael, 27
Welch, Major Patrick, 266-67
White Paper on policy in Pales-
    tine, 75-77, 78, 84, 90, 109-
    10, 111, 153, 168, 191
Wilkins, J. J., 242
Wingate, Captain Orde, 87
World War I, 85, 86
World War II, 82, 83, 154
World Zionist Movement, 46

Yair, Eliezer ben, 105
Yehoshua, Rabbi, 194
Yitzhaki, Arieh, 58, 60, 61, 80-
    81
Yizernitsky, Itzhak ("Rabbi"
    Shamir), 20-22, 35, 60-61,
    93, 124-25, 126, 127-32,
    133, 139, 140, 148, 151-52,
    155, 156, 160, 177, 180,
    181, 184, 185, 189-92, 206,
    212-13, 223, 224, 231, 279-
    80, 282
YMCA building, Jerusalem, 137-
    38
Youth movements, 49-50

Zaki, Colonel Selim, 28-29, 30,
    31-32
Zionism, 33, 46, 48, 83, 102-03,
    186
Zurabin, Shalom, 69-70

317

ABOUT THE AUTHOR

Gerold Frank covered the trial of Lord Moyne's assassins while he was serving as a war correspondent in the Middle East during World War II. He had earlier been a newspaperman in Cleveland and New York. He has collaborated on many books about Israel and the Middle East, including Bartley Crum's Behind the Silken Curtain *and Jorge García-Granados'* The Birth of Israel. *More recently he has written, and jointly signed, Lillian Roth's* I'll Cry Tomorrow, *Diana Barrymore's* Too Much, Too Soon, *Sheilah Graham's* Beloved Infidel *and Zsa Zsa Gabor's* My Story. *Of these last four books, more than 6,000,000 copies have been sold in hard and paperback editions.*